HARNESSING THE POWER OF COLLECTIVE LEARNING

What were new ideas thirty years ago, such as the concepts of participatory develop-ment and systems thinking, are now accepted norms in international development circles. The majority of professionals engaged in rural development accept the prop-osition that the people who participate in development should play an active role in defining, implementing and evaluating projects intended to improve their productiv-ity and lives. However, this goal remains unrealized in many development programs.

Harnessing the Power of Collective Learning considers the challenges and potential of enabling collective learning in rural development initiatives. The book presents eleven case studies of organizations trying to develop and implement collective learn-ing systems as an integral component of sustainable development practice. Through systematic reflection on action and experience, key lessons and themes emerge regarding the nature of voice, participation, feedback loops, accountability and trans-parency, which will be useful for many others in the development community.

This book is a useful resource for academics, practitioners and policy-makers in the areas of international development, sustainable development, organizational development, philanthropy, learning communities, monitoring and evaluation, and rural development.

Roy Steiner is Director of Learning and Impact of the Omidyar Network and was the former Deputy Director of the Agricultural Development Initiative at the Bill & Melinda Gates Foundation's Global Development Program.

Duncan Hanks is Director of Organizational Learning and Development at the Baha'i National Centre in Canada, a global board member of the International Environment Forum and, since 2007, an independent consultant to the Global Development Program of the Bill & Melinda Gates Foundation (Agricultural Development).

"*Harnessing the Power of Collective Learning* is an encouraging and valuable contribution for those in the development community who believe in the immense power of people and communities to transform themselves. It highlights new possibilities for collective listening and learning to drive rural development, improve lives and make the world a better place."

Kofi A. Annan, Chair of the Kofi Annan Foundation,
Former Secretary-General of the United Nations (1997–2006)

"All development practitioners should read this book. In a dozen case studies it brilliantly distils the powerful experience of collective learning involving donors, NGOs and rural people."

Sir Gordon Conway, Professor of International Development,
Imperial College, UK

"Sustainable development requires collaboration, but creating and maintaining collaboration is hard. This book presents important approaches to building the shared understanding, personal and collective alignment, trust, and ongoing community participation essential to improving lives around the world."

Peggy Dulany, Founder and Chair, Synergos, USA

HARNESSING THE POWER OF COLLECTIVE LEARNING

Feedback, accountability and constituent voice in rural development

Edited by Roy Steiner and Duncan Hanks

Routledge
Taylor & Francis Group

LONDON AND NEW YORK

First published 2016
by Routledge
2 Park Square, Milton Park, Abingdon, Oxon OX14 4RN

and by Routledge
711 Third Avenue, New York, NY 10017

Routledge is an imprint of the Taylor & Francis Group, an informa business

British Library Cataloguing-in-Publication Data
A catalogue record for this book is available from the British Library

Library of Congress Cataloging-in-Publication Data
Names: Steiner, Roy, editor. | Hanks, Duncan, editor.Title:
Harnessing the power of collective learning : feedback, accountability
and constituent voice in rural development / edited by Roy Steiner
and Duncan Hanks.Description: New York, NY : Routledge, 2016.
Identifiers: LCCN 2015035530| ISBN 9781138121119 (hb) | ISBN
9781138121126 (pb) | ISBN 9781315651248 (ebook)Subjects: LCSH:
Rural development projects--Citizen participation--Case studies. | Rural
development projects--Management--Case studies. | Communication
in rural development--Case studies.Classification: LCC HN49.C6 H38
2016 | DDC 307.1/412--dc23LC record available at http://lccn.loc.
gov/2015035530

ISBN: 978-1-138-12111-9 (hbk)
ISBN: 978-1-138-12112-6 (pbk)
ISBN: 978-1-315-65124-8 (ebk)

Typeset in Bembo
by GreenGate Publishing Services, Tonbridge, Kent

This publication is dedicated to the memory of Nura Faridian Steiner who committed her life to the realization of the oneness of humanity, and to the 500 million smallholder farmers worldwide—women, men, adults, youth and children—that feed a large portion of the people on the planet. May their voices be increasingly heard and their service increasingly valued.

CONTENTS

FIGURES

TABLES

BOXES

ABOUT THE EDITORS

Roy Steiner is a highly experienced senior global agriculture and global development leader. He served for nearly a decade at the Bill & Melinda Gates Foundation, culminating in a position as Deputy Director and Founding Member of the Agricultural Development Initiative. He managed a professional team responsible for a $400 million grant portfolio in the area of sustainable farmer productivity that included irrigation and water management, seed systems, agronomy, farmer organizations, gender, human capital and information and communication technology initiatives. Moreover he was integral to the development of innovative initiatives including the Alliance for a Green Revolution, the Agricultural Transformation Agency in Ethiopia and the Digital Soil Map of Africa.

Duncan Hanks is an experienced community development professional and facilitator in the fields of education, governance, youth empowerment and ICT. For over twenty-five years he supported tutorial learning and social action programs for youth, leadership training, and the use of participatory methodologies in development throughout Latin America. He currently works as the Director of Organizational Learning and Development at the Baha'i National Centre in Canada. He supports the United Nations' work in sustainable development, climate change and the Post-2015 development agenda, is a member of the board of directors of the International Environment Forum and served as an independent consultant to the Global Development Program of the Bill & Melinda Gates Foundation (Agricultural Development) from 2007–2015.

ABOUT THE CONTRIBUTORS

Chapter 2: Digital Green

Rikin Gandhi is chief executive officer of Digital Green. His interests include sustainable agriculture and technology for socioeconomic development. Rikin received a master's in aeronautical and astronautical engineering from MIT and a bachelor's in computer science from Carnegie Mellon University. Rikin is a licensed private pilot and received patents for linguistic search algorithms that he helped develop at Oracle. Born and raised in the USA, Rikin ventured to rural India to start up a social enterprise to develop biofuels. He then joined Microsoft Research in Bangalore, India, as a researcher in the Technology for Emerging Markets team that incubated Digital Green. Digital Green is now an independent, not-for-profit organization with support from the Bill & Melinda Gates Foundation, DFID, USAID, Google and others.

Shreya Aggarwal is a former senior program manager at Digital Green. She has worked in India and Africa building partnerships with governments and non-profit organizations and facilitates trainings on community-based learning and data management. As a public policy analyst, she has authored articles on education policies in India emphasizing the need for learning-based indicators for school assessment. Currently she is a student at the Harvard Kennedy School, completing a master's in public administration.

Remya Sasindaran is a program manager at Digital Green. She has worked as a communications specialist with several international public health organizations. A key focus of her career has been to use her skills in behavior change communications to connect communities with easily adoptable health best practices. She has a Bachelor of Arts in advertising from Assumption University, Bangkok, and a Master of Arts in media communications from RMIT University, Melbourne.

Chapter 3: Grameen Foundation

Whitney Gantt is responsible for Grameen Foundation's mobile agriculture strategy and leads the expansion of mAgriculture initiatives in new markets. She brings multiple years' experience designing and implementing mobile agriculture programs in East and West Africa and South and Central America. Prior to joining Grameen Foundation, Whitney worked in the public and non-profit sectors in education, civil society, and national resource management in the USA and abroad. She excels in building and leading cross-functional teams who work closely with end-users and public and private sector partners to co-design and co-implement solutions to reduce poverty. Whitney holds a bachelor's degree in cultural anthropology from Colorado State University and a master's in international public affairs from the University of Wisconsin, where she led research on resiliency and natural disasters, participatory conservation, and gender in water management in the development sector.

Chapter 4: Farmer Voice Radio

Philip R. Christensen has lived and worked in Africa since 1980. While on the continent he has inaugurated a pioneering online education company in South Africa and managed six multi-million-dollar, donor-funded educational development projects covering fifteen countries—most recently as Regional Project Director for Farmer Voice Radio, a six-year initiative funded by the Bill & Melinda Gates Foundation. He currently consults on a variety of international development initiatives. He focuses on designing learning systems that improve lives, with a particular interest in how information and communication technologies (ICTs) can enhance outcomes. He holds a bachelor's degree in social psychology from Harvard University and a doctorate in education from the University of Massachusetts.

Dwight W. Allen is Emeritus Eminent Scholar of Educational Reform at Old Dominion University (ODU). As Stanford University's director of teacher education he helped develop a teacher internship program which is still offered. As Dean of Education at the University of Massachusetts, he implemented award-winning teacher training programs and reforms combating institutional racism. At Old Dominion University he was the principal investigator for a $1.3 million grant to improve the technology training of teachers. He was the founding coordinator of NewPAGE, ODU's environmental education class required for more than 2,000 freshmen. For sixteen years he worked with the World Bank and the United Nations Development Program as chief technical advisor and international advisor for the largest UNDP education programs in China. For seven years (2007–14) he consulted with the Bill & Melinda Gates Foundation to help devise strategies to bring better information to smallholder farmers in South Asia and Africa.

Katharine N. Tjasink is a social development professional with substantial experience working in complex development environments in Uganda, Tanzania, Kenya, Malawi and South Africa. For five-and-a-half years, she worked with a radio- and ICT-based agricultural program funded by the Bill & Melinda Gates Foundation, Farmer Voice Radio (www.farmervoice.org). As Regional Technical Coordinator, she supported this project through the coordination of program activities among twenty-one African sub-grantee implementing partners, international partners, and thirty-six radio stations in four countries in East and Southern Africa. Currently, she is Senior Associate in the Education and Social Development Division of Khulisa Management Services, a monitoring and evaluation firm based in Johannesburg, South Africa.

Chapter 5: Keystone Accountability

Andre Proctor is a founding partner and current Programme Services Director of Keystone, working on its groundbreaking Impact Planning, Assessment and Learning (IPAL) methodology. He also co-leads the development of Keystone's Comparative Constituency Feedback Survey methodology.

David Bonbright is founder and Chief Executive of Keystone. Over the past three decades, as a grantmaker and manager with Aga Khan Foundation, Ford Foundation, Oak Foundation and Ashoka, David has sought to evolve and test innovative approaches to strengthening citizen self-organization for sustainable development as an alternative to prevailing bureaucratic, top-down models of social service delivery and social value creation.

Chapter 6: PRADAN

Anirban Ghose is part of the leadership team at PRADAN working on rural transformation directly with more than two million people in over 7,000 villages across seven of India's poorest states. He is currently co-leading an ambitious initiative around large-scale, multi-dimensional transformation of villages in India with a large number of civil society organizations, government and philanthropic organizations.

Chapter 7: CARE USA

Maureen Miruka, PhD, is Team Leader of the Pathways Program at CARE USA.

Emily Hillenbrand is Senior Technical Advisor for Gender and Livelihoods at CARE USA.

Chapter 8: One Acre Fund

Andrew Youn is Executive Director of One Acre Fund. He co-founded One Acre Fund in 2006 in Kenya, along with John Gachunga. He graduated magna cum laude from Yale University and worked as management consultant to Fortune 500 companies for four years with Mercer Consulting. He received an MBA from the Kellogg School of Management at Northwestern University before starting the One Acre Fund program. He currently lives in Rubengera, Rwanda.

Matthew Forti is Managing Director of One Acre Fund USA. He has been involved with One Acre Fund since the organization's founding in 2006, serving as its first Board Chairman. He joined One Acre Fund's staff in 2013, as the director of One Acre Fund USA. Prior to joining One Acre Fund's staff, he was a Manager and Co-Head of the Performance Measurement Practice at the Bridgespan Group. He received an MBA from the Kellogg School of Management and graduated summa cum laude and Phi Beta Kappa from Northwestern University.

Chapter 9: IDEO.org

Jocelyn Wyatt is Co-Lead and Executive Director of IDEO.org, the non-profit design organization that she co-founded in 2011 after leading IDEO's social innovation practice. She sorts out the vision, strategy, funding, and growth plans for IDEO.org, and heads up partner development with foundations, non-profits, and social enterprises. Prior to joining IDEO in 2007, she worked in Kenya as an Acumen Fund fellow, VisionSpring's interim country director in India, and worked for Chemonics International. She also serves as a program advisor to the Clinton Global Initiative, an advisory board member to Marketplace, a board member for Whitaker Peace and Development Initiative, and an Aspen Institute First Movers Fellow. She has an MBA from Thunderbird School of Global Management, and a BA in anthropology from Grinnell College.

Chapter 10: Synergos

Synergos is a global non-profit organization that helps solve the complex problems of poverty and inequality by promoting and supporting collaborations among business, government, civil society and marginalized communities. It creates the conditions for these partnerships to be successful by building trust, designing and implementing change processes, enhancing the effectiveness of bridging leaders and institutions, and sharing its knowledge and experience.

Chapter 11: FOSCA

Fadel Ndiame is Head of AGRA's Regional Team in West Africa. Previously, he was the Lead Coordinator of the Farmer Organization Support Center in Africa (FOSCA), and spearheaded the institutionalization of FOSCA within AGRA.

Prior to joining AGRA he was Program Director at the W.K. Kellogg Foundation in Southern Africa, and led the conceptualization and content design of the Foundation's investment program in Southern Africa, with a particular focus on economic opportunities and agricultural investment programs. He has also worked as the Executive Regional Director of the West Africa Rural Foundation (WARF), Program Coordinator at the Local Organization Support Program (LOSP), and a Program Coordinator of the Senegalese Institute of Agricultural Research. He holds an MSc in agricultural economics from Michigan State University and is completing a PhD in sociology with a focus on rural development from Wageningen Agricultural University.

Emma Kambewa is Program Officer for AGRA's Market Access Program. Before joining AGRA in 2010, she had over eighteen years of experience in agricultural and natural resource commodity value chains and marketing especially in developing countries, working as an Institutional Capacity Development Coordinator for EU- and DANIDA-funded projects. She has a PhD in social sciences and marketing, an MSc in agricultural economics and a BSc in agriculture majoring in rural development.

Mary Njoroge is Program Officer of FOSCA's M&E and Knowledge Development area, and Capacity Building Officer of the United Nations Development Program. Prior to joining AGRA she was the Head of Monitoring & Evaluation at African Capacity Building Foundation (ACBF), in Harare. She had also worked as a Director, Program Management Division, at UNDP-managed basket fund for Public Service Reform in Kenya. She holds a bachelor's degree in economics and sociology, a Master of Science degree in economics and a Master of Education in entrepreneurship development.

Pauline Kamau is Program Officer within the Private–Public Partnerships (PPP) unit of AGRA where her work is focused on ensuring the role of farmer organizations (FOs) in the context of AGRA's refreshed strategy. She is a former Program Officer for the Farmer Organization Support Centre (FOSCA), and Executive Officer within the President's office at AGRA. She has over fifteen years' experience in project management, financial management and budgeting and human resources, and worked with the Rockefeller Foundation, Africa Regional Office. She holds a Bachelor of Commerce (BCom) degree and a Master of Business Administration (MBA) specializing in strategic management.

Samuel Sey is Program Officer in AGRA working with service providers. Prior to joining AGRA, he worked with CARE International Ghana as the Manager of the Natural Resource-Based Enterprise Development Project. He is also a former Senior Programme Officer with the Centre for Biodiversity Utilization and Development (CBUD) of KNUST. He has an MSc in natural resource management and a BSc in agriculture.

Chapter 12: Kenya Markets Trust

Mike Field has over twenty years' experience of designing, assessing, implementing and training on leading-edge private sector development approaches. Through his work, he has played a key role in setting learning and research agendas in the field of systems approaches. He continues today by regularly training and presenting on how to manage systems programs, as well as contributing to various learning networks dedicated to improving the application of systems and complexity concepts. He recently finished an assignment as the technical lead on a DFID-funded market development project in Kenya.

Anna-Paula Jonsson specializes in private sector development for pro-poor growth in East Africa, with a niche focus on M4P and market systems approaches. Currently a member of ASI's Africa office in Kenya, she is in charge of developing knowledge and learning material, including case studies and articles, as well as project and financial management of agricultural projects in East Africa. Her experience includes private sector and infrastructure projects in Kenya, Rwanda, Botswana, Nigeria, South Africa and the Dominican Republic; and business development of new projects in Africa and Asia.

Mehrdad Ehsani is the Team Leader for the multi-donor-funded Kenya Market Assistance Programme and concurrently serves as the CEO of Kenya Markets Trust which seeks to catalyse inclusive growth in various market systems. He has expertise in ecosystem approaches to value chain development in agriculture and rural development and its implications in adaptive management. Over the past twenty years he has worked with numerous businesses, associations and non-profits in East and Southern Africa, Israel, Canada and Costa Rica.

PREFACE

As we climbed the steps up to the presidential palace of Ethiopia I noticed that the grounds were strangely quiet and there was no one to guide us to our meeting with the Prime Minister. My Gates Foundation colleague, Khalid Bomba, and myself were scheduled to present the findings from a nine-month study of the Ethiopian agricultural extension system, conducted at the personal request of the now late Prime Minister Meles to Melinda Gates, and I was doing my best to manage the trepidations going through my mind.

After a few minutes wandering about we came across a room full of machine gun-festooned guards who ushered us into a waiting room, furnished with over-stuffed chairs and unexpectedly scented with House of 4711, a cologne that happened to be my Swiss grandfather's favorite fragrance, and I couldn't help but think about what his advice to me would be at this moment.

My grandfather was a fearless newspaper editor, a champion of human rights who stood up to the Nazis in World War II and never wavered in his dedication to justice. Here was his grandson working with someone many considered a dictator in order to ensure food security for smallholder farmers living on less than $1 a day. I was trying to navigate a world where means and ends, principles and motivations were not easily disentangled.

My trepidation stemmed from two sources. First, we had tried to ensure that the process we used in the diagnostic reflected our deeply held beliefs about the purpose of this enterprise we call development. Rather than a quick three-week consulting approach typical of many donors, we had opted for a deep participatory process that had engaged hundreds of stakeholders, from farmers to extension workers to the private sector over nine months. We had acted based on our belief that true development consists of building the capacity of people to make their own decisions and we viewed them as protagonists in the process and not passive bystanders. The report that we were about to deliver could easily be seen as a threat to Ethiopia's authoritarian system because it recommended increased autonomy for extension workers, greater accountability to farmers, systematic feedback from communities and changes to performance measures.

The second source of trepidation was the fact that we were engaged in a process that made many people at our Foundation uncomfortable. The initiative we had embarked upon was primarily focused on participatory processes, improving governance and building capacity within specific institutions and populations— radically different from the technology-focused grants for which the Foundation was well known. We were clearly going off-strategy and if this failed we were the ones accountable.

Fortunately my trepidations were never realized. Perhaps because the participatory process we used had fully engaged the government, and perhaps because the robust data we had collected strongly supported our case, the Prime Minister fully endorsed the findings and requested that the same methodology be applied to other critical agricultural systems (seed, water, markets) which took us another 18 months to complete. Over the course of these successive diagnostic studies and intensive consultations with partners in Ethiopia, a new initiative called the Agricultural Transformation Agency (ATA) was conceived as an institution to support strategy development, implementation and coordination in critical areas of the agricultural sector for Ethiopia to achieve its ambitious 2015 targets of doubling agricultural production with a focus on smallholder farmers. Today, the ATA is a public agency based in Addis Ababa with a staff of 250 with financial support of the Ethiopian government and ten+ bilateral, multilateral and private foundation donors. While it is still too early to pronounce the ATA an unqualified success, its impact has been significant and it became an important factor in the Gates Foundation's shift to more country-based strategies.

One of the consequences of the perceived success of the ATA was that a host of other countries and donors wanted to "adopt the model." What that usually meant was adoption of the final structure (in the form of a public agency reporting directly to the head of state) rather than the process by which that solution was developed. For those of us involved in the formation of the ATA it was the process of helping stakeholders understand and trust each other, collecting real data to reveal system challenges and building the feedback and learning orientations that were the keys to success, yet those seeking to adopt the model were less interested in this process. At the risk of misusing a technology metaphor, they wanted hardware, without understanding or appreciating the need for software. The experience in Ethiopia where we tried to foster a participatory process with intentional feedback loops as well as dozens of other projects over the nine years I served at the Gates Foundation and my decade of living and working in Africa have convinced me that we in the development community need to be more systematic in enabling a collective learning process—the software of development.

Roy Steiner

ACKNOWLEDGMENTS

The editors wish to thank all the contributors and their organizations for their ongoing and thoughtful participation throughout this learning process, and the Bill & Melinda Gates Foundation for its kind support in creating the space and conditions to reflect on action and experience. We also extend our heartfelt appreciation to the many friends at Routledge Earthscan for their willingness to publish these initial conclusions thereby widening the circle of potential participants in this ongoing learning process about harnessing the power of collective learning. Lastly, we wish to thank those many friends who helped edit the various sections and to Reza Mostmand for producing the graphics in Chapters 1 and 13.

ABBREVIATIONS

AEPMS	Agriculture Extension Performance Management System
AGRA	Alliance for a Green Revolution in Africa
ALINe	Agricultural and Learning Impacts Network
ANC	antenatal care
APHLI	African Public Health Leadership Initiative
ARC	American Refugee Committee
ASA	Action for Social Advancement
ATA	Agricultural Transformation Agency
BGAK	Banana Growers Association of Kenya
CDP	Cooperative Development Program
CKW	Community Knowledge Worker
COCO	Connect Online | Connect Offline
CoP	community of practice
CPI	Capacity Performing Index
CSISA	Cereal Systems Initiative for South Asia
CV	Constituent Voice
DA	Development Agent
FFBS	Farmer Field and Business School
FO	farmer organization
FOSCA	Farmer Organization Support Center for Africa
FTC	Farmer Training Centre
FVR	Farmer Voice Radio
GED	Gender Equity and Diversity
GEF	Global Environment Fund
ICRW	International Center for Research on Women
ICT	information and communications technology
IFPRI	International Food Policy Research Institute

INR	Indian rupee
IPTT	Indicator Performance Tracking Table
ISFM	integrated soil fertility management
KENFAP	Kenya National Federation of Agricultural Producers
KIP	Key Performance Indicator
KMT	Kenya Markets Trust
KVTC	Kilombero Valley Teak Company
LARA	Local Agricultural Radio Agenda
LDF	Leadership Development Forum
M&E	monitoring and evaluation
MAP	Market Assistance Programme
MGNREGS	Mahatma Gandhi National Rural Employment Guarantee Scheme
MHI	Maternal Health Initiative
MLE	measurement, learning and evaluation
MoA	Ministry of Agriculture
MoHSS	Ministry of Health and Social Services
MTR	mid-term review
NARA	National Agricultural Radio Agenda
NPA	Net Promoter Analysis
NRM	natural resource management
PI	Presencing Institute
PPT	Participatory Performance Tracker
PS	Permanent Secretary
REO	Radio Extension Officer
SC	Scheduled Caste
SHF	smallholder farmer
SHG	self-help group
SII	Strategic Impact Inquiry
SME	small and medium-sized enterprise
SMS	Subject Matter Specialist
SSA	sub-Saharan Africa
ST	Scheduled Tribe
USAID	United States Agency for International Development
WEAI	Women's Empowerment in Agriculture Index

1

THE DEVELOPMENT CONUNDRUM

Roy Steiner and Duncan Hanks

Introduction: enabling a process of collective learning

The discourse on developing effective feedback and learning systems is not new. In the past seventy years development practitioners have been experimenting with approaches, methods, instruments and technologies all designed to alleviate poverty and create conditions of social justice. Along the way, much has been learned, systematized and diffused. There are a growing number of vibrant communities of practice, knowledge networks and learning platforms that have been established worldwide—a living testimony to the centrality of knowledge in the struggle for development. And throughout this journey, profound questions about learning processes and how new knowledge is generated in the context of development have been asked and explored.

Reflecting on the past decades of development work and discourse, it is clear that incremental learning, often through trial and error, has been a primary mode of operation. In an effort to appreciate the important role that a collective learning process plays in rural development, the Gates Foundation invited eleven of its most innovative, agriculture-related grant recipients to reflect about their different organizational experiences on this theme. In essence, the Foundation invited these practitioners to participate in a collective meta-learning process about what they have discovered over the years about how to effectively involve their collaborators and partners in learning and how to radically improve project outcomes through interactive learning and systematically listening to feedback. Participants were asked to write a case study outlining a successful experience of their organization and to share it with a small group of colleagues. A two-day workshop was convened in May 2014 at which each participant presented key lessons learned, while representatives of the other organizations listened, asked probing questions, reflected on what they were hearing and shared their own perspectives. Over the course of the workshop the participants saw certain patterns emerging of cause and effect, of challenge and response that were largely consistent with each other. The workshop itself was intended as a safe space for reflection and sharing of experiences. It served to jump start an important conversation that is still unfolding amongst these practitioners.

This learning process began with an appreciation for several key insights regarding the nature of voice, participation, feedback loops, accountability and transparency, among others, all of which have been gaining importance in the world of development dialogue and practice over the past decades. Resisting the temptation to define what "enabling a collective process of learning in development" entails, the group decided it would approach the topic from an experiential perspective that allowed meaning to emerge through engagement with each other and comparison between helpful and less helpful lessons learned.

Among the initial discoveries was the recognition that the participants and their organizations had conceptually moved away from the notion of delivering services to the poor. Progressive development workers no longer speak of beneficiaries or recipients as objects (targeted others) to be developed. Rather, they are now learning to speak, think and act in more inclusive ways. They are struggling to respectfully conceptualize those involved in the process not merely as stakeholders, but as constituents—as co-creators—of processes that result in improved well-being. The collective, therefore, in "collective learning process" implies that all the participants have a significant role to play in the innovation of development. They are all co-creators and constituents (beneficiaries), each with the same rights and obligations to participate in the generation and use of knowledge to improve well-being.

In reflecting on the idea of "collective" it appeared hard to separate it from broader discussions about participation and voice. The value of participation has been maturing in understanding and growing in complexity over the past decades. It has been explored through various approaches, methods, models, techniques and technologies. What has repeatedly come to the surface is the imperative nature of participation as a prerequisite for development to occur. It operates across cultures and continents as a guiding principle and core value. At the heart of participation lies the notion of voice, not to be given or taken, but rather to be expressed freely and openly in a variety of spaces (informal and formal), and at different levels from the grassroots to the highest levels of decision-making.

The notion of "process" was never understood to be unconcerned with material outcomes or outputs, organizational efficiencies and effectiveness. Rather, the notion of process implied an ongoing exploration of issues sometimes causally linked, and other times seemingly random, but somehow always with the intention of progress. The idea of enabling a collective learning process for development therefore welcomes and requires a diversity of thought and perspective. It is never about a singular process that may encourage dichotomized thinking, but rather a constant and evolving approach that welcomes complexity and values diversity.

At the heart of the discussions around feedback loops, accountability, transparency, constituent voice and participation, is an appreciation that knowledge is being generated. A key question is therefore the degree to which this knowledge is being used to improve decision-making. Debates on local versus external knowledge, expert versus traditional knowledge, scientific versus cultural (religious/traditional) knowledge, etc., all begin to fall away when the co-constituents operate in a learning mode and exhibit a humble attitude of learning towards the development work they are learning to carry out together.

It is here that the case studies presented in this book find common ground. While diverse in their expression and experience, the case studies presented in this publication share a common acknowledgment that operating in a collective learning mode both stimulates and releases new capacities that benefit all of the co-constituents in different but entirely coherent ways.

Becoming co-learners

Each of the case studies in this publication sheds light on how organizations and their partners are learning to be co-constituents by reinventing their relationships with each other, by exploring new organizational arrangements that call for higher degrees of mutual accountability, and that celebrate the diversity of voices involved in the search for progress through development (Figure 1.1).

One quick illustration of this point is shown in Figure 1.2, which is also outlined in Chapter 10 that shares Synergos' story, and describes how creating a culture of "co-learning" only happens when efforts are made to:

- *build leadership capacity* to help people come together across divides and work as partners;
- *build collaborations* that involve and respect the contributions of all stakeholders;
- *focus attention* on systems thinking—identifying root causes, system blockages, the interrelated factors that affect outcomes and the resources needed for continuous improvement;
- *use personal reflection* to connect people to their core values—enabling them to be open-minded, open-hearted, trusting and most importantly open to learning. Success is more likely when there is a shift from "fixed mind-sets" to "growth mind-sets."

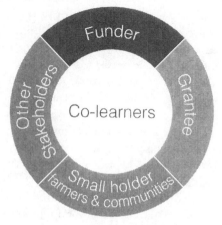

FIGURE 1.1 Constituents as co-learners

FIGURE 1.2 Creating a culture of co-learning

This book highlights eleven projects that, like Synergos, are actively engaged in different collective learning experiments that use feedback and accountability in new ways. Most of the case studies are grantees of the Gates Foundation and were selected because they had: (a) rich experience on the ground; (b) a track record of successful innovation; (c) a learning orientation; and (d) willingness to be candid about the challenges of implementing new learning paradigms and processes, including where they got it wrong and how they adjusted. Although we make reference to them, we have not included case studies of outright failures, an omission some readers may find problematic, especially when so much can be gained by reflecting openly and honestly on our failures. In point of fact, removing the fear of failure is an essential component of operating in a learning mode. Nonetheless, the development literature is overflowing with case studies of failure; therefore, we wanted to provide ideas and inspiration to donors and development practitioners as an antidote and as encouragement to those who wish to introduce collective learning processes within their organizations and among their partners.

Learning to participate

This book is not focused on headline-grabbing global issues, although its insights are relevant to solutions at many scales. Nor does it rely on carefully designed experiments to reveal clear causal determinants for success. Rather it describes a process of enabling collective learning in development initiatives. It is motivated by years of observing, participating and funding development projects that too often failed to deliver the sustainable impact that was intended.

What were new ideas thirty years ago, like the concepts of participatory development and systems thinking, are now accepted norms in development circles. The majority of professionals engaged in rural development accept the proposition that the people who participate in development should play an active role in defining, implementing and evaluating projects intended to improve their productivity and lives. We have observed that systematic participation and feedback can often contribute (although not always) to better-targeted, locally owned and hence more sustainable projects. Over the past few decades, various approaches and research methodologies have been introduced to transform top-down projects—in which farmers are the passive "recipients" of donor-driven programs—to approaches where farmers become the co-developers and co-owners of projects intended for their benefit. Ideal initiatives are where constituents (no longer beneficiaries) and implementing organizations work hand-in-hand in a joint learning process through which they become mutually accountable for results. Accountability then becomes omni-directional, because implementing organizations are accountable to farmers to deliver results and farmers and communities are accountable for the roles they have agreed to play.

This introductory chapter will explore some key elements of an emerging conceptual framework for sustainable development that arises out of the experience of practitioners enabling collective learning. It outlines some of the organizational barriers that produce inadequate feedback systems that essentially undermine accountability and transparency. Feedback, its agents, process, purpose and how it functions as a system are further explored. The chapter then presents technological and organizational innovations that can produce new dynamics resulting from collective learning that significantly change feedback mechanisms for the better.

Real participation and collective learning in rural development projects remain a difficult challenge in concept and practice, despite the insights gained through recent experience in the field. Donors like the Gates Foundation are geographically and culturally distant from rural communities in Africa and South Asia, and there are rarely easy ways to collect information and engage directly with constituents. Organizations receiving funding from donors, or grantees, whether in the public, private or NGO sectors, are ultimately more responsible to the donors who fund them than to the farmers they are supposedly serving.

Unlike the private sector where you go out of business if you don't listen to your customer, or government where you get voted out of office if you don't listen to your electorate, the international development enterprise lacks an equivalent feedback mechanism. If one wanted to design an accountability-averse system it could easily be modeled after the current development approach. Despite this disconnect, the development industry is replete with practitioners earnestly engaged in trying to generate new understandings about development that make a permanent, sustained and positive difference. These thoughtful practitioners typically work in very difficult environments, addressing the challenges of real accountability in two broad categories: (1) organizational barriers and (2) inadequate feedback/accountability systems and tools.

Organizational barriers

1 *Short time frames and funding cycles*: The development process is a notoriously difficult, complex and long-term effort. Practitioners often need to experience several cycles of success and failure before patterns emerge that can help organizations shape better programs or approaches. However most funding cycles are not long enough to permit such learning and when there is enough time most organizations don't have the feedback and learning processes in place to institutionalize or embed that learning throughout all levels of the

organization, let alone build and spread best practices with their partners and beyond. Project cycles are often three-to-five years in length and in many donor organizations staff are routinely moved after three years ensuring that all process history and knowledge gained will have to be rediscovered and relearned by the next program officer.

2 *Incentive systems*: Many grantees are incentivized against responding to farmers due to pressure from donors and others to: (a) show progress is "on track" and without problems; (b) show success in terms of short-term cycles rather than in terms of commitments to bigger socioeconomic and political changes; (c) keep costs down; and (d) not complicate already complex development work. There is very little reward for discovering the real problems that are blocking progress with a project and using this feedback to improve project impact. Some grantees simply don't want to know about complicated and/or ugly truths and are content to move on to the next funding cycle. In donor organizations incentives are often given to move money through a complicated, sometimes confusing system to meet annual goals, and are only weakly linked to long-term impact. On the other hand constituents need to be given ample opportunity to give feedback that will make a difference without fear of retribution. Unfortunately, these conditions are often not met on the ground and in the field. The traditional hierarchies, lack of education and imbalances of power can often make real bottom-up feedback next to impossible.

3 *Design–implementation accountability gaps*: Often the people tasked with designing a development intervention are different from the team tasked with its implementation. As a result, feedback and lessons learned from the implementation process are not systematically incorporated into the design of future development initiatives. Even where feedback is collected, organizations face challenges. How can they effectively use the information to adapt the project by re-conceptualizing ends and means and guiding decisions about organizational processes? To complicate matters, in instances where external evaluations are conducted, that knowledge may not find its way back into the macro or micro decision-making processes; project designers and implementers end up flying blind and therefore real learning simply cannot take place.

4 *Thematic "fads" in funding*: Grantees may be unable to act on their own indigenous and context-based learning and expertise when donors have abruptly moved on to different priorities.

Inadequate feedback/accountability systems and tools

1 *Reach/cost*: It is very expensive for grantees and implementing organizations to communicate regularly with constituents, like rural smallholder farmers, who tend to be geographically difficult to reach. Traditional surveys can cost several hundred thousand dollars and this limits their frequency and utilization.

2   *Representation*: Smallholder farmers include large populations with diverse economic, social, demographic, environmental, linguistic and behavioral conditions that make accurate representation difficult. Who represents the community in these kinds of circumstances? Given this complexity, what determines a robust feedback system is often ambiguous.

3   *Measurement*: Short-term gains are frequently more highly valued than longer-term change processes. Measurement approaches often focus on impact assessment, capturing material and technological improvements instead of values or behavior change (i.e. asking people who are intended to benefit from social change what they think about plans, performance and results). Measuring critical "accountability" and "sustainability" variables is typically difficult, in part because the factors that influence this type of project performance are hard to identify and analyze. A better balance between these material/technological improvements and the values or behavioral change implications needs to be struck.

The consequences of poor feedback systems and learning-averse organizational cultures include wasted effort and squandered resources, loss of good will and lost opportunities for empowerment. A few disheartening examples include the following:

- A large African NGO spent almost $1 million on baseline surveys that in the end were never used in their monitoring and evaluation (M&E) system.
- A research organization spent ten years developing a higher-yielding bean variety only to learn farmers did not want to grow it because women found that it took too long to cook.
- When offered extra funds to implement a monthly feedback system using mobile phones to conduct quick market research, an NGO turned down the offer because they didn't feel they needed to improve this aspect of their work. Recently this NGO's community projects collapsed because they were not meeting market demand and as a consequence failed to empower community leaders.
- One grantee whose work was extremely innovative and showed huge promise had their funding cut when their program officer was transferred.

Every development professional can add additional examples of development disasters to this list. The problems described above are not new, and a plethora of papers have been written about them. These obstacles interfere with inclusive learning and up to now have obstructed the capacity of development professionals, community leaders, government officials and businesspeople to unify their efforts. What is different now, however, is that technological and organizational innovations are today creating new opportunities that have the potential to overcome many obstacles.

Defining feedback and accountability

The terms feedback, accountability and collective learning appear quite frequently throughout this publication, and it may be useful to address each of these concepts in greater depth.

Feedback contributes to collective learning. It is multi-faceted and for this reason it may be helpful to distinguish three dimensions that help unpack the concept, namely (1) agents, (2) type and purpose, and (3) project stage.

1 *Agents in the feedback process*
Within rural development initiatives we typically identify four types of feedback loops between agents in the system (Figure 1.3). They include:

> *Donor–grantee*: Donors usually begin their interaction by identifying grantees that are expected to achieve a development objective. Given the power dynamics, grantees listen very carefully to the donor—who controls the money—and adjust their activities to ensure continued resource flows. Unfortunately, donors are typically less interested in listening carefully to their grantees because they do not think of themselves as being accountable to them. Honest feedback from grantee to donor is therefore difficult to obtain and often not appreciated.

> *Grantee–constituents*: Grantees or grant receivers are usually actively engaged with constituents (often referred to as beneficiaries) but the nature and quality of feedback vary dramatically depending on the organizational culture of the grantee and the capacity of cooperating communities to inwardly and outwardly manage their own affairs.

> *Donor–constituents*: This kind of feedback is very rare because it is difficult for donors to communicate directly with community-based beneficiaries, and grantees generally do not like the idea of unmediated feedback going directly to donors because such information can be misunderstood or reflect poorly on the project.

> *Development project–other stakeholders*: Development projects are part of a larger socioeconomic and political system and it is essential to pay close attention to feedback from boundary partners and external agents such as:

- consumers;
- competitive agents/market processes;
- political and social/civil society actors; and
- media systems.

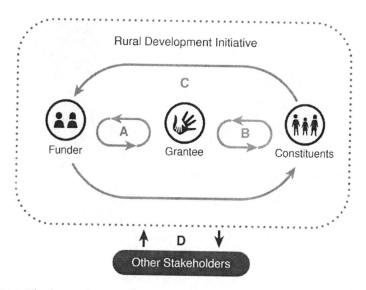

FIGURE 1.3 The four main agents and their feedback loops: funder, grantee, constituent, and other stakeholders

2   *Type and purpose of feedback*

Feedback comes in many forms and serves a variety of purposes. As illustrated in Figure 1.4, it is usually intended to:

> *Improve decision-making*: This consists of the feedback that helps project managers and participants arrive at adaptive decisions and provides information that allows grantees to take corrective action (e.g., farmers don't like the varieties being sold or they are not receiving market information in a timely manner). This is the kind of feedback that management needs to make good decisions and upon which good project performance depends.
>
> *Increase social capital*: In many cases, the most important effect of feedback is to build social capital[1] because it creates a sense of ownership and strengthens the constituent's sense of agency (self-determination), particularly if they see how their voice and participation in decision-making positively contribute to new knowledge that in turn leads to more successful outcomes. Positive feedback can also be used to encourage players and participants in the struggle for development. Such encouraging feedback is needed to counteract setbacks and contribute to creating a culture of encouragement that can mean the difference between success and failure.

Often the same feedback mechanism can serve both purposes, improving decisions and building social capital.

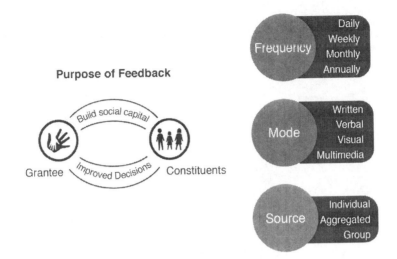

FIGURE 1.4 Types of feedback as distinguished by purpose, frequency, mode and source

Feedback systems can also be characterized by other attributes:

Frequency/timeliness: Feedback can occur in a range of time frames from daily to annual. In general real-time or near real-time feedback is most useful but often the most difficult to implement.

Mode: Feedback can take many communication forms including written, verbal, visual and multimedia. The most appropriate form depends on context, cost and purpose of the feedback.

Source: Is this from an individual, an aggregation of a number of individuals or does it represent a collective viewpoint from a defined group?

Follow-up: Feedback that is not followed up has minimal impact and can be damaging to long-term relationships.

3   *Stage in project lifecycle*
The types of feedback and the respective roles of agents within the development initiative can vary by the stage within the project:

Design/initiation: This stage usually takes a lot longer than expected and as a result some donors call it "the lost year." However, this is a misperception because the quality with which projects are designed and launched establishes culture and norms that ultimately determine the success or failure of the initiative.

Operation: Projects rarely unfold as they are first designed and envisioned. Development is an organic process occurring in highly dynamic environments and the ability to adjust to and learn from changing circumstances requires well-developed feedback systems and organizations willing to be flexible.

Evaluation: End project evaluation is rarely done in a way that fully includes all constituents. Furthermore, it is often done late and almost as an afterthought. The feedback on failed or lackluster projects is typically done to minimize failure and therefore is not very useful to future projects. If external evaluators are used, there often are additional challenges generated by cultural gaps in perception, difficulties of translation, and the authority and will to ensure adoption and acceptance of lessons learned.

With this preliminary overview as the starting point, one can start to visualize how feedback systems vary from project to project depending on culture, government, collaborators, implementation capacities of the different constituencies and willingness to operate in a learning mode. As illustrated in Figure 1.5, for example, critical feedback loops with important constituents are typically weak or missing at key stages of the initiative.

Traditional M&E systems clearly overlap with our definition of feedback systems and certainly when they are well designed and implemented they can contribute to healthy and productive collective learning. However, M&E systems are usually designed as a reporting mechanism for the donors and, because of the learning-averse cultures of many organizations and the lack of effective, timely and low-cost feedback tools, the impact on collective learning is usually weak. This is changing, however, as M&E systems become more advanced and address the organizational barriers to learning.

There is a growing body of literature and research on accountability, but for our purposes we will define it as the obligation of an individual or organization to account for its activities, accept responsibility for them and to disclose the results in a timely and transparent manner.[2] It also includes the responsibility for money or other entrusted property. In general accountability relationships overlap with the feedback loops illustrated in Figure 1.5.

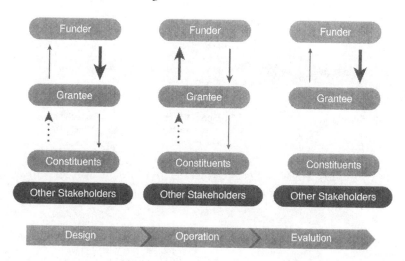

FIGURE 1.5 Traditional feedback loops with important constituents

Technological and organizational innovations

1   *The impact of new information technologies:* The exponential proliferation of new communication technologies now reaching even the most remote and poor areas of the planet is completely changing the cost structures of market research and project feedback mechanisms. As a result, the very nature of feedback and learning systems is being revolutionized. One simple example that illustrates this massive shift is shown in Figure 1.6.

2   *The design-thinking and organizational learning movement:* A vibrant community of practice is emerging around the application of design-thinking to development efforts (IDEO.org, Feedback Labs, etc.). New methodologies to create learning cultures in development organizations are today being actively experimented with, perfected and applied in the field (e.g. Synergos, Keystone).

3   *Big data informatics and predictive analytics:* Multiple and diverse flows of data create opportunities for predicting and learning about human behaviors under different conditions. Our ability to integrate and generate quantitative and qualitative inferences from this data can create insights about how to inclusively enrich and benefit large numbers of people.

These dynamics reinforce each other and are creating the potential for innovations that until recently have been impossible to even imagine let alone implement. As a result of a growing appreciation for collective learning in development, the potential positive impacts of these innovations can now be seen.

Feedback Tool	Sample cost	Time to collect & Produce report	Potential frequency in a project
Traditional paper survey - 1000 participants	$150,000	One month to collect, 3-6 months to analyze and report	Every 3 years
Tablet based survey	$80,000	One month to collect, 1 week to analyze and report	Every year
SMS based survey	$1,000	One day to collect, 1 day to analyze and report	Every month, week or even daily

FIGURE 1.6 Impact of new technologies on cost structures of market research and feedback mechanisms

Exploring innovations and alternatives

The first section of the book focuses on four case studies that illustrate the use of new information technologies in feedback and collective learning:

- *Digital Green* is an NGO in India at the cutting edge of using video-based agricultural extension to dramatically reduce the cost of reaching farmers with improved practices. Their approach has proved to be ten times more cost-effective than traditional extension. They have developed a system of collecting information down to the farmer level and using well-designed feedback systems to track progress in real time. The rapid evolution of their products and services reflects a high-frequency feedback system that enables rapid collective learning.
- *Grameen Foundation* and their Community Knowledge Workers program initiated in Uganda has pioneered the use of a mobile phone extension advisory service combined with trusted community members to provide another alternative to traditional agricultural extension.
- *Farmer Voice Radio*, a South African-based organization that initiated a radio consortium in four African countries that innovate with new forms of agricultural radio programs using the power of mobile phones to make the traditionally one-way media into a two-way interactive platform. Their focus and much of their learning have been on "baking in" sustainability right from the beginning as well as innovative ways of introducing course corrections that will prove useful to others.
- *Keystone Accountability* was set up in 2006 for the specific purpose of exploring and developing ways in which the views and experiences of those intended to benefit from development initiatives (the primary constituents) can meaningfully and systematically influence the way that programs undertaken in their name are designed, implemented, managed and evaluated. Their chapter cites an example in Ethiopia that tried to overcome the top-down, bureaucratic management behavior that seems to characterize government systems in general and turn the agriculture extension system into a much more "farmer-driven" service that responds dynamically to farmer needs. They also explore how this project tried to overcome the high levels of demoralization and frustration expressed by frontline extension staff and inculcate a responsive "performance culture" in the extension system.

The second section of the book highlights four cases studies of NGOs that are evolving new community engagement models that ensure farmers are the primary protagonists in rural development programs and that all of the stakeholders (co-constituents) get an opportunity to reimagine and define themselves as co-creators of their progress:

- *PRADAN* is one of the most experienced community development organizations in India and has done pioneering work with women's self-help groups among the poorest and most marginalized members of Indian society. Their methodologies focus on building a "sense of agency" and have proved to be transformative in multiple environments.
- *CARE*'s case study describes their Pathways to Secure Livelihoods Program that focuses on increasing poor women farmers' productivity and empowerment in more equitable agriculture systems in five countries, along with impactful ways of changing their own organizational culture to enable conditions to support women's empowerment.
- *One Acre Fund* works in East Africa building highly efficient and effective agricultural input supply chains. They adopt and innovate user-centric approaches to research and product development—starting with surveys, but moving rapidly into immediate "market testing" that creates products and services that meet the real needs of smallholder farmers.
- *IDEO.org* is the non-profit arm of one of the leading design firms in the world whose founder helped birth the human-centered design-thinking movement. Their chapter describes how they developed the human-centered design toolkit to assist grantees and other development actors to more effectively listen to and co-design with the constituents being served.

The third section of the book highlights three grantees that are using system-level approaches that work across regions and sectors, and which enhance collective learning:

- *Synergos* has worked for almost thirty years supporting initiatives that build collaborations between business, government, civil society and marginalized communities. Their chapter describes experiences in both Ethiopia and Namibia and the lessons learned in shifting mind-sets and behaviors in large bureaucratic organizations.
- *Farmer Organization Support Center for Africa* (FOSCA) is a program within the Alliance for a Green Revolution in Africa (AGRA) and works to build the capacity of farmer organizations to more effectively serve their members. Their chapter explores the concept of accountability and the inherent tensions in the competition for resources that characterize many development organizations. They illustrate their approach to creating alignment and supporting learning with a value chain base program in Mozambique.
- *Kenya Markets Trust* manages the Market Assistance Programme (MAP) which is a multi-donor-funded initiative that aims to reduce poverty in Kenya by making markets work for the poor. They describe how their approach maps out the system dynamics of a market and uses feedback loops to alter behavior and incentives in order to create a more inclusive market value chain.

Following the presentation of the case studies, the concluding chapter will offer some initial reflections on each of the three sections of the book. These reflections provide a synopsis of the case studies and some key areas of learning identified by the contributors. When seen together with other experiences, certain patterns, trends or commonalities appear. It is important to note, however, that while certain case studies have been chosen to illustrate reflections for each section, this does not preclude the possibility that the case studies have something significant to offer to enhance our understanding of the other sections as well.

The emerging connection of ideas and experiences leads into the penultimate section on Emerging Elements for Collective Learning in Development, which presents some of the common elements identified by the contributors at a reflection gathering held at the Gates Foundation in May 2014. These emerging elements, while not definitive, illustrate the commonality of seemingly separate paths of learning. The shared experiences and discoveries speak to the inescapable reality of our common humanity. The levels of convergence observable in the midst of such a diversity of actors using different methods, approaches and technologies in geographically dispersed areas of the planet, speaks to the ever greater levels of conceptual coherence gradually being achieved by co-learners around the globe.

At the reflection gathering it was evident that there was an obvious and intentional use of language and terminology by the participants that is not typical or universal in the development field. Much of the language stems from the participants themselves striving to use language that more accurately states what they are learning about. Also, ideas were being expressed with a certain degree of reservation with a specific concern to not overstate, embellish or jump to conclusions. The sense of humility in this regard was palpable, as the contributors recognized that they were only scratching the surface of some very deep issues, and didn't want to appear prescriptive or didactic in the manner in which they describe their work. It is this same sense of concern that prevents presenting the common elements as a defined conceptual framework—it is simply too early.

As this publication is more practitioner-based than academic, the "voice" of the contributors is not uniform, and no effort was made to restrict the mode of expression of each contributor.

The publication concludes with some final remarks and suggestions for future research.

Notes

1 Social capital also refers to: (1) relations of trust; (2) reciprocity and exchanges; (3) common rules, norms and sanctions; and (4) connectedness in networks and groups. Strong feedback loops have the potential to positively influence social capital in all its dimensions and to forge synergies amongst and between them.
2 Source: www.businessdictionary.com/definition/accountability.html#ixzz3622Clgk0 (accessed September 20, 2015).

2

DIGITAL GREEN

Enabling a collective process of learning in rural development

Rikin Gandhi, Shreya Aggarwal and Remya Sasindaran

SUMMARY

Digital Green is at the cutting edge of using video-based agricultural extension to reduce the cost of reaching farmers with improved practices. Their approach has proved to be ten times more cost-effective than traditional extension systems. This case study illustrates how they have pioneered a system of collecting information down to the farmer level and use well-designed feedback systems to track progress in real time. The rapid evolution of their product and services reflects a high-frequency feedback system that enables rapid collective learning. Their approach allows for iterative improvements in project design, operation and evaluation by capturing data and feedback from all its constituents including individual farmers. This data is recorded in a proprietary software called Connect Online | Connect Offline (COCO) that allows for near real-time analysis on open-access analytics dashboards. Analytical data is enhanced by face-to-face interactions to check data quality and verify adoption claims through spaces for reflective dialogue between farmers, community workers, partners and wider agricultural extension community. These meetings are facilitated monthly using participatory approaches.

Digital Green is gaining insights into how collecting and presenting data are not the same as using it. Collecting timely, appropriate and segmented data, which can be freely accessed through customized presentations and made sense of through regular engagement with clear incentives, can drive programmatic improvements.

Reflection through collaborative and participatory spaces builds trust, helps to align values and allows unequal power dynamics between collaborators to be examined. This in turn strengthens the quality of those relationships. Building a culture of learning, ownership and accountability by both institutionalizing systemic changes and building capacities can drive sustained impact. Greater equality and unity and diversity of voice promote mutual accountability and innovation when catalyzed through an infrastructure of networks, knowledge platforms and communities of practice.

Our caravan of vans rolled up to the field office on a strip of road flanked by farmsteads and a patchwork of fields on each of its sides. The gleam of our vans against the late morning sun made our arrival seem otherworldly. The vans that got lost in the traffic of the high-tech city of Bangalore just 50 kilometers away now seemed sufficiently novel to create a stir of attention. From the tinted windows of our vans, we caught the glances exchanged between the field staff and members of the community, as they got themselves organized for our visit.

I was eager to be part of this trip with the director of the small non-profit leading the intervention in the village, as it was one of my first to check out the action in the field, but the discussions that we had now seemed obvious. The field staff shared reports on the trainings that they conducted and members of the community described the practices that they had taken up as a result: from setting up vegetable gardens to conserving local seed varieties. There were, of course, challenges like a long dry spell and grievances of field staff not getting adequately paid; however, the conversation felt somewhat contrived.

We essentially heard what we wanted to hear. The field staff and community members had been part of this routine before. They weren't intentionally lying or withholding information, but they were complicit to a code in which community members showcase their work to field staff, field staff to their leadership, leadership of development organizations to donors and policy-makers. The incentive is often stronger to align accountability to those decision-makers at the top of this hierarchy rather than enabling farmers to achieve aspirations of their own.

Our approach

When we began to develop what would eventually become the Digital Green approach (Figure 2.1), we made a conscious effort to see how this dynamic could be flipped, a decision arrived at both by design and necessity. Initially incubated as a research project at Microsoft Research, our group of engineers and economists had little experience in grassroots-level agricultural development. As technologists, we could only serve as enablers for organizations and individuals already working in the field.

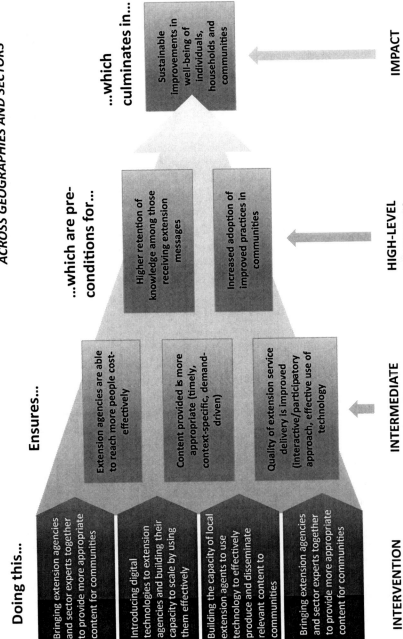

FIGURE 2.1 Digital Green's theory of change

The prevalent agricultural extension systems in most developing countries can be costly, slow and limited in effectiveness. Classic "training and visit" programs generally involve an extension agent traveling from village to village, door to door, and speaking with a select number of individuals in a village, usually males who own larger farms. Farmers may be slow to adopt external extension trainers' techniques due to several factors: external agents often do not possess location-specific knowledge; their visits can be infrequent and erratic; and their information rarely reaches farmers with the lowest yields, who often are women. Alternatives to the "training and visit" mode, such as farmer field schools, are believed to have a better impact but at a dramatically higher cost. Cost-effective solutions are rare.

At Digital Green, we combine technology with social organization. We partner with and train organizations that exchange agricultural technologies and techniques with smallholder farmers in parts of South Asia and sub-Saharan Africa. Farmers, our primary constituents, remain at the center of the intervention.

In the villages where we work, groups of farmers come together to view short how-to videos on agricultural practices. These videos are screened using battery-operated mobile projectors and are mediated by trained members of the community, who are mostly farmers themselves. These mediators answer questions, facilitate discussions to encourage group-based learning and motivate farmers to adopt new technologies. We have found that even more than technology, it is human mediation and group processes that drive learning and behavior change.

A separate cadre of members of the community are trained to produce videos. They create stories, and shoot and edit videos, which feature local farmers. The topics are identified with inputs from farmers and domain experts based on their needs and priorities. One of our early insights was the level of excitement among rural community members when they watched videos featuring peers. Before considering the economics of a practice, farmers would often first ask for the name of the individual featured in the video and the village he or she was from to determine its relevance. Compared with their past experience of receiving advice from extension agents which they often could not relate with, most farmers viewing the videos expressed their comfort and interest in receiving information from a source they could identify with. A small-scale controlled trial of our methodology suggested that it is ten times more cost-effective than the classical agriculture extension methods.

Initiating processes for collective learning

From our research-based inception, we realized that to be accountable to our mission, we needed to be accountable to the farmers that we serve. That is why Digital Green, from the very start, purposefully designed mechanisms to collect data and seek feedback from farmers at an individual level. Since data and feedback are especially useful when collected, presented and analyzed on a timely basis, we developed the near real-time system of data management.

In each village, we trained extension agents to collect data using paper-based forms that could be filled in at each farmer interaction at the time of producing a video, attending a video screening or adopting a practice. Simple forms, no longer than a page, were used to capture the details such as name and gender of individual farmers, their attendance during video disseminations, interests, questions and the change in their agronomic behaviors gauged through their adoption of new practices. Farmers can be quite vocal, sharing everything from the challenges they face on their farms to their entertainment preferences.

To analyze trends, track activities and assess our intervention outcomes, we needed to aggregate this individual feedback through a management information system. We developed a web-based application called COCO, which supports data entry even in locations where Internet connectivity is limited or intermittent.

BOX 2.1 DASHBOARD

Built on the COCO database, Digital Green's Analytics suite of dashboards provides near real-time information on field operations, performance targets and other metrics relevant to the organization. The system is freely available and accessible online. You can visit the Analytics dashboard at: www.digital-green.org/analytics/overview_module (accessed September 22, 2015).

Collection and entry of data are useless without its analysis and presentation being accessible to individuals who can reflect and be informed by it. We developed systems to visualize data on our open-access Analytics dashboards (Box 2.1) using tables and infographics showcasing monthly screenings, rates of adoptions, gender-wise participation and qualitative feedback on videos, viewed per geography, partner and time. This data helped assess the performance of partners and community workers, inform decision-making, and drive iterative improvements in content and programmatic processes. This programmatic data provides transparency among partner staff at state and national levels on the progress of activities in the field, while community feedback and adoption statistics for each video inform those involved in producing or exchanging content at district or block levels. Additionally, we have found that this open-access dataset can stimulate collaboration and, at times, healthy competition among partners reviewing the progress of peer organizations.

Our Analytics dashboards feature rich aggregate data, but we also realized the need to analyze the engagement of individual farmers with us. We developed Farmerbook (Box 2.2), an open-access site showcasing the timeline-based activity feeds of the videos that each farmer has watched, the questions they asked and the farming practices that they tried for themselves on a geo-located map. This data not only helps us validate the authenticity of the data through on-farm quality checks but also provides a mechanism for frontline extension agents and farmers to reflect on their own performance and that of their peers and to identify opportunities for potential collaboration and sharing. Since the idea of Farmerbook is

BOX 2.2 FARMERBOOK

Farmerbook is an open-access platform which displays detailed timeline-based activities of each farmer Digital Green works with along with the villages plotted on a digital map. The application highlights the integrated nature of the practices that individual farmers adopt on their fields as well as stimulates healthy competition among partners, village facilitators and community members through the sharing of performance data and community feedback.

Use of Farmerbook also supports transparency and accountability in existing extension systems and enables the development of non-monetary incentive structures among stakeholders participating in them through mechanisms such as leaderboards.

You can visit Farmerbook at: http://farmerbook.digitalgreen.org (accessed September 22, 2015).

to connect the seemingly impersonal statistical data on our Analytics dashboards with the faces of the real farmers behind them, the question of privacy also became important. That was addressed by seeking consent from all farmers engaged with Digital Green. We envision that with the spread of mobile technology and Internet access, farmers would soon be able to track their progress and see themselves with respect to one another on dynamically generated leaderboards using Farmerbook.

Through these systems, we have witnessed the development of an iterative cycle of knowledge creation and feedback exchange between those providing information and those receiving it. This break from the usual top-down approach to extension was making way for a platform in which those who typically make decisions—NGOs, government officials and researchers—could engage with farmers on a more individual level to include their feedback into programmatic decisions. From simply being the target of generic development messages, farmers are gaining a voice that can be heard.

Since data is only useful if we can trust its quality, a key focus has remained on quality assurance checks on the regularity and accuracy of data collection and entry through regular visits conducted by partners and our staff. Similar visits help maintain quality of videos, disseminations and adoptions when observed and verified with the help of simple forms that rank quality of activities. Identifying videos, screenings and adoptions through random selection ensures neutrality and prevents selection bias. We have found that discussing the observations with appropriate extension agents during the visit itself helps close the feedback loop and enables stakeholders to together make sense of the findings while also creating common benchmarks for quality.

At Digital Green, we have been finding ways to triangulate data received via COCO, quality assurance visits and monthly program monitoring site visits. Our head office initiates monthly calls with regional and partner teams based on consolidated findings from quality assurance observations to track specific issues and identify appropriate actions. Using such data to assess and, where appropriate, incentivize performance of video production teams and community mediators has also helped improve data quality and timeliness.

Learning: collecting, presenting and using meaningful data

Those who work closely with data know that collecting and presenting data are not the same as using data to inform programmatic decisions. Though we had developed our data management system to present appropriate, high-quality and timely data, we found that sometimes our partners and even our staff did not access this data at all.

With support from IDEO.org, we considered how capturing more meaningful and relevant data could provide insights that would better inform our decisions and those of our stakeholders. The design process involved a series of in-depth workshops, interviews and iterative prototyping with potential users among our stakeholder community. This process helped question some of our implicit assumptions of putting data into use, both on what is captured and what is used.

We found that there were cases where data was being captured unnecessarily, resulting in needless burden on partners, loss of interest and delays in data collection of up to two-to-three months. On the other hand, we also found that potentially useful data was lost or not reviewed. For example, some of the extension agents who would visit farmers' fields to record the practices that they had adopted from the video screenings would note the challenges that individuals faced while adopting practices and the innovations that some had made with them, but we had not included a designated place that could be used to capture this data in our existing forms. We are now working to streamline the forms that are used to capture data and are piloting forms that have approximately 20 percent fewer data points than before with no negative effect on project monitoring or evaluation. We also learnt that individual-level farmer feedback was not always necessary and that it could be more cost-effective and at times more insightful to capture collective feedback from extension agents.

In addition, we found that our extension partners who had limited experience with data could be overwhelmed by having to navigate through a series of search and navigation parameters on our Analytics dashboard to find an indicator that they were interested in. We found it critical to segment these views to the dataset for each stakeholder based on their specific interests and abilities to derive utility from them. Our partners and team members, for instance, have mostly used this data for administrative tracking, but we have seen that, given the richness of the data being captured, there is an opportunity for this data to better support a process of reflection and review by the extension agents who produce and screen videos and potentially even the communities themselves. We are now looking to generate curated, customized reports that address the specific needs and interests of each stakeholder including extension agents and farmers. We are also increasingly embedding in our trainings a way to build the competencies of our constituents in reading and making sense of these reports, while creating systems to engage with the findings focused towards follow-up.

Since we now engage with a much wider set of stakeholders that extends beyond extension agents and farmers, and now includes a combination of extension systems, research agencies, donors and the general public, we have sought to see how our data management can be leveraged to support each of these groups in areas that might extend beyond tracking the production and distribution of videos. For example, we are working with the Indian government's Ministry of Rural Development to customize COCO to capture and analyze data on the mobilization of self-help groups, bank linkages, recruitment of human resources and other initiatives.

Learning: reflective practice for strengthening relationships

Just as a collective learning process can be used to inform programmatic decisions, it can also be used to strengthen relationships within and between institutions. Strong relations in turn perpetuate a mutually reinforcing cycle of learning, especially when there exist collaborative and participatory spaces for reflection.

The Digital Green approach represents a combination of a top-down and bottom-up approach. Community members drive the content production and distribution processes; however, these activities are embedded within the operations of an existing extension system, which provides coordination and technical support to ensure that these efforts lead to positive outcomes. At the village level, the mediated screening of videos seeks to affect the agricultural practices applied by farmers. At an institutional level, the broader Digital Green approach seeks to affect the existing extension system of our partners.

Like any new practice, the changes that our approach introduces have a learning curve associated with their acceptance and integration with our partners. Unlike some systems that expect information and communication technology alone to deliver useful knowledge to marginal farmers, our approach has focused on amplifying the effectiveness of existing, people-based extension systems. These extension systems bring significant domain expertise and experience that can link information with the actions that farmers can take across an agricultural value chain. They also have trust already established among groups of farmers that they have helped organize and typically have a network of extension agents recruited to support their interventions. Our approach builds on these foundational interventions; however, it also brings about significant structural change within our partners. This includes aspects like systematizing the knowledge base of extension agents, regularizing schedules for training farmer groups, and a mechanism to capture data and feedback from individual farmers to inform the direction of program interventions.

When we began as a research project, we approached organizations that were willing to experiment with our idea. This was a necessary and useful first step to prototype and gain insights around issues like the type of individuals that should appear in the videos and the mode of distributing videos. We organized workshops to share the concept of our approach among our partners to build mindshare for it. Despite these steps, several of our early partners had an impression that this video-enabled initiative belonged solely to Digital Green. These groups initially considered any issue connected to videos as being the responsibility of Digital Green and had a limited sense of institutionalizing the end-to-end approach for themselves. Often, we would receive high-level interest for our approach among the senior leadership of our partner organizations. However, we also found it critical to get buy-in from the mid- and grassroots-level staff of these agencies, since they would be the ones to implement and benefit from the approach. We also sought to see how they could become not just adopters of the Digital Green approach but to also contribute, and even champion, its adaptation and evolution more broadly.

With growing demand for these exchanges, we broadened our collective learning agenda to expand beyond the voice of our primary constituents to include those of our partners, who had until then only used informal structures for feedback. We initiated a process of bringing together a variety of stakeholders to define a shared vision. We organized a series of workshops at multiple field sites: first with members of the farming community, then with the extension agents working with them and finally with staff members of our partners. In contrast to a typical stakeholder interview or survey, the aim of these workshops was to collectively reflect on the journey of our collaboration and the relationships between stakeholders, and to strategize the direction of the intervention. Role-playing, games and mapping exercises were used to make participants comfortable, build trust, avoid judgment and collectively reflect on feedback. Moderators were trained to be sensitive to inherent power dynamics and translators briefed to be precise, quick and accurate.

These exercises corroborated some of our early insights, such as the criticality of socializing content in the local context, and also revealed new ones, such as the limitation of relying on monitoring data alone to assess project performance. These discussions with stakeholders provided a richer, more holistic view on several issues, such as the interests of farmers, the growing aspirations of extension agents, and the flow of communication between us and partner staff.

To continue to develop our partnerships, we have committed to building our own team's capacity as relationship managers through an appreciation of concepts such as being of service, coaching and supportive supervision, and we are imbibing a shared vocabulary for creating safe spaces and active listening. Beyond these workshops, we are now developing survey tools to assess the health of our current partnerships as well as checklists to help identify new collaborators with a shared vision. This includes ensuring that we agree upon a common set of principles—in particular, localized content production, mediated dissemination, and data and feedback mechanisms—that guide our work while remaining open to learning and adaption. To stay accountable to our ever-increasing number of partners, we are also seeking channels to facilitate anonymous feedback and to learn from failures.

Learning: building a culture of learning, ownership and accountability

To strive for sustained impact, there is a need to build a culture of learning, ownership and accountability in organizations and their collaborators. One way is to strengthen relationships. We have found that both institutionalizing systemic changes and building capacities can also do this.

At Digital Green, we've developed our team to optimize collective learning. With our initial partners, we embedded members of our staff in their offices to provide handholding support to drive the project forward. We found that this often limited partners' ownership towards the approach and inhibited cross-learning. In response, we restructured ourselves by establishing regional offices to provide the necessary orientation and backstopping support to our partners in a particular geography from an appropriate distance. We found that this approach not only increased the level of ownership of our partners, but that these offices also served as centers for exchanging learning among our partners and even members of our own team. As we established regional offices to support our partners, we also set up directorates within the team to focus on aspects of quality assurance, research and learning, and training that could cut across all of our programs. Like most organizations, our team comes together through a variety of meetings. As we have grown, we have found that there is a need to give dedicated space for reflection and learning so we now set aside one day every month for the organization to come together to do so in a conscious manner.

As our team has grown, there has been an increasing need to create neutral spaces to air concerns, provide feedback and seek direct guidance from different levels of the organization. This was felt deeply during a recent retreat in which the number of team members who had joined in the last year outnumbered those who had been with the organization longer than that. We have sought to institutionalize an open-door policy, dedicated weekly open-house slots with senior management and set up a web-based forum for anonymous feedback from the staff.

We have also found that enhancing the confidence and skills of staff, partners and constituents in an appropriate manner is key to developing a culture of learning, ownership and accountability. Indeed, one of Digital Green's central roles is to build capacities. Rather than training farmers directly, we train extension agents involved in the extension systems of our partners to produce videos, mediate group screenings, and capture data and feedback. For those involved in facilitating the screening of videos, this training includes a combination of technical aspects, for instance, handling a projector, and softer elements, such as how to ask open-ended questions and the importance of maintaining eye contact with a group. For a long time, we contended with the question of how to build the capacity of video producers and mediators so that they feel accountable and responsible to their peers in their respective communities.

Initially, we emphasized the building of their technical competencies. Though extension agents would learn how to operate a projector or how to perform a particular farm practice, we found that they did not always see how those skills could enable them to become agents that could catalyze change more broadly in their own community. We found that some would combine their existing extension activities, like farmer field schools and on-farm demonstration programs, with the video screenings, while others focused solely on disseminating videos. Many of these individuals had not had an opportunity to reflect on their role within the community and its aspirations for development. These insights emerged from conversations that we facilitated between some of our partners and the extension agents they work with to map the history of their relationships and the vision they had for themselves. This exercise essentially enabled these extension agents to see the set of tasks that they were trained on and incentivized for, in the context of a bigger picture that they could help define.

Based on these preliminary discussions, we sought to see how elements of this reflection process could be institutionalized. We modified our training program to provide time and space for extension agents to deliberate on their understanding of their current role as well as their vision for their communities. We designed activities to help participants link the change they wanted to see in their community with the individual impact that they could help trigger. In one such activity, groups of trainees follow a set of instructions to complete a task that are communicated either orally, through a document or via a video. By enabling extension agents to see for themselves the support that technology can provide, we have found that they developed a greater sense of ownership for utilizing it to complement their existing work on a day-to-day basis.

We also found that extension agents were motivated to work to improve the welfare of their fellow community members when they could visualize how this could tangibly take place. With this in mind, more sessions were added to enable extension agents to reflect on the fact that they are not just channels for routing messages to communities, but they are also active agents who can facilitate, probe and encourage their peers to take up improved agricultural practices through discussion and debate. The training also encourages them to reflect on how the quality of the video and the manner in which its screening is facilitated can impact the response and ultimate adoption of the practices by farmers in their community. We have found that extension agents that have participated in these exercises have felt empowered as thought leaders within their own communities.

The re-conceptualized training program for extension agents has also translated into a change of perceptions among the farmers that they work with. Extension agents who have undergone our training sessions listened more, judged less and were more inclusive in group discussions compared to those involved in earlier programs. The farmers also felt that their point of view was increasingly heard and understood, and their questions were being answered. For many farmers, this represented the first time in a development intervention in which their feedback was proactively requested and responded to.

To further improve trainings, we have started capturing data through post-training tests, feedback forms and trainer-to-trainer observations, which are analyzed through an online system for tracking the performance of trainers.

Learning: catalyzing voices through networks and knowledge platforms

As the scale of our approach expands, we have become increasingly conscious about our role as a facilitator in bringing together a disparate set of stakeholders toward building a shared vision for improving the lives of rural communities. We have found that we can serve as facilitators to build an infrastructure of networks, knowledge platforms and communities of practice that promote equality, unity and diversity in voice.

For instance, we found that we could serve as a catalyst to link agriculture research and extension so that the messages disseminated to farmers return sustained, positive value. In the state of Bihar, we partnered with an NGO, Action for Social Advancement (ASA), which promotes a variety of sustainable agricultural practices. Around the same time, the International Rice Research Institute was working on a large-scale program to improve grain production through the Cereal Systems Initiative for South Asia (CSISA). CSISA had developed a package of practices that had shown success in the field. ASA, however, expressed reservations in taking this information directly to the farmers that they were working with.

We had to develop a process to avoid undermining the voices of both CSISA and ASA by leveraging both ASA's expertise and experience of working with communities and the latest technologies and practices that CSISA had identified. We facilitated a process for CSISA to review the prevalent practices followed by farmers as well as the ones promoted by ASA to identify areas where CSISA's expertise would represent an improvement or fill a gap. Next, CSISA showcased the utility of their practices by adapting and demonstrating them on the fields of farmers that ASA was already working with. This approach respected the existing practices of farmers and ASA's interventions, ultimately increasing ASA's ownership to produce videos on the practices that CSISA introduced.

One of the practices CSISA recommended sought to address a concern that farmers expressed on not having adequate mechanisms to properly store grain and seeds. We worked with ASA, with support from CSISA, to produce videos on the use of "super bags," which could be used for safe storage. As the practice was shared more widely, on review of farmer feedback in our data management system, we learned that the video did not precisely answer where farmers could purchase super bags, how much they would cost or what the precise benefits would be. At the same time, another group of farmers wondered whether the super bags, which were designed for protection against insects, would also be robust protection against rodents, which they perceived as a greater menace. Such feedback helps inform the production of new videos to address frequently raised issues. In this case, it also informed CSISA's research agenda, and the team began a process of identifying an alternative solution, thus closing the loop to the iterative cycle of knowledge creation.

Feedback from farmers themselves cut through the rhetoric of ideologies that often hamper action in agricultural development and engendered a sense of humility by working from the perspective of farmers. For us, at Digital Green, this experience also served to remind us that although we could serve as a facilitator to bring organizations together, our partners would ultimately need to drive this process forward to create long-term impact.

As we grow, we are keen to enable the process of building networks and shared learning in a manner that supports the unique interests of each stakeholder while ensuring that these partnerships are mutually edifying in nature. This includes, for instance, linking the extension agents that graduate from our training programs, the extension and research partners, and the donors and policy-makers that we work with to learn and share with one another. We are also building networks with the wider extension community and the general public. With the increasing coverage and bandwidth of telecom networks, we are developing an online–offline courseware platform not only to engage researchers, extension professionals and farmers to view and comment on videos but also to drive greater transparency and accountability for the knowledge and data being exchanged. We are also developing a virtual training institute, a resource for training extension agents using videos. This has the potential of building a culture in which the same approaches that are used to exchange practices among farming communities can also be used to develop a community of learning among extension agents.

We have also helped constitute communities of practice, both within Digital Green and with our partners, to reflect on the variety of ways in which our approach supports the efforts of each stakeholder.

Conclusion

The Digital Green approach facilitates shared learning in agriculture. To some extent, that can be attributed to our focus on enabling processes for collective learning across our organization and our partners.

Looking back at our journey, we have made some progress in the use of data and feedback and successfully emphasized the need for reflective dialogue between key constituents. This to us is evident through our increasing ability to take informed decisions that account for the voices of all stakeholders while strengthening relationships.

Despite these successes, there is still substantial room to develop a systemic culture of learning and create platforms and networks for sustained knowledge exchange among all of the stakeholders that we engage with. As we go forward, we are confident that only by institutionalizing our core values of humility, excellence, accountability, empathy and integrity can we continue to learn with the ultimate aim of enabling every individual to live a life of dignity (Box 2.3).

BOX 2.3 DIGITAL GREEN AT A GLANCE

Digital Green is a non-profit organization headquartered in India and the USA, which promotes the use of participatory videos developed by, of and for rural communities to exchange good agricultural practices to drive improvements in productivity and well-being.

Founding date:	2008
Annual budget 2015:	$7m
Countries of operations:	India, Afghanistan, Ethiopia, Ghana, Niger and Tanzania
Current number of staff:	100
Videos produced:	3,765
Villages reached:	7,826
Farmers engaged:	680,797

Source: Digital Green Analytics dashboard, July 2008 – July 2015.

LEARNING SUMMARY

Digital Green values the process of collective learning to make iterative improvements in project design, operation and evaluation by capturing data and feedback from all its constituents including individual farmers.

Processes and tools for feedback:

- In each village, we collect individual farmer details, attendance, expressed interest, adoption of videos and questions at each of the weekly or fortnightly interactions during screenings and adoption verifications through paper-based forms.
- We record this data in a software called COCO which is analyzed in near real time as per geography, partner and time visualized on open-access Analytics dashboards.
- We assess quality of activities and performance of extension agents through monthly observations of randomly selected videos and screenings, checks on data quality and verification of adoptions.
- We develop spaces for reflective dialogue between farmers, community workers, partners and the wider agricultural extension community through facilitated monthly meetings and participatory workshops.

Lessons learnt:

- Collecting and presenting data are not the same as using it. Collecting timely, appropriate and segmented data which can be freely accessed through customized presentations and made sense of through regular engagement with clear incentives can drive programmatic improvements.
- Reflection through collaborative and participatory spaces can help build trust, align values and account for power dynamics between collaborators in development and in turn strengthen relationships.
- Building a culture of learning, ownership and accountability by both institutionalizing systemic changes and building capacities can drive sustained impact.

Equality, unity and diversity in voice can promote mutual accountability, innovation and complementarity when catalyzed through an infrastructure of networks, knowledge platforms and communities of practice.

3

GRAMEEN FOUNDATION AND LEARNING WITH COMMUNITY KNOWLEDGE WORKERS

Whitney Gantt

SUMMARY

The Grameen Foundation, through its Community Knowledge Worker (CKW) program, has pioneered a model that combines mobile-enabled advisory services with networks of trusted community members to complement traditional agricultural extension systems.

Grameen Foundation's CKW concept, in which a network of village-level farmer intermediaries are equipped with mobile phones, enables the flow of information between farming communities and research organizations, government extension agencies, buyers, NGOs, and other groups working with farmers. The model described in this case study creates a dynamic, two-way feedback loop between farmers and the organizations serving them and enables sector-wide learning.

The use of mobile devices within last-mile agent networks promotes participatory, iterative, real-time dialogue between development stakeholders and farmers, a fundamental component in enabling a collective learning process. Establishing feedback loops alone is rarely sufficient to spur action or ensure accountability for the information exchanged. It is also critical to build analytic capacity to derive meaning from feedback and to develop the institutional systems and incentives to ensure that learning leads to action.

Undoubtedly, collective learning requires bidirectional feedback channels. Building these channels to facilitate dialogue with farmers was just the beginning. Only through multiple cycles of learning and, admittedly, some failure along the way, did the Grameen Foundation gain insight on how to develop the organizational capacity needed to consistently derive meaning from the feedback channels created and ensure that the unique insights that the CKW model enabled translated into improved services for farmers.

Introduction

In the summer of 2008, Grameen Foundation received a call from the Bill & Melinda Gates Foundation inviting us to come over from our Seattle offices for a whiteboarding session. The goal was to learn from our efforts using technology to reduce poverty and to brainstorm about how mobile phones could be employed to improve the delivery of agricultural services to poor farmers. Our hypothesis was that farmers could use mobile phones to create dynamic two-way feedback loops between the communities they lived in and the organizations providing services to those communities. We stipulated that these feedback loops would enable farmers to articulate their needs directly to agricultural organizations in the public and private sectors. These feedback channels would help bridge the research–extension divide, fostering an ongoing dialogue between farmers and organizations working in agricultural development.

In the collaborative sessions that ensued, we discussed how mobile technology might be deployed to address "last-mile" challenges in agricultural extension, including high agent-to-farmer ratios, the difficulty of providing regular outreach in remote areas, and the high-cost, low-accountability nature of the traditional one-way training and visit model. We hypothesized that mobile technology could dramatically increase the viability of reaching remote, off-the-grid communities, improve the cost-effectiveness of interacting with farmers regularly, and provide a channel for much-needed feedback, allowing farmers not only access to accurate, up-to-date information but also a channel to articulate their challenges and priorities. Speaking with other agricultural extension practitioners, our staff, and partners on the ground, we evaluated what type of model would best facilitate farmer voice. Ensuring farmer participation and promoting a two-way interchange with farmers became fundamental principles of the model that emerged.

At the time we began these discussions, we had been working in the mobile-for-development space for six years. In 2002, we had launched Village Phone in Uganda, a business-in-a-box in which micro-entrepreneurs offered calls and SMSs for a fee to those who didn't own a phone or have airtime. We had sold our stake in the Village Phone joint venture in 2006 after it was established as a profitable business line of a major telecom company. We were also developing five SMS-based information services in agriculture, health, and markets in collaboration with Google and a major telecom company in Uganda. Through this work, we had seen that mobile technology had huge potential to be leveraged as a tool in international development. We were also getting our first glimpse of the importance of thinking about what types of individuals could serve as effective intermediaries to help make mobile phone-based information services discoverable, usable, and relevant. We understood from these early experiences in Uganda that the technology was the easy part; ensuring that the technology would actually be used, and that its use would lead to beneficial outcomes for poor farmers, posed a greater challenge. Specifically, we grappled with how to increase the accessibility of agricultural extension, improve extension service quality, and make the entities serving farmers more responsive to their needs and more accountable for results.

With these goals in mind, we developed the CKW concept, in which a network of village-level farmer intermediaries would be equipped with mobile phones and would use these phones to facilitate the flow of information between farming communities and research organizations, government extension agencies, buyers, NGOs, and other groups working with farmers. The CKW, we hypothesized, would be critical to the functioning of this feedback loop. As members of farming communities, the CKW would help introduce farmers to mobile information services, teach them how to use the services, contextualize information, and ensure that the information was accessible—even if the farmers weren't literate, couldn't speak English, or didn't have a phone or airtime. The CKWs would play an equally important role in gathering data on farmers' needs and transmitting that information to agricultural organizations. To complete the two-way feedback loop, we would also have to develop partnerships with the actors providing services to farmers. Finally, we recognized that we would need to develop a business model to incentivize the CKWs to provide services over time. Given the focus on monitoring and evaluation in the development sector, we hypothesized that we could sell data collection services to a range of entities. Offsetting the costs of providing extension services, the revenue could then be used to remunerate the CKWs.

The CKW model

Years of research have documented the benefits of using an inclusive approach to extension in which farmers are active participants in designing, delivering, and critiquing extension. Using insights from this research we established a channel for farmer voice, recruited farmers to extend information, and facilitated linkages between farming communities and agricultural organizations. Not surprisingly, collective learning emerged as a fundamental component of the model, with a multitude of actors using the CKW channel to communicate with farmers and learning from these interactions to address farmer needs.

As seen in Figure 3.1, the CKW theory of change articulates this learning cycle. The cycle begins by engaging communities to select a farmer who will serve as the village change agent, occupying the center of the model. Next, the CKW collects baseline data to better understand farmers, including their adoption of sound agricultural practices. This data then informs how information services are developed and targeted to farmers. Ongoing monitoring and evaluation efforts are used to track farmers' feedback on service value and to monitor how farmer behavior changes. Finally, farmer feedback is analyzed to design and deliver new and improved services.

The evolution of the CKW model: from pilot to expansion

Validating the model

After developing the CKW concept, the next step was to test the model's potential to deliver value to poor farming communities in Uganda. We embarked on

Targeted information services and technical assistance

1. Regular CKW visits and group training
2. Menu-based reference guides
3. SMS and voice message curriculum
4. Video demos
5. Real-time, location-based advice and information on prices and weather
6. Radio programming

Farmer profiles and farm management plans

1. Poverty and food security assessment
2. Farm characteristics
3. Production practices
4. Certification readiness evaluation
5. Access to finance and financial practices

Community Knowledge Worker

Regular data collection and monitoring

1. Good agriculture practice adoption tracking
2. Farm management plan monitoring
3. Production and quality tracking
4. Certification compliance monitoring
5. Sales tracking

Analytics for targeting services, mid-course correction, and transaction facilitation

1. Monitoring and evaluation
2. Agent performance management
3. Production forecasting
4. Certification tracking
5. Output aggregation
6. Product sourcing and traceability

FIGURE 3.1 CKW learning cycle

an intensive, six-month pilot in which we recruited 40 CKWs in two distinct cultural, linguistic, and agro-ecological zones. Each month we prototyped a new information or data collection service with the CKWs and farmers. We innovated rapidly, co-designing and deploying the services with the CKWs. On a monthly basis, we solicited feedback from farmers, CKWs, and partners concerning the value and relevance of the information services, the usability of the technology, and the utility of the data. During this period, we had fast iteration cycles in which we tested rough concepts as opposed to robust products, trialed multiple mobile devices and channels, and relied heavily on the qualitative feedback from CKWs, with whom we remained in constant contact. We responded quickly to feedback. For example, we eliminated basic phones and SMS-based data collection when we realized that smartphones' utility and value far outstripped that of basic phones once we factored in the cost of SMS data transmission. We experimented broadly, relying not only on the feedback we gathered from farmers but also on our own observations as to farmers' usage of different mobile channels and their demand for different information topics.

It was a period of intensive learning. Initially, we harbored our fair share of doubts. In our first training we focused on helping CKWs learn how to use a mobile phone. Some CKWs had never owned a phone; other older CKWs could barely read the screen because they didn't have reading glasses. The CKWs' hands were weathered by working in the field, meaning that they, in their own words, had "big thumbs" that made the error rate typing on tiny keyboards high. Despite fears that because many CKWs could barely send a text message, they would never master the phones' more complex functionality, the CKWs quickly proved us wrong.

Early in the pilot, we hosted a group of leaders and donors in the field and invited CKWs to discuss their experiences. As we began the discussion, the visitors took out their cameras and started taking pictures; the CKWs, in response, took out their phones and began taking photos of the visitors. At this point, it had already become evident how comfortable the CKWs had become with their phones; for example, many had downloaded additional applications, one regularly filmed church services for the sick and elderly, and another bought a projector that he connected to his phone to create a village movie hall. The CKWs had independently adapted the technology to create additional value. Watching the CKWs and the visitors filming each other was an ironic reminder of our innate ability to learn and our natural tendency to innovate.

In addition to initial doubts about the CKWs' ability to master new technology, we wondered whether farmers would find the information useful, whether they'd trust CKWs, and whether the data CKWs collected would be accurate enough to convince organizations to pay for data collection. Within the short pilot, each doubt was refuted. For example, working with the Institute for International Tropical Agriculture and a national research body, we tested a diagnostic survey that enabled CKWs to help farmers identify which banana disease they had present on their plantation and use that diagnosis to teach farmers how to control the disease. Farmers found the diagnostic surveys and disease control information so useful that CKWs had to travel outside their sub-counties to meet farmer demand. Over a period of two months, 38 CKWs collected 2,991 geo tagged surveys with disease photos. Follow-up visits and lab tests revealed that CKWs generally accurately diagnosed the disease correctly using the diagnostic survey but misestimated incidence, likely because of their reliance on farmer reporting. The data gathered was compared with similar data collection activities and the collection process was found to be roughly one-tenth of the cost. The combination of these findings suggests that when overseen by official research bodies that ensure quality control, CKW community disease surveillance may be a cost-effective complement to official monitoring efforts to identify outbreaks early.

At the same time CKWs played an important role in educating farmers on prevention and control recommendations for the different diseases and provided important insights into farmer knowledge and behavior. For example, data collected via CKW surveys illustrated that 43 percent of farmers had never heard of Panama disease despite its prevalence in Uganda and that farmers often confused the symptoms of banana bacteria wilt and Panama disease. In addition, surveys showed that the methods for controlling banana bacterial wilt, which has had a devastating impact on farmer livelihoods in some parts of Uganda, were not understood by farmers and that the easiest control method, removing male flower buds to prevent insect transmission, was often not being used or was being conducted in a way that spread the disease to other plants through the use of non-sterilized tools.

Despite our initial doubts, these encouraging results boosted our confidence about the model's fundamentals. Due to the pilot's iterative nature and small scale, we had the ability to be highly responsive to farmer feedback delivered via the model. As we moved to scale the program, we had to make major shifts to formalize the feedback loops the CKW model enabled. Although it was much more difficult to capture and act on that feedback at scale, we continued to use the feedback captured to adapt program design, and, with time, we internalized the learning to make modifications to deepen the value farmers received.

Scaling the model

During the scale-up of the program in Uganda, we realized a number of achievements that further validated the CKW approach. For example, over four years we deployed 1,300 CKWs who generated more than 1.5 million interactions with farming households, proving the ability to scale and setting the CKW approach apart from the many ICT-for-development pilot projects in the sector. We developed a robust set of mobile tools, delivered over multiple channels, that we offered to development partners. We responded to farmer information demands by building out our content base, eventually covering 58 farming enterprises (i.e. crops, livestock) and providing market prices at more granular levels than other providers. In addition, a wide range of industry clients commissioned CKW data collection. There was also substantial demand for services by extension organizations and farmers. In total, over a four-year scale-up period, we generated $1,108,085 in earned revenue through our CKW extension and data collection services.

Most importantly, we saw positive indications that CKW services could effectively influence farmers' adoption of good agricultural practices and improve their price realization. The International Food Policy Research Institute conducted an evaluation of CKW services, finding a 17 percent increase in farmer knowledge of best practices, a 22 percent increase in price realization in maize, and a 34 percent increase in access to extension services. In partnership with Palantir Technologies,[1] we also performed internal analyses of dairy farmers served by CKWs under our partnership with a consortium of dairy-related NGOs and found a positive correlation between farmers' adoption of best practices and usage of CKW services.

The challenges of scaling-up and implications for learning

Although these results were encouraging, we realized that we were receiving feedback that suggested new opportunities to deepen the model's value. Equipping village-level intermediaries with mobile devices did create dynamic, two-way feedback loops, but we found less-than-anticipated gains in accountability and improvements in our own and our partners' service delivery. Internally, we acted on feedback to improve our information services and to refine the CKW operating model. However, we did not make more substantial modifications to deliver greater value to farmers and partners as quickly as we hoped. This was in part because the necessary changes required substantial shifts in our strategy, and in part because we did not initially have the all the pieces in place to link insights to action. We also recognized that in some cases we were not listening to what the feedback was telling us.

With time, we gained insights on what changes we needed to make to ensure that we were learning from our efforts and maximizing the value we were delivering. As the quantity and sources of data increased, we needed to invest in more powerful analytic tools—and more skilled data analysts—to sort through the data and extract meaning. We needed to simplify the data and make it more accessible through automation and visualization and we needed to ensure it was embedded in our own processes, as well as those of our partners, so that we could act upon it. We also needed to shift our approach to working with partners from providing turnkey solutions to embedding the technology and the CKW network within their businesses. In addition, we needed to adjust our operational model and organizational structure to promote greater responsiveness to farmer needs and increased accountability to our partners and donors. The feedback and results we saw during the initial scale-up period also made it clear it was time to go back to our strategy and evaluate the impact we were delivering, how we could maximize it, and the importance of measuring and proving our impact as a precursor to scaling and sustaining the model. We used the lessons from our successes and failures during the scale-up period to improve our accountability for results, refine our strategy, modify our approach in Uganda, and design initiatives in new geographies.

Expanding the model

Expanding the model to new geographies provided a number of opportunities to adapt and improve our model. The agility offered by again being in pilot mode, without aggressive sustainability and scale targets, allowed us to test new service components. In Kenya, Grameen Foundation worked with a local microfinance institution and an agricultural NGO, to adapt the CKW model to deliver an e-Warehouse solution designed to mitigate smallholders' dependence on seasonal cash flows, which force farmers to sell when prices are lowest. E-Warehouse is a virtual warehouse receipt-lending and bulk-buying platform that enables farmers to use their stored grain as loan collateral while assisting them to maintain the quality of their stored grain at the farm, group, or village level. Farmer groups are also able to bulk and sell their grain through the e-Warehouse solution, which provides payment processing to individual farmers via mobile money or directly into farmer bank accounts. CKWs register farmers in the system before the season begins and then provide training on good agricultural practices, post-harvest handling, and localized storage techniques throughout the growing season to increase productivity. Following these practices reduces the risks of harvest spoilage that deter lenders from providing financing to farmers. CKWs also provide information and education on loan products. At harvest time, CKWs visit registered farmers and complete a harvest survey which determines the loan amount that individual farmers are eligible to receive—equal to 50 percent of their crop value at current market prices. These loans smooth out farmers' incomes, allowing the farmers to hold grain until they can fetch higher prices.

In Latin America, we have used learning from what worked and didn't work in the original CKW program in Uganda, to deliver three solutions that leverage the CKW model and mobile tools. In our Cafeteros Connectados (Connected Coffee Farmers) program, we rolled out a network of CKWs with a targeted mandate to drive productivity increases, promote Fairtrade certification and Starbucks' CAFE Practices verification, and improve quality. Partnering with Starbucks and coffee producer cooperatives in Colombia and Guatemala, we profile cooperative members (as shown in Figure 3.2) and then use the needs surfaced during profiling to help producers develop farm management plans. These plans help farmers get on track for certification schemes and identify ways that farmers may adopt better practices to boost productivity. In addition to targeting producers and assisting cooperatives to deliver more effective technical assistance, Cafeteros Connectados aims to deliver value up the value chain by increasing the visibility of coffee production levels, quality, and certification compliance among buyers, exporters, and other key market players.

In Colombia, we also work with a horticulture association, which sells 77 different products to six supermarket clients, each of which has its own quality standards and packaging requirements. On a daily basis, the association consolidates orders for each crop from the grocery stores and sends the orders to their farmers. There is frequently a mismatch between supply and demand, and produce that does not

LAC Farmers Details Detail

| Edit | Delete | Clone |

▽ Información básica

Image

Farmer Code   3144597

▽ Perfil de productividad

Total Farm Area	4.00
Coffee Planted Area	4.00
Variedades	Castillo, Colombia, otro
Productivity	2829.25
Production	11317.0
Certifications	C.A.F.E. practices

FIGURE 3.2 Producer profile of a coffee farmer in Colombia

meet quality standards is rejected. As a result, farmers miss the opportunity to sell more of their crops and lose revenue on the rejected produce. The association performs the ordering, fulfillment, and reconciliation manually using pen and paper, whiteboards, and by calling farmer leaders who then call farmers in their network to fill the orders. Given these inefficiencies, it takes farmers weeks to get paid. It is also difficult for the association to expand its farmer base because it doesn't have a clear picture of fluctuations in supply and demand for each crop or knowledge about the individual farmers who supply produce. To address these challenges, Grameen Foundation worked with farmers and the association to design a mobile sourcing solution. Working closely with association staff, we digitized sourcing processes and equipped farmer group leaders with mobile devices. Farmer leaders now use the mobile device to view and fulfill orders, track farmer contributions by crop and grocery store chain, reference quality requirements, and order packaging materials.

Finally, we work with a government partner in Colombia, MANA, which focuses on improving food security and nutrition for close to 30,000 of the poorest households in the region. In this case, the intermediaries are managed by government contractors and provide inputs and training on how to establish backyard gardens and how to improve household nutrition. The intermediaries use mobile devices to register households, track the delivery of inputs, log trainings, and provide information on agricultural techniques and nutrition practices. They also use mobile phones to monitor food security and track household food consumption. The government uses the system to manage the performance of its contractors and their intermediaries, evaluate which interventions are delivering the most value, link program recipients to other government programs, and monitor how household nutrition is changing over time.

Leveraging mobile phones to enable feedback loops

Our experience with the CKW program has demonstrated that mobile phones provide a highly appropriate and effective tool for reaching more farmers at the last mile with far greater frequency than possible via traditional extension methods. The mobile channel has also enabled us to capture farmer feedback on a regular basis. In the CKW program, we used the mobile phone to engage communities in providing feedback via three primary channels: (i) mobile surveys; (ii) a real-time, two-way feedback application called Pulse; and (iii) a field force management application that enables Grameen Foundation and partner organizations to track field agent performance. In addition, we conducted analyses on usage statistics of information services including a mobile reference guide called CKW Search, SMS campaigns, and our farmer call center. These feedback channels and tools are outlined in Table 3.1.

Farmer registration is one of our most important tools for capturing feedback and has been administered by CKWs to the over 200,000[2] farmers we reach today in Uganda—an achievement that would have been cost-prohibitive using most other channels. The registration form asks questions designed to assess the probability that a household is below international and national poverty lines using Grameen Foundation's Progress out of Poverty Index tool and to evaluate food security. It also captures basic farm characteristics, such as farm size and primary enterprises, and details about individual farmers, such as gender and age. Capturing this data allows for market segmentation and needs assessment oriented toward different groups, such as the very poor or women-headed households. As a result, the farmers we serve are visible as individuals with specific needs. This is a substantial and important development, as the rural poor are too often regarded as a single, generic market even though they may constitute 80 percent of a developing country's population.

We also use mobile forms to conduct annual farmer surveys, using feedback from these surveys to prioritize the development of content, design new services,

TABLE 3.1 Tools for enabling feedback loops

Tool description	Purpose	Data collected	Frequency
	Mobile surveys		
Industry surveys	Understand farmer needs/ demands	Policy topics, e.g. access to services, farmer needs	On demand
Farmer registration	Create a system for tracking farmer demand and behavior	Poverty, gender, agriculture enterprises, food security	Ongoing
Partner surveys	Monitor changes in impact indicators	Change in knowledge, attitude, practice	Baseline, endline
Adoption survey	Track changes in farmer knowledge, attitude, practice	Adoption of practices and use of CKW services	Annual
Farmer satisfaction survey	Gauge program quality	Satisfaction with program and CKW service delivery	Annual
Farmer group participation survey	Track CKW outreach	Farmer participation and topics	Weekly
	"Pulse"		
Two-way, real-time data messaging channel linked to ticketing system	Answer CKW and farmer questions on agronomic and program topics	Payment and performance Program feedback Content requests Complaints Technical issues	Ongoing
	Field force management		
Mobile "jobs" split activities into distinct tasks to be completed with specific farmers	Program and coordinate field activities	Task list and instructions	Monthly
Real-time target setting and tracking on phone/web portal	Set and track field targets and target field support	Performance targets	Monthly

and to address pain points in the field. In addition, we collect farmer adoption surveys on good agricultural practices for the extension partners with whom we deploy CKWs. These surveys enable our partners to track behavior change and assess and improve the effectiveness of their extension efforts. Finally, we historically conducted monitoring and needs assessment surveys on topics such as water resource management for industry clients outside the agriculture sector, for example the World Bank. Clients used the information to evaluate their programs, scope interventions, inform policy, and develop new services.

In addition to collecting data, we also use the mobile channel to solicit direct feedback from farmers on service quality. We have created a two-way, real-time data channel called Pulse that lets CKWs send in questions, comments, and challenges. This channel provides farmers with a voice to share their perceptions of the program. At any point, farmers and CKWs can submit a comment through Pulse or by calling our farmer call center. Dedicated customer service agents and call center operators address feedback from Pulse and use a ticketing system to direct each query to the relevant Grameen Foundation team member so that they can be resolved, documented, communicated back to the CKW, and closed. As illustrated in Figure 3.3, farmers have provided various types of feedback via Pulse, for example, suggesting topics they'd like covered in the information services (e.g. bee-keeping), pointing out where the information provided was insufficient (e.g. disease control in plantain crops), and offering ideas for new products and services (e.g. a directory of agrochemicals on sale from the local banana company). CKWs have also used the channel to raise challenges with operational issues such as phone repairs and payments. These qualitative channels are critical sources of feedback as they enable us to have a dialogue with farmers in real time on a regular basis.

Frequently this qualitative feedback has been easier for staff to digest and act on than the survey data we collect. We've also shared this qualitative feedback with our research and extension partners, and then fed new content from those partners back out to farmers.

In addition, we have leveraged mobile technology to support and promote accountability among the dispersed networks of field agents and staff serving farmers in remote areas. Often agents themselves are disconnected from the organizations they work with; agents frequently are not accountable or recognized for the work they do, have few channels for communicating with their organizations, and receive little guidance on how to perform their work. Recognizing mobile technology's potential to remedy these challenges, Grameen Foundation created a separate unit that focuses exclusively on developing mobile applications for social business clients. The product suite, called TaroWorks, includes a mobile field force application that allows organizations to remotely task agent work and set and track performance goals. Agents use the mobile application to view and track targets while field supervisors use a web portal to set, assign, and monitor agent projects. Today we use this application to create a series of jobs with sub-tasks that CKWs need to carry out with specific farmers, whose identities are logged into the system and shown with pre-populated data fields (such as farmer names and IDs). We are able to track the overall performance of different agent groups and individual CKWs and our partners can see performance hotspots at a glance via dashboards. Using this capability, we are better equipped to track challenges in the field, monitor which intermediaries need support, and identify opportunities for improving field force accountability.

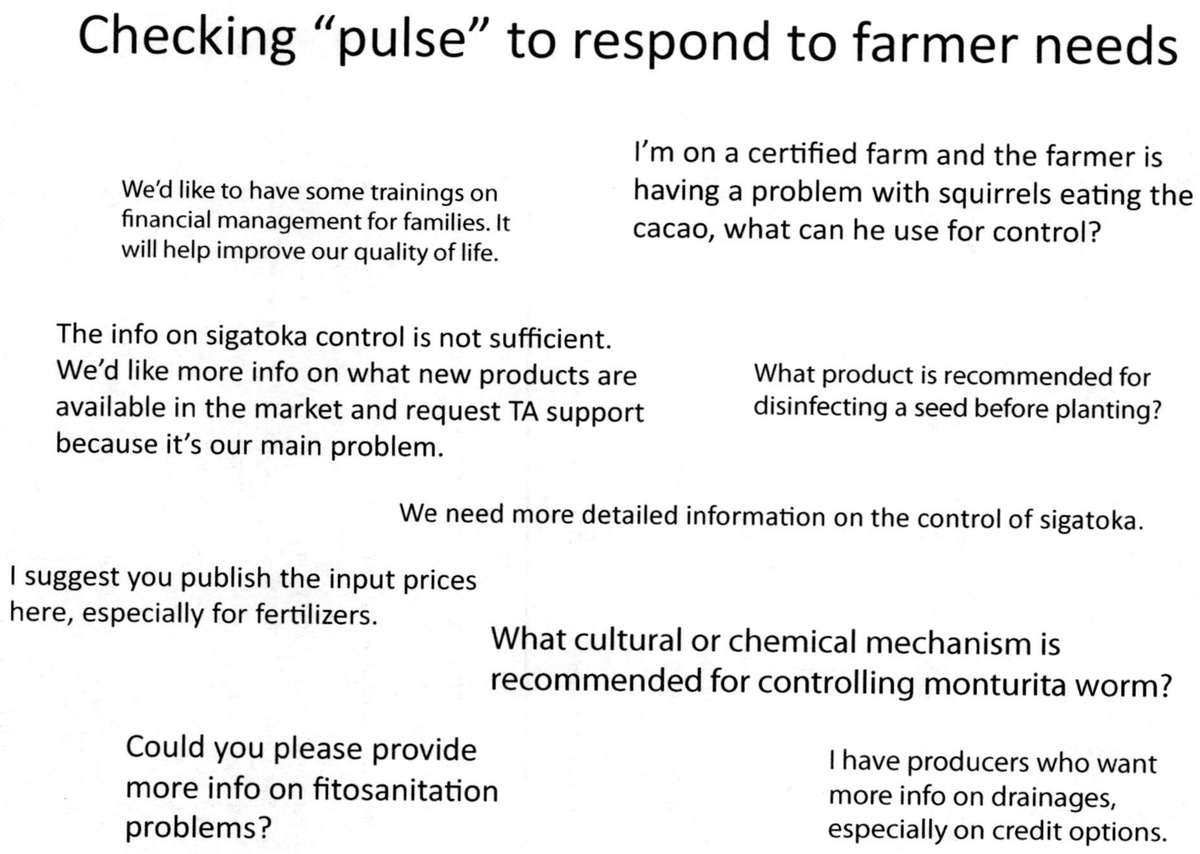

Checking "pulse" to respond to farmer needs

I'm on a certified farm and the farmer is having a problem with squirrels eating the cacao, what can he use for control?

What product is recommended for disinfecting a seed before planting?

We need more detailed information on the control of sigatoka.

What cultural or chemical mechanism is recommended for controlling monturita worm?

I have producers who want more info on drainages, especially on credit options.

We'd like to have some trainings on financial management for families. It will help improve our quality of life.

The info on sigatoka control is not sufficient. We'd like more info on what new products are available in the market and request TA support because it's our main problem.

I suggest you publish the input prices here, especially for fertilizers.

Could you please provide more info on fitosanitation problems?

FIGURE 3.3 Feedback from CKWs illustrating farmer demand

As these examples demonstrate, mobile technology can be incorporated into program design not only to accomplish direct objectives—such as training farmers and collecting crop data—but also to make systems more transparent. Mobile devices provide a mechanism for communities (and individuals) to evaluate the services they receive and to provide qualitative feedback (Box 3.1). Mobile devices also make it easier to monitor and support field agents, providing more consistent guidance while promoting accountability by tracking extension outreach and quality. Figure 3.4 shows a dashboard illustrating the purpose and location of farmer visits of a public extension agent.

BOX 3.1 LEARNING ON HOW TO LEVERAGE THE MOBILE CHANNEL TO ENABLE FEEDBACK LOOPS

Use the two-way capability of the mobile channel to create dialogue with end-users. It can be tempting to focus on only information dissemination or data collection, but once the channel has been established there's substantial value in ensuring two-way information flows. This two-way capability is essential in facilitating inclusive feedback and participatory learning.

Leverage the basic phones already in the hands of users *and* deploy smartphones with intermediaries to balance the reach of basic phones with the rich feedback and content that smartphones enable.

Track and analyze mobile services usage to gain additional insights into demand and interest that users may not state outright.

Leveraging networks of local change agents to enable feedback loops

Scaling the CKW program, we learned that while the mobile channel is an excellent mechanism for capturing feedback from farmers, it also plays an important function in delivering value back to communities. One element that promotes this value exchange is the use of village change agents. From our work on SMS-only initiatives, we learned that mobile solutions are rarely sufficient to create responsive and effective feedback loops that lead to learning and improved results. Enlisting a local intermediary is an essential ingredient; Figure 3.5 shows a government technician in Colombia.

A critical element of the CKW approach is the CKWs' relationship to the communities they serve. The CKW's role as a trusted representative of the community not only ensures that feedback loops are as close to the end-user as possible, but also that farmers will have confidence in the system—both receiving assistance and providing valuable feedback. An intermediary increases accessibility for those who aren't literate, who don't own a phone, or who are less comfortable with technology. By living in the communities in which they work, CKWs are also accessible

Assessment of
the health of
dairy cow

Routine advisory visit to
monitor farmer performance
AASP Visit
For: NAADS
null

Name: Edward Omaido
Subcounty: Labori

Call to diagnose disease and
offer technical advice

Assessment of the health
of the bulls and check
on the progress of the
farmer.
AASP Visit
For: NAADS
null

Name: Edward Omaido
Subcounty: Labori

Call upon to
treat the calf
AASP Visit
For: NAADS

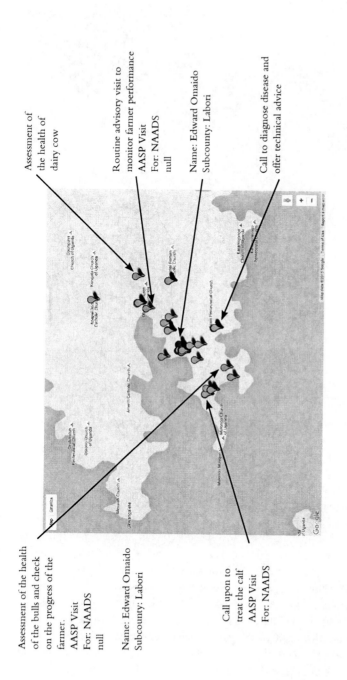

FIGURE 3.4 Dashboard illustrating agent outreach to farmers

Source: www.google.ca/earth/outreach/stories/grameen.html

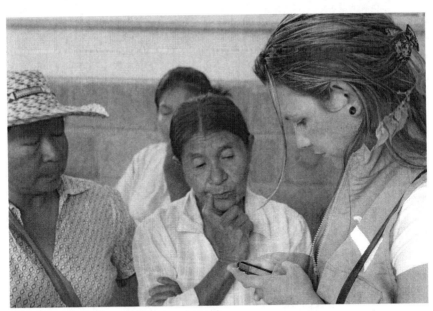

FIGURE 3.5 MANA technician serving a farmer

to farmers in their own settings, whether at the market, in the field, or at a social gathering. These quotidian interactions encourage ongoing dialogue and avoid the power dynamics that an outsider introduces.

The selection of CKWs is arduous, as illustrated in Figure 3.6. After soliciting lists of eligible candidates from our partners, our teams go village by village to select the CKWs with the participation of the individual communities. We publicize the nomination process on radio stations and in other social forums (such as churches and mosques) and solicit wide community participation. In the selection meetings, we share our learning on what makes a CKW effective and then provide the initial list of partner-nominated candidates. We then encourage the communities to debate who would make the best CKW.

To ensure that a CKW will be effective we encourage communities to select someone who is trusted by the community, has a deep commitment to community service, has some leadership experience, is a permanent resident and a farmer, is literate in English, and has the time and mobility to visit farmers. These criteria have been developed through years of observing which CKWs tended to be successful in the program. Some demographic groups are less likely to be eligible for the CKW position or, if eligible, to stick with it. These groups include recent graduates (who often drop out of the program when they receive full-time job offers or move to other locales), the elderly (who are less mobile), and women and the poorest (who are less likely to be literate in English and have less time available because of other household requirements).

While these criteria were developed to maximize program effectiveness, we recognize that they may exclude certain already-marginalized groups and might

FIGURE 3.6 CKW recruitment

further exacerbate power dynamics by bestowing influence on individuals who already enjoy more resources. To mitigate these risks, we monitor the percentage of poor and poorest who access the services, set targets for the participation of women as CKWs, and speak about the importance of using the services for community gain during CKW selection and training. While political interests and power dynamics do surface, our facilitators remind the communities of the criteria, and communities usually select CKWs who serve with success and receive high farmer satisfaction ratings.

Given the high costs associated with soliciting community input at the selection stage, we tried to cut out community participation in later iterations of the model. However, we reverted back to our original approach as we learned that participatory selection plays an important role in validating the CKW's position. A community's trust in the CKW—and long-term participation in the feedback process—depends on meaningful involvement in the selection process.

This trusted relationship between the CKW and the community touches almost all elements of the CKW's work. It also creates a social contract in which the community expects the CKW to deliver value in return for receiving its trust. To maintain the delicate balance between the CKW and the community, the mobile channel should be used bilaterally: not just to gather data on farmers but to provide useful information back to them. Communities also expect us (and our partner organizations) to be responsive to the feedback they raise. Sharing useful new information on, for example, Newcastle disease in chickens, after a farmer has requested it, deepens the trust between the CKW and the community. A CKW's prominence in a community also serves as an incentive in sustaining the two-way flow of information. CKWs receive social prominence through selection and their ongoing visibility in the community; this provides motivation for them to serve their community and reach the community's poorest members.

Applying the model to new geographies, we saw that these core principles—creating a trusted relationship between a CKW and the community, and involving the community in the selection process—hold across cultures, continents, crops, and languages. However, fostering a trusted relationship between a CKW and the community needs to adapt to fit local cultural norms. For example in Côte d'Ivoire,[3] it was less acceptable for a female farmer to deliver information to male farmers. There, we worked with local stakeholders to develop the concept of a "couple CKW," as seen in Figure 3.7, in which the husband and wife would work together to serve their community.

The CKWs also serve as important agents in the learning system, identifying new ways of interacting with their communities and adapting the mobile services to deliver value. That active role in interpreting the program's value at the village level creates a bridge between the communities, Grameen Foundation, and our partners. The CKW reduces the divide between the service provider and the beneficiary, promoting a greater sense of ownership for program results in the community in which the CKW lives. CKWs not only bring feedback loops within reach of farmers but also make it more likely that farmers trust the information exchanged and, in turn, more likely that they act on the information. Box 3.2 outlines these findings.

FIGURE 3.7 "Couple CKW" in Côte d'Ivoire

BOX 3.2 LEARNING ON LEVERAGING TRUSTED CHANGE AGENTS TO ENABLE FEEDBACK LOOPS

Leveraging trusted change agents at the last mile to enable feedback

Leverage existing village-level networks to ensure agents are accessible on an ongoing basis.

Involve the community in the selection of agents to ensure that the community will trust the agent and provide candid feedback an outsider might not be able to capture.

Select agents who have a commitment to serving their communities and use incentive schemes that tap into and reward this intrinsic motivation by showcasing CKW contributions to their communities.

Using data to drive insight and learning

Examples of data analyses enabled through the CKW channel in Uganda

Employing mobile devices opens up tremendous opportunity to analyze data to inform learning and improve service delivery. In the case of the CKW model, our farmer registration system enabled us to analyze farmer behavior at scale to glean insights on farmers and how to improve the services we offered. Once a farmer is registered in the system, we can track farmer demand for mobile information services by monitoring which types of users access which topics and at what frequency. Each time a farmer interacts with a CKW, either by asking a question about farming or completing a survey for a partner or client, the farmer ID is logged. Analyzing usage data against farmer registration data has enabled us to identify trends and tailor services more effectively for different types of farmers. This ability to observe behavior by monitoring usage trends is a powerful mechanism for understanding demand. For example, we observed that 60 percent of queries in the first year were related to pest and disease management, market prices, or weather. This data helped us realize that the on-demand channel works particularly well for dynamic information that changes regularly and for responding to a challenge or threat on the farm. However, it was less effective at changing behavior on other good agricultural practices, as farmers were less likely to proactively ask about those topics. In those cases, sending information directly to farmers on their own phones was a better tactic to build awareness and drive behavioral changes. Based on this insight, we used targeted SMS campaigns and CKW-led farmer group meetings to promote greater adoption of practices such as post-harvest handling. Monitoring farmer queries can also be used to develop early warning insights, as illustrated in Figure 3.8, which shows how disease queries were used to identify disease outbreaks.

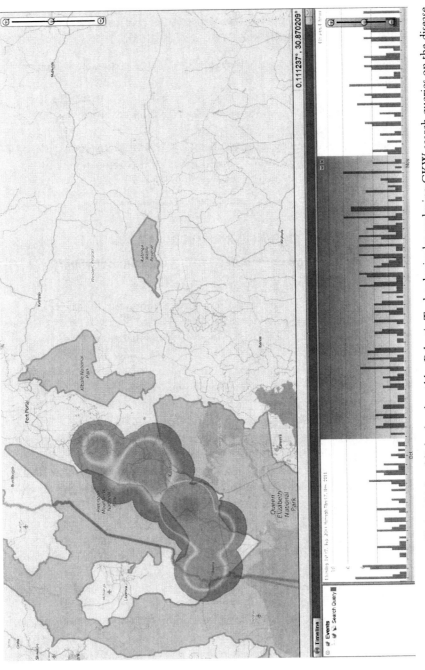

FIGURE 3.8 Heatmap of baby chicken blight developed by Palantir Technologies by analyzing CKW search queries on the disease

We also correlated usage analyses against CKW performance data to better understand how CKW characteristics such as age and gender impact outreach. We observed that CKWs who were effective at disseminating information were not always as strong at collecting data. For example, more elderly and female CKWs were likely to be lower performers when it came to data collection because of the time commitment and travel it required, but were quite effective at disseminating information—particularly in reaching more disadvantaged users, such as female-headed households. Despite their strength as educators, these CKWs were penalized in the performance management system. Using this information, we created a tiered CKW structure in which those who were high performers in data collection—and presumably had time and ability to travel to survey locations—were assigned more surveys and paid more for the additional work. This structure provided a role for CKWs who might not be able to collect as much data but who were champions in providing information to disadvantaged farmers.

Challenges with data and its analysis

During program scale-up, we encountered challenges that led us to learn more about what metrics to employ and, more crucially, how to visualize, automate, and embed data analyses in organizations to promote learning and change. Because the mobile channel generates and makes it easy to collect large quantities of data, data analysis can become unmanageable if there is not an accompanying investment in analytic capacity on a human and technological level. The sheer quantity of data we collected and number of data sources, including over 1.5 million logged program interactions, initially made it difficult to store and analyze the data. Storing that much data in the cloud was costly and required exporting it from local servers to data analysis tools, which often took hours; exports frequently timed out requiring our analysts to start again. In addition, correlating data from multiple different sources to identify trends required specialized software. It also meant that there were many more possible analyses that could be run and more potential for "noise." Although this was not a problem in itself, it required greater staff expertise to design appropriate analyses to derive meaning from the data.

We also struggled to develop a reliable unique identifier for individual farmers and households that farmers were able to remember. It is essential to have a unique identifier to track farmer interactions with CKW services, which then provides insights on behavior, demand, and pain points. In some countries where we work, national ID systems are available and farmers know their numbers; in many other countries (including Uganda), national ID systems either do not exist or, if they do, many individuals do not have IDs or cannot remember their numbers. We considered using farmer phone numbers but we saw that over 50 percent of our farmers didn't own a phone; those who did would often change SIM cards to take advantage of carrier deals. This problem was specifically challenging because CKWs need to register and interact with farmers offline and may not connect with the system for days, meaning that it was not possible for us to auto-generate an ID without significant investment in the mobile application.

To address this challenge, we developed an ID system in which CKWs provided farmers with a physical card with a unique ID that they could reference when using CKW services. CKWs were instructed to provide these cards to farmers at the time of registration. However, a number of challenges quickly arose. It was difficult and costly to ensure CKWs maintained a stock of ID cards, and when farmers would lose their card or forget their IDs, CKWs would sometimes register the farmer in the system again. The ID issue was also problematic when farmers addressed CKWs in a group setting where it was time-consuming to register a new farmer and disruptive to enter each individual farmer's ID. As a result, CKWs would sometimes use one farmer's ID to answer all questions in the group. Overall, the ID system was burdensome for CKWs and farmers alike, leading to duplicate registrations and misattributed searches. The result was "dirty" data that required significant cleaning and quality control investment by staff and created challenges when trying to correlate the usage of CKW services with changes in farmer behavior. As a result, despite our wealth of data, we weren't able to extract enough meaningful indicators of program impact and communicate them to key decision-makers.

Partially related to challenges associated with extracting meaning from the data, the CKW program in the early years emphasized activities, outreach, and financial indicators, which tended to be significantly easier to automate and visualize, over metrics that were more closely tied to value, such as changes in adoption of specific good agriculture practices, productivity gains, or improved prices. Not surprisingly then, we focused the automation of our analytics on outreach and output indicators, such as the total number of surveys completed, what percentage of our users lived on less than $2.25 per day, and how many farming households CKWs had reached. While these statistics were useful in telling us whether or not we were achieving operational and equity goals, they did not tell the full story on the impact we were delivering.

We did include two metrics in our electronic dashboard in Uganda that were more closely tied to the value the system was delivering: farmer adoption rates and repeat usage. In an annual adoption survey, CKWs ask farmers to report if they have adopted one or more practices they learned about through CKWs over the past year. Our adoption surveys have consistently shown farmers reporting around 70 percent adoption rates.[4] The repeat usage rate is calculated automatically via the technology platform, measuring if a farmer asks a CKW more than one question per quarter. Our repeat usage rates range between 20 and 25 percent per quarter. Both of these statistics are encouraging, especially in agricultural extension, where a farmer often sees an extension agent no more than once a year and often not at all.

However, we still struggled to use these indicators to inform program modifications. In the case of annual adoption surveys, the breadth of topics we covered made it difficult to derive meaning from the adoption statistic. Largely in response to farmer demand, we provide a broad set of information services and have partnerships that span multiple value chains, subsistence crops, and livestock. With over a thousand best practices spanning the 58 enterprises we cover, it was difficult to track changes in adoption or productivity for specific practices and crops. The blanket adoption statistic we regularly reviewed did not capture which practices were delivering the most value to farmers, or how those adoptions affected farmer livelihood. In order to take action to deepen value, we needed more specific information. At the partner level, we did measure adoption statistics specific to the value chain or intervention in which the partner worked via baseline and endline surveys conducted by CKWs. However, this more meaningful adoption indicator was not reviewed at management levels. Further, due to the challenges of analyzing disparate data sources and challenges with farmer IDs, it was difficult to effectively correlate farmer usage of CKW services against changes in farmer behavior.

Examples and lessons on how to conduct data analysis to drive value

Based on these lessons, we have made adjustments that allow our partners and us to measure value in a way that wasn't possible before. From our initial experiences working with the data collected via the CKW program, we have learned how to design data collection, data analyses, and reporting to drive learning and deliver value. For partners to act on the collected data, they require a handful of simple but specific indicators that quantify the impact their programs are delivering. They also need data analytics that are delivered in real time, within their decision processes, in easy-to-digest visual graphics that allow them to easily extract meaning. Understanding what data our partners were already collecting and how that data fit into their business processes and decision structures enabled us to co-design dashboards and reports. Using that information, we configured our technology platform to run automated analytics and visualize key indicators in dashboards that are directly accessible to our partners. For example, we developed an automated food security scoring tool using Freedom from Hunger's methodology. The system automatically provides a score for each household, and that score is then visible at aggregate and household levels through a web portal as seen in Figure 3.9. Designing reports that map to specific points in iterative decision cycles that staff can reference on a regular basis is another way to promote data use. These findings highlight the importance of training partner staff on how to create and use data analytics.

In Colombia, for example, we work in partnership with the government of Antioquia. Prior to the partnership, the government's food security program, MANA, collected data on all of its participants yet only analyzed data on 10 percent of households due to the costs associated with digitizing paper forms and performing analysis manually. It would often take six months to a year to answer a particular question given the time it took to collect, send, digitize, and analyze data. Today, the program has access to data on all the households it serves in real time and uses automated reports to improve programming and operational efficiency. For

Clasificacion de Seguridad Alimentaria LB

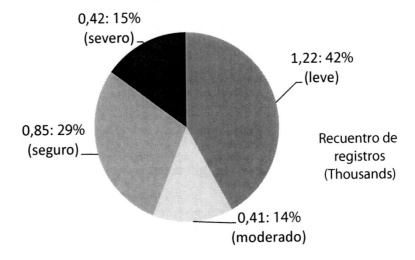

0,42: 15% (severo)

1,22: 42% (leve)

0,85: 29% (seguro)

Recuentro de registros (Thousands)

0,41: 14% (moderado)

Recuentro de registros (Thousands)

FIGURE 3.9 Automated food security analytic

example, analyzing surveys and matching them to government databases and food security scores revealed that some of the families originally included in the program were neither poor nor food insecure. In these cases, the government has used the data to require that operators include only those families that meet program criteria. Data analysis also brought attention to the fact that the chickens being provided to households to serve as a source of ongoing protein (by egg consumption) were being consumed within a few weeks of delivery. In response, the program no longer includes chickens as part of the backyard garden kit, focusing instead on inputs that have proven more effective in driving positive nutritional outcomes. The government program could only take this kind of ownership over the information once staff members had direct access to the data. This experience has illustrated that learning gleaned from data can only be used to improve service delivery to poor communities if it is accessible.

In the case of the m-Sourcing program in Colombia, the data that is collected is now automated and aggregated in reports by grocery store client, farmer cooperative, farmer, and product, thereby substantially reducing the time it takes to pay farmers. Previously, a full-time staff position was dedicated to manually generating reports from paper receipts that were issued daily and had to be collected from each farmer cooperative. Today, this task has been eliminated and the time reallocated to technical assistance. The data has also allowed the association to track when stores reject produce, in order to identify which farmers and cooperatives require more support to reduce future losses. With this new visibility into its operations, the association has learned where farmers face challenges, has tracked demand and supply fluctuations over time, and has developed plans to expand its business to new stores and additional crops using this information.

Lastly we learned from our early struggles with data collection and analysis to improve our monitoring and evaluation of CKWs in Uganda. We designed a new feature on the mobile reference guide for capturing farmer IDs. This feature enables a CKW to begin to type a farmer name on his or her phone and then select the appropriate farmer from a list that is associated only with that particular CKW. This new capability has enabled improved farmer tracking and follow-up and resolved many of the data analytics challenges we experienced earlier. In addition, we now generate monthly quality reports that incorporate a handful of operational and adoption indicators that are shared with management; these indicators cover CKW performance, duplicate interactions, call center logs, and observed versus reported adoption of specific GAP. This increased visibility has helped improve results; for example, 95–97 percent of CKWs now consistently perform in the highest performance category and farmer adoption is now observed on farm and checked at the individual practice level for each focus value chain, enabling more responsive follow-up. Figure 3.10 shows an adoption dashboard developed in partnership with Palantir.

Embedding feedback loops and analytics for results

Why feedback didn't always lead to improved results

Although we co-designed CKW deployments with partners in the scale-up period in Uganda to accelerate the success of their interventions, after the initial design

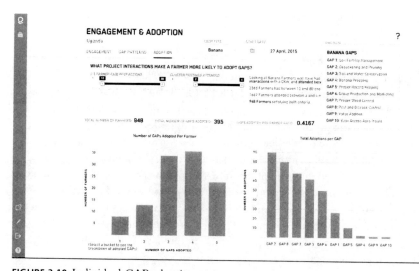

FIGURE 3.10 Individual GAP adoption report

was complete, Grameen Foundation did the vast majority of the "heavy lifting" to get a CKW project running. We offered a turnkey solution in which we recruited, trained, supported, and monitored the CKWs, we input partner surveys and content into the system, and we performed all data analysis ourselves. Although partners were very active in providing inputs and designing content and surveys, they usually didn't have direct access to the technology platform and were multiple steps removed from the CKWs in the field. This meant that the CKW services were never embedded in a partner's infrastructure and partners ultimately didn't take ownership of the CKW services. While partners usually perceived value in the services CKWs provided, they weren't always able to pinpoint that value; they felt little ownership for the results and did little to adapt the services to drive additional value. As a result, the feedback the system generated was less apparent to partners, making it less likely that they would learn from the feedback.

In addition, the learning the CKW program generated was often divorced from the partner's decision-making and operational infrastructure. During the initial scale-up, we would present findings from data analyses to partner management in quarterly steering committee meetings that covered multiple agenda items. We would spend a short time reviewing findings and move on. Often the staff responsible for the areas highlighted in the data analyses were not in the room or, when they were, they were skeptical of the results and saw the data as a threat introduced by an outsider, rather than a tool they could use themselves to improve program results. Ultimately, the majority of the feedback coming in through the model was going to Grameen Foundation rather than to the partner and was therefore disconnected from the day-to-day decisions and actions of partner staff. This lack of ability to present where a partner's intervention was succeeding and failing made it difficult to prove the full value of the model.

Linking learning to action by embedding feedback loops in a partner's systems

Based on this experience, we recognized the importance of not only designing services with the partner but also embedding the technology and the last-mile, mobile-enabled agent network within a partner's infrastructure. By embedding the model components in partner systems, we promote both ownership of the feedback loops and greater accountability for using information exchange to drive results. This shift towards embedding solutions within the core business of our partners, whether public or private, demands that we, at Grameen Foundation, be more flexible and agile in our approach so that partners can adapt the technology and methodology to fit their own needs. We have had to modify our technology to make it more modular and standardized so that it can be configured to meet the specific needs of a particular partner. This also holds true for our approach to leveraging agent networks. The basic fundamentals of the trusted intermediary remain the same, but the specific tasks that an agent performs vary, as does who that agent is within a partner's ecosystem. For example, in our mobile sourcing program, an agent's primary role is still to facilitate two-way information flows; however, agents have shifted their focus to connecting farmers to markets, as opposed to delivering extension advice.

To embed effectively, we involve the partners in program design, deployment, and support, identifying key staff members who will own and operate the technology and field agent components. Partner staff are not only involved in designing services but also trained on CKW methodology and how to be tech system administrators. They learn how to build mobile surveys, create and run reports, and input content for information services. Similarly, although we offer standard tools for the value chains we work in, we help partners to digitize the forms and content they are already using. Partner field agents, who previously did not receive CKW kits, are now not only equipped with mobile devices but also use the mobile phone to perform their existing work. If a partner chooses to deploy additional village-level agents, those agents are recruited, trained, monitored, and supported by the partner field staff.

Because the services are embedded in the partner's systems, partner staff are better situated to internalize and act on the learning generated by the CKW approach. For example, partner staff have identified ways to use the services to drive additional value that Grameen Foundation would not have otherwise proposed, illustrating the type of adaptation and adoption that is needed to sustain services on a long-term basis. For example, by analyzing the system's data, MANA staff realized that 50 percent of children under six in their program, or 9,750 children, were not benefiting from the government's infant feeding program, which provides milk and fortified biscuits to malnourished children. MANA now uses that data to enroll eligible households that had previously been excluded.

Cultivating a learning culture

In addition to developing feedback loops, we realized that we would also need to promote a learning culture to ensure that we were constantly attuned to where we were succeeding and failing as an organization. Proving our assumptions and getting the operational model right would be critical during the pilot and initial scale-up and would require active learning and mid-course correction. Due to its pilot nature, learning was an innate component of the original CKW pilot and it emerged dynamically and organically as we tested different approaches. Listening, and responding, to farmer needs became more difficult as we scaled. By examining the points at which we fell short in internalizing our learning and acting on it, we have been able to glean insights around how to enable collective learning. In this section we explore why we initially fell short in internalizing feedback and what adjustments we've made to increase our accountability and responsiveness to farmers, donors, partners, and other stakeholders. We will also outline how we've used that learning to modify our strategy to deepen the value we deliver.

Obstacles to internalizing and acting on feedback generated from the CKW model

In the case of mobile information services, which were relatively easy and low cost for us to develop, we were able to quickly pivot to respond to farmer feedback. In other cases, we did not always directly address the needs that farmers articulated. For example, one of the pain points CKWs raised was the time it took to get phones repaired. We hadn't developed an effective system for tracking broken phones and repair times, it was not a metric that was highly visible to our management team or partners, and responsibility for the issue's resolution sat across multiple functional groups (including technology, account management, and network and training units). It has also been difficult to respond to farmer requests to address obstacles at the sector level, for example access to inputs or finance, that prevented farmers from acting on the information they received via the program because of the lag time associated with making strategy pivots and the additional resources needed to do so.

Another challenge was that our initial hypotheses around the business model did not play out. While there was demand for data collection services and we saw a greater willingness to pay for embedding CKW services in existing extension efforts than we anticipated, it was still not sufficient to sustain the overall CKW program. We had made commitments to reach 60 percent sustainability by the close of the grant cycle and hit revenue targets as key milestones, which meant that we dedicated much of our energy and focus toward trying to figure out how to fill the revenue gap when our original assumptions fell short. It also meant that our learning culture was particularly sensitive to the financial health of the program, sometimes to the detriment of evaluating the program's impact metrics and the value generated for farmers and partners. Because of our persistent optimism in believing we could achieve these targets—and because we did not have strong internal monitoring structures—we did not communicate as transparently as we could have as signals began to indicate that we might fall short of revenue targets. In many ways, we jumped directly from a promising pilot to scaling a sustainable business without fully understanding what the value drivers would be for the latter.

Similarly, the demands of scaling the agent network meant that our operations and account management teams struggled to respond to feedback from farmers, CKWs, and partners as they grappled with expanding the CKW network while maintaining and supporting existing CKWs. With so much of our focus on scaling and achieving what proved to be unrealistic revenue targets, and without strong measurement systems in place with clear protocols for addressing and resolving feedback, it was more difficult to identify challenges in the field, hear grievances from partners, and track whether they had been addressed and resolved.

How our learning led us to shift strategy

In response to our own learning, as well as feedback from farmers, partners, and our donor, we modified our strategy to drive more value. These modifications include addressing farmers' needs more holistically by bundling access to information with access to finance and markets; targeting and more deeply contextualizing solutions for specific value chains; more deeply embedding the model with long-term business owners; and differentiating between sustainability and commercial viability.

Although some of our extension partners provided access to markets and inputs, the extent to which our partners offered farmers an integrated solution was inconsistent and, when available, often disconnected from the services CKWs delivered. As a result, farmers told us that there were a number of obstacles that prevented them from acting on the information services CKWs delivered. They lacked access to finance, and the recommended inputs were not always available locally or affordably, and were often of questionable quality. Farmers' incentives to act on the information was also diminished when there was not a guaranteed market that rewarded them for investing in practices that would deliver higher productivity or improved quality.

Today, our strategy aims to address these challenges by bundling mobile-enabled information services and CKW-facilitated technical assistance with access to finance and inputs and outputs markets. Pairing extension information with other agricultural services makes it more likely that farmers have the incentives and resources to manage their subsistence crops more productively and operate their farming businesses in a more profitable way. We work with long-term business owners in the public and private sector to deliver these integrated solutions within the contexts in which farmers transact. The early feedback we're receiving shows higher value for both farmers and the organizations serving them, as well as a much tighter and more responsive feedback loop between the two.

For example, in our mSourcing solution, we have focused on how we can facilitate transactions that ultimately address the barriers that prevent value chain players from including smallholders in their supply chains. Over $600,000 in sales have been facilitated through the platform and 100 percent of orders are now digitized, enabling the horticulture association to track order completion and transaction history by farmers and reducing payment time from 40 days to seven days. The association has saved on average 14 days per month in preparing monthly liquidation. The solution has also led to a 90 percent reduction in order allocation errors and the association has agreed to pay for the services post-pilot, while a national restaurant chain has committed to using the sourcing platform to engage more smallholders directly.

In designing solutions, we also learned that we needed to focus our efforts to more effectively drive behavior change. We have adopted a much more targeted approach to designing and delivering information services for the specific value chains and enterprises of our farmers and partners. Today, we utilize multiple channels to transmit information on a regular basis to farmers, including via SMS campaigns that are timed to a specific cropping calendar, CKW-facilitated farmer group meetings, mobile interactive guides, and videos. (We also continue to offer information on demand via CKW Search and the call center.) In Uganda, these insights were reflected as modifications to the CKW program. For example, the program now targets adoption via SMS campaigns and CKW-facilitated farmer group discussions delivered regularly to farmers in the coffee, banana, and maize value chains.

Cafeteros Connectados in Colombia and Guatemala is another example of how a more focused approach enables tighter and more responsive feedback loops between value chain players and farmers. The program's baseline includes a full battery of good agricultural practices for coffee, socio-demographic information, food security indicators, farmer attitude questions, and farm characteristics such as size, coffee variety, and the previous season's production information. This expanded, detailed baseline captures adoption levels of specific agronomic practices and adherence to certification standards, allowing coffee cooperatives to evaluate where the greatest opportunities are for improving productivity (for example, in soil management and nursery establishment) and to drive faster certification to open up opportunities for farmers to sell to higher-paying markets. The more comprehensive baseline has also enabled producer organizations to identify which farmers are most likely to respond positively to interventions through attitude segmentation and analysis on the economic viability of coffee farming at the household level.

We also see through Cafeteros Connectados how involving farmers in setting and tracking targets helps promote farmer accountability for learning. The CKW meets with farmers on a bimonthly basis to discuss their progress on farm management plans. Farmers set their own targets in the plans, giving them more ownership and accountability for using the information to improve outcomes on their farms. Showing the farmers how they benchmark against other farmers has proven to be an important motivator for behavioral change and has helped farmers learn how they can improve their own practices. Similarly, CKWs regularly facilitate trainings. They use a tablet to show more in-depth, curriculum-based information, including videos and other multimedia presentations, mapped to the cropping calendar. These modifications have driven faster learning for farmers, producer organizations, and other value chain players.

Through a partnership with Opportunity Bank in Uganda, we are testing the value of delivering bundled financial and extension services. The bank uses CKWs to collect "know your client" data to identify credit-ready farmers. Under this partnership, the delivery of financial services is paired with agronomic information delivered by CKWs to maximize the farmer's return on investment and to reduce the bank's default risk. We are also strengthening our partnership with the government of Uganda with the aim of embedding the model within the national extension agency for long-term sustainability, rather than pursuing a commercial model.

E-Warehouse is another example of how farmer demand for access to financial services and markets changed the way we deliver the CKW model. By providing extension and financial services in tandem, we were able to generate more value for the farmer and provide opportunities for commercial players such as banks and buyers to offer services to farmers where they had before been unwilling. Although the pilot included only 90 farmers in the loan and/or bulk buying services, the results have been encouraging; farmers who held grain through the program received on average 47 percent higher prices.

How we used learning to modify our operations and promote a learning culture

We have also modified our approach to cultivate a responsive learning culture and to increase our accountability by investing in analytics and M&E capacity; systematizing our tracking of key impact metrics and elevating their regular review; phasing learning objectives over time and multiple grant cycles; having honest, data-/evidence-based conversations with donors about the time needed to achieve results (especially related to program sustainability); and institutionalizing learning capture and knowledge sharing. Through a collaborative dialogue with our donor, we have shifted course to focus on validating the model's impact and prioritizing the delivery of high-quality extension, rather than generating revenue. Critically, we are no longer pursuing a commercial model to attain sustainability. This has given us both the space and the mandate to fine-tune our operational model and quantify the value we are delivering.

We have adjusted our approach in Uganda to promote more rapid learning cycles and greater accountability. For example, we found that we sometimes didn't listen to or act on feedback from CKWs and farmers because accountability for problem resolution was spread across multiple functional areas. To address this accountability gap, we reorganized the management team into two primary areas that include service delivery and account management. Consolidating responsibility with a single manager for service delivery and for partner account management has led to improved coordination and accountability for resolving field issues such as equipment maintenance while also improving responsiveness to partner concerns. In addition, we are currently hiring a seasoned M&E expert in Uganda and contracting an M&E firm to help us design a system that can analyze data from various sources to better evaluate impact results. We are also partnering with Palantir Technologies to analyze our existing data and to build automated dashboards that can pull data from disparate sources, including farmer registrations, mobile surveys, and SMS and call center logs, so that we can understand whether the CKW program as a whole is driving behavior change. These analyses also enable us to assess which services deliver the greatest value and are most effective in changing specific behaviors.

We have also institutionalized channels for learning that map our organizational culture to make pathways for action more visible. Our staff bring experience from multiple domains, including finance, technology, and international development, and we borrow methodologies from across these domains to understand our clients and listen to our users. A drive toward innovation permeates Grameen Foundation's organizational culture. This organizational affinity for innovation has influenced how we learn from our clients, including poor farmers served by the CKW program. Gathering user insights and requirements directly from our clients—using human-centered design principles, prototyping tools and services, and frequent iteration in line with lean methodology—are all standard approaches we use to cultivate insights that drive innovation. Similarly, our learning culture incorporates tools from the private sector, such as balanced scorecards and key performance indicators, alongside more traditional development tools, such as results frameworks, that link back to our theory of change. Program teams conduct annual and multi-year strategic planning and collective visioning sessions. These teams then assess progress against targets and evaluate results in weekly management meetings and quarterly off-sites. We have also introduced mechanisms for better measuring and tracking key indicators that roll up to senior leadership review, for example through quarterly program reviews and an organization-wide balanced scorecard that tracks operational and impact indicators, which is shared with our Board. This collective process of setting and tracking goals provides a forum for organizational learning and promotes accountability at multiple levels.

Learning from the original CKW program delivered insights that enabled us to pivot in Uganda and innovate to drive additional value in new programs. Our learning continues to deepen as we expand our initiatives. This expansion brings a new challenge of ensuring that learning is being shared between geographically diverse teams; we are just beginning to address this by promoting more structured knowledge exchange to institutionalize learning. For example, we recently created an mAgriculture Council comprised of leaders running our country programs where we discuss challenges and insights. We also have a knowledge exchange initiative in which we send out monthly communication on program learning as well as providing webinar spotlights on particular programs that allow teams to share their insights. We have found that having a local champion in each office who works as part of a larger knowledge exchange group has helped drive participation; conversely, we have seen that without senior-level buy-in and support of the initiative, attendance suffers. These lessons, summarized in Box 3.3, reflect how we have evolved to promote a responsive, learning-oriented, organizational culture.

Conclusion: insights on enabling collective learning

In piloting, scaling, and expanding the CKW model, we created a two-way dynamic feedback loop between farmers and the organizations serving them. This feedback loop presented tremendous opportunity for enabling sector-wide learning. Sometimes, however, we missed the chance to fully deliver on that potential. With time, our experience scaling and adapting the CKW model generated insights that not only have led us to deliver on this potential, but also have guided us toward becoming a more responsive and accountable organization.

We've seen that the use of mobile devices within last-mile agent networks promotes participatory, iterative, real-time dialogue between development stakeholders and farmers, a fundamental component in enabling a collective learning process. However, establishing feedback loops alone is rarely enough to spur action or ensure accountability for the information exchanged. In our experience, it was

BOX 3.3 LESSONS ON ENABLING COLLECTIVE LEARNING

Phase the development, testing, scaling, and commercialization of new innovations to ensure there is sufficient time to refine the operating model, prove the innovation's impact, and articulate and quantify the value proposition before introducing aggressive revenue targets. Include business model innovation and rigorous business assumption testing during pilot and scale-up stages to distinguish between those innovations that may be commercially viable and those that can be sustained via government funding.

Develop shared ownership for results among stakeholders, including implementers, communities, and donors, and at different levels of an organization, to help promote open and honest dialogue about results, challenges, and failures. Position feedback channels as a tool for improving outcomes for those who are responsible for driving results.

Align incentives and build accountability structures that elevate the visibility of impact and value indicators to tighten the link between feedback and course correction.

Package learning in language that resonates with stakeholders and organizational culture.

Co-design, with stakeholders, indicators that measure operational health and end-user impact, and invest in the capacity to automate and visualize analytics to derive meaning and promote action.

critical to build analytic capacity to derive meaning from feedback and to develop the institutional systems and incentives to ensure that learning leads to action. In particular, we needed to elevate the visibility of and accountability for value indicators to tighten the link between feedback and course correction. It was also important to create sufficient runway to prove program value and impact as well as rigorously test the potential for commercial viability before introducing aggressive revenue targets. Sharing overall CKW program accountability amongst leadership and across the team created an atmosphere in which failure was something that was both owned at the highest level by the organization and was a part of the learning process. Similarly, with our partners, it was important to position CKW feedback as a learning tool rather than an auditing mechanism.

Another key take-away was designing our operational structure to insulate our field and services team from the pressure of achieving sustainability so that they could focus on listening to farmers and shifting course as needed. Capturing and communicating learning in a language that resonated with our organizational culture—in our case, tying it closely to innovation and "private sector speak"—made it more likely that we would internalize and act on insights. We had to invest in our analytical capacity and prioritize rigorous M&E. Developing automated analytics was one of the highest return investments to drive learning internally and with partners. Embedding analyses within the decision-making process of those who were responsible for resolving challenges and driving results was also a key factor in ensuring data is used to improve results. Similarly, embedding feedback loops and analytics within partner organizations led to greater ownership of the services and promoted accountability for using the information gleaned from CKWs to respond to farmer needs and to improve service delivery.

Undoubtedly, collective learning requires bidirectional feedback channels. In our case, building these channels to facilitate dialogue with farmers was the easy part. It was through multiple cycles of learning and, admittedly, some failure along the way, that we gained insights on how to develop the organizational capacity needed to consistently derive meaning from the feedback channels we created and to ensure that the unique insights that the CKW model enabled translated into improved services for farmers.

Notes

1 Palantir Technologies builds software products that enable organizations to solve their hardest data problems and overcome their most complex operational challenges. To achieve this, they build platforms for integrating, managing, and securing data on top of which they layer applications for fully interactive, human-driven, machine-assisted analysis. Grameen Foundation has been partnering with Palantir Technologies under their Philanthropy Engineering initiative since 2011.
2 Although we have over 300,000 farmers registered in the system, based on our challenges using unique identifiers (more on this later), we expect to have reached 200,000 farming households based on calculations and analyses of CKW outreach.
3 In Côte d'Ivoire, we recruited 150 CKWs but ultimately did not deploy the network due to shifts in the political landscape in the cocoa sector.
4 Data validators back-check a percentage of those surveys to assess if there is a statistically significant difference between the adoption reported to a CKW versus that reported to an external verifier.

4

FARMER VOICE RADIO AND MULTI-LEVEL COLLABORATION TO ENGAGE FARMERS EFFECTIVELY

Philip R. Christensen, Dwight W. Allen and Katharine N. Tjasink

SUMMARY

Farmer Voice Radio (FVR) initiated consortia in four African countries that use new forms of agricultural radio programs, combined with the power of mobile phones, to make the traditionally one-way medium into a two-way interactive platform that ensures meaningful feedback. Much of the learning and experience described in this case study focuses on "baking in" sustainability right from the beginning as well as discovering innovative ways of introducing course corrections that will prove useful to others. FVR has learned that true collaboration arises only when stakeholders at all levels plan collectively and embrace the value of in-flight corrections. Technology-based feedback mechanisms can prove expensive and complex, yet simpler feedback mechanisms can raise concerns about data quality. For this reason, delivery systems using broadcast media such as radio must aggregate feedback to learn from audience responses, even if audience members tend to expect personalized responses to their individual feedback. External support can impede fully honest collaboration when one party's budget depends on another party's funding. Long-term sustainability requires innovative strategic thinking, scrupulous avoidance of buying short-term gains with unsustainable operational support, and more time than most donors are willing to invest.

Introduction[1]

Let this analysis of collective learning within FVR begin, as it should, with the voices of farmers themselves[2]:

[FVR] has helped me great[ly] … Before this program, I was not able to feed my family through the year since I had no knowledge of mixed farming, but with this program I was able to hear voices of my fellow farmers, their testimony, and this encouraged me to practice the information given out by agricultural experts, hence increase production output and increased finances.

Concy Omandi, multiple crops and livestock farmer

FIGURE 4.1 Concy Omandi

I have tried deworming of sheep and cattle. I used to wait for veterinary officer to do it for me but after listening to the radio *and* learning how to do it, when and how, I do it myself … My animals are now healthy because I learnt about deworming and vaccination. I collect more milk from them because they are healthy and all milk is good for sale and consumption … I was recorded and broadcast on air … My experience managed to reach many [more] farmers than I could ever reach.

Mateke Eliphaz, livestock farmer

FIGURE 4.2 Mateke Eliphaz's livestock

At the heart of FVR lies the premise that we, as implementers, do not have "the solution." We have never believed that FVR should exist within a vacuum—internally consistent yet externally disconnected—but rather that it should fit within, and complement, existing structures. To accomplish this, we developed innovative approaches to enhancing feedback and accountability for the purpose of collective learning from the very beginning of our work. Learning did not evolve to become central to this process. Rather we designed the process itself to foster continuing learning.

We set out from the start to build a system in collaboration with the ultimate users of, and actors within, that system. This began through consultations in five sub-Saharan African countries with smallholder farmers[3] themselves, as well as with national stakeholders representing government extension services, farmer organizations, and civil society. Combining the learning from those discussions with a landscape survey of technology-based innovations in agricultural extension, we presented a set of design principles to the donor—with whom we then worked jointly to develop an initial model. This model, in turn, evolved over time as we reflected with all stakeholders on what had been discovered in practice.

We discovered much about what does, and does not, work in promoting feedback, accountability, and collaboration with smallholder farmers to enable learning and improve livelihoods. The fact that so many aspects of the FVR model were never conceived prior to the start of implementation testifies to this reality.

The FVR concept

FVR rests on the premise that conventional models for providing advisory services to farmers no longer work well enough. Many factors underlie this dilemma, but they do *not* include lack of knowledge. Much of what farmers need to believe, know, and do in order to enhance productivity, reduce food insecurity, and improve livelihoods already exists. What *is* lacking is effective support for taking yield-enhancing practices to scale. Severe capacity constraints on government agricultural extension services contribute significantly to this challenge.

The rapid expansion of information and communications technologies (ICTs) throughout the global South offers some hope for finding alternative solutions. Yet many ICT-based extension strategies face significant limitations. Some operate independently of public advisory services, without taking advantage of these important resources. Many focus only on specific interventions, rather than supporting a complete, continuous extension system. Some technologies (for example, video and Internet), while offering robust media channels, simply cannot reach the majority of rural famers. Perhaps most important, yet rarely addressed in any practical manner, is the reality that most ICT-based initiatives are not sustainable. When external support ends, so do their benefits.

FIGURE 4.3 Radio recording

FVR was designed to address all of these challenges, beginning with the selection of radio as its primary delivery medium and including support from other technologies, especially mobile phones. Often overlooked as an ICT strategy, broadcast radio remains the lowest-cost, most accessible, and most trusted medium in rural Africa. In the four countries where FVR was introduced, baseline surveys showed almost 80 percent of households had access to radios, two-thirds of farmers used radio as a source of extension, and more than 80 percent of those farmers trusted radio extension messages. There is very little marginal cost for a farmer to listen to a radio program, while FVR's systematic programming strategies increase the ease of doing so.

FVR began its fieldwork from 2009 in two "flagship" countries: Kenya and Malawi. Two additional countries, Tanzania and Uganda, were added in 2011. The FVR concept rests on three major ideas: building a full extension-delivery system around radio, putting farmers at the center of this process, and designing for true sustainability. Each of these has significant implications not only for FVR's technical approach in general, but specifically for the process of collective learning.

1   *A full delivery system.* Since the standard "training and visit" model of delivering advisory services to farmers has largely broken down, an appropriate response requires a complete, alternative delivery system, not just limited interventions. Many ICT-based innovations, while effective, reduce their focus to a few issues of immediate donor or corporate interest. Others take a scatter-shot approach, without any systematic planning. Farmers, on the other hand, need broad, continuous support to improve their practices and livelihoods— throughout every year (according to the agricultural calendar), and across the full range of their needs (different crops or livestock, different points in the value chain). Their conversation, their contributions, and their challenges are not limited to a single priority or intervention. In this context radio, as with any technology, serves as a means rather than an end. FVR uses radio as a tool for delivering extension services that foster learning, action, and reflection on an ongoing basis.

2 *Farmers at the center.* Older models of agricultural extension tended to see the farmer as an empty vessel in need of filling from external fountains of knowledge. This perspective ignores the fact that farmers themselves possess valuable expertise and experience. Furthermore, they trust other farmers. Therefore, FVR adopted a community-of-practice (CoP) approach. We set ourselves a goal of using radio to facilitate discourse among farmers, the narrower CoP, while including farmers in the broader CoP of agricultural experts. This laid the foundation for learning collaboratively with farmers. To accomplish this goal, FVR incorporates the farmer's voice at every stage of the process, from needs assessment to radio broadcasts to feedback systems. Farmers become proactive constituents rather than passive recipients.

FIGURE 4.4 LRAAC meeting in Kenya

FIGURE 4.5 Production team at work

3 *Designing for true sustainability.* Successful innovations must continue in order to make a lasting difference. Most externally funded projects, therefore, have "sustainability plans." Yet in practice, true sustainability has proven elusive as donors and implementers choose short-term success over long-term impact. FVR, therefore, chose to "bake in" sustainability from the start—understanding the risks involved in taking more time than other approaches that pay incentives and operational costs. By addressing this issue up-front and showing

each partner a value proposition that supports its own objectives, FVR shifts the development paradigm from dependency to collaboration and ownership, using no donor funding to purchase airtime or to top up extension officer salaries. Instead, we make a business case to the respective agencies. We demonstrate to radio stations (local, regional, and national) and mobile network operators how enhancing the quantity and quality of their services to farmers can increase the size of their audience and market share while reducing churn through greater user loyalty. Radio stations also gain access to accurate agricultural content that would otherwise prove difficult to obtain. We explain to extension services how redefining the duties of some experts as Radio Extension Officers (REOs) can allow them to serve significantly more farmers. The successful continuation of FVR at multiple sites in Kenya and Malawi, two years after the end of funding, proves the robustness of this approach.

In implementing these principles, FVR links agricultural and radio experts in production teams to create actual programming, while including farmers throughout the process. As shown in Figure 4.6, this begins with farmers and extension specialists prioritizing topics for the following quarter as National and Local Agricultural Radio Agendas (N/LARAs). Production teams then plan programming for those topics and record farmer voices to include in the broadcasts. Farmer feedback on those broadcasts, collected at station research desks, drives programming improvements and future planning.

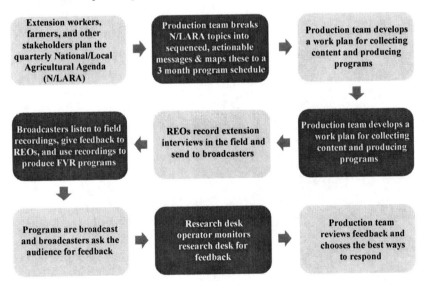

FIGURE 4.6 Production process

Multi-level collaboration in FVR: why and how?

FVR was conceived as a developing conversation among farmers and practitioners at all levels and stages of an evolutionary process. Without such a broader context, one-way systems for feedback and accountability risk reinforcing old power dynamics. Single-direction feedback and accountability also preclude effective application of lessons learned, recording what works and what doesn't without reflecting on why this happened and what all partners could improve by working together. Two-way feedback and accountability, on the other hand, represents one step towards shifting the fundamental paradigm of development from top-down interventions to collaborative accompaniment. We learned that thoughtful response is critical to enhancing collaborative learning in this context. We need to hear what is being said and respond in meaningful ways. Feedback on its own does not promote learning. It is what we do with this feedback that counts. In the same way, providing donors and other stakeholders with evidence may promote accountability but does not ensure learning. Acting on this evidence, and using it to shape the way forward, is what makes a difference.

Although FVR, by design and in name, focuses on farmers, we found it necessary to consult at multiple levels to cooperate effectively with them. We found that the most useful learning arises from effective collaboration at all three of these levels: the farmers themselves; implementing partners (national and regional); and donors. Collective learning with farmers benefits from, and offers benefits to, all collaborators. Interactions among actors at each level, and also across levels, proved vital to achieving impact in the field—even more so than we originally anticipated.

Specifically, we sought collaborative learning at three levels (Figure 4.7), with feedback and accountability operating between each:

1   *The smallholder farmer*: the *raison d'être* for FVR, the target of support efforts, a valuable source of expertise, and the ultimate determinant of success or failure.
2   *Implementing partners*: the intermediaries between donor funding and farmer practice, divided for FVR purposes into three sublevels:
    • Core alliances: sustainable partnerships on the ground between REOs and radio station personnel.
    • National consortia: collaborative relationships among government, knowledge partners, civil society, and the private sector.
    • Regional Office: liaison between the donor and the field, coordinating activities, providing technical support, overseeing a centralized measurement, learning and evaluation (MLE) system.
3   *Donor*: providing funds, approving overall goals and direction, providing consultative support, assessing progress.

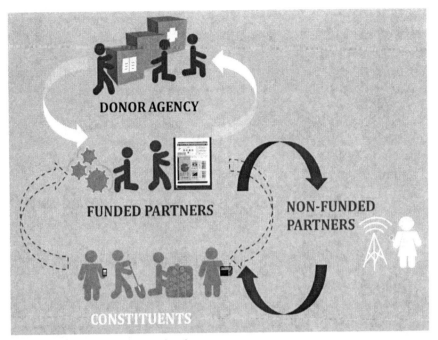

DONOR AGENCY

FUNDED PARTNERS

NON-FUNDED PARTNERS

CONSTITUENTS

FIGURE 4.7 Three collaboration levels

Two guiding principles shaped learning in this context: collaborative planning and in-flight corrections. If external experts start by offering all of the answers (which, in any case, we did not have at the beginning of our own work), how can actors at different levels chart a course together through consultation? If plans cannot be adjusted along the way, sometimes to a significant degree, how can learning be incorporated into implementation?

To systematize collaborative planning and learning, we used a "dual-workshop"[4] model. Over the course of four years we trained 105 extension officers plus staff from 36 radio stations during 25 workshops in four countries. Workshops were held at least once every quarter. The dual-workshop approach addresses the lack of true feedback and accountability in standard workshop design. Typically participants attend a single workshop to receive training. They then return to their normal working environments, where any benefits gained soon dissipate from lack of practice, responsibility, or institutional support. Instead, the dual-workshop model addresses capacity development in a broader, educational sense—as part of an ongoing process. Not only are participants engaged during the event as collaborative learners, they commit to follow-up assignments. At the next workshop, they report back on their progress (accountability) and what they learned (feedback).

We found that this format helps to foster a community of practice among implementers at all levels. It gives the Regional Office and national consortia an opportunity to learn directly from the field. It also gives core alliance teams the chance to learn from one another. As implementers put their heads together, they co-create solutions that are contextually relevant. Learning becomes multi-directional. We listened, learned, and adjusted our plans accordingly. In adopting this stance, where we as the implementers are not "the solution" but rather are co-contributors to a system that is designed and implemented collectively, we created an organizational culture where feedback is valued and where it truly impacts decisions.

Turning to the second principle, since the waters of FVR implementation had never before been navigated we had only sketchy maps to guide us: core principles, based on proven theories and practice, around which we built our initial proposals to the donor and from which we developed preliminary implementation plans in collaboration with colleagues from our two flagship countries. We then used "in-flight corrections" to chart our course—not as an inadequacy for which apologies would be necessary, but as an opportunity to be embraced.

As we engaged with the donor, implementing partners in each country, and farmers, we shared our questions and uncertainties as well as our vision, promising them that some things would need to be modified and asking for their patient collaboration along the way. Course correction was not a one-off exercise for FVR. Instead, such modifications were integrated into all dual workshops and were acted upon either directly during the workshops or in a follow-up phase.

This approach allowed relatively rapid adjustments when initial ideas proved sub-optimal or external circumstances changed. It also facilitated a steady stream of new ideas. In fact, most of the innovative and successful alternatives pioneered by FVR, from AgTips (one-minute spots presenting sophisticated content that is easy for farmers to hear and learn, and for stations to schedule repeatedly) to radio farmers (ordinary farmers who engage repeatedly with an REO so that their learning can be followed over time) emerged through such collaboration, rather than from our initial proposal. Collective learning was made possible through this iterative approach. We are certain that many of our most successful concepts would not have emerged had we simply implemented a typical project work plan, without allowing for course corrections in near real time.

Collaboration at the farmer level

While radio represents FVR's primary delivery technology, it remains only a means to the end of capturing the farmer's voice at every stage of the process. Collaboration begins by listening as farmers participate fully in discussions about what issues should be addressed each quarter, through the development of Local Agricultural Radio Agendas with full farmer participation. REOs and radio producers then record farmer voices in the field to include in programs. For example, a smallholder farmer who has implemented a new practice might explain why she did so, how she went about it, and what she learned—taking on the role of advisor to her peers. Alternatively, the interaction between an REO and a farmer who has not yet attempted a new practice, or who encountered problems along the way, could be recorded so that other farmers can benefit by listening to the learning process. Once the programs go on air, farmers are encouraged to provide feedback to production teams.

One mechanism that we tested to support CoP collaboration involved an updated version of the listener-group model. Originally developed in an era when farmers had to share radio access by listening together, FVR modernized this approach to emphasize its peer-learning element and rebranded it as "Farmer Voice Radio Clubs." Even when farmers listen individually to FVR broadcasts, they still find value in meeting to discuss what they have learned and how to apply it. In Malawi, for example, some FVR Clubs developed formal structures—with a chairperson, a secretary to record minutes and review actions on decisions, and an emphasis on collective trials of selected new practices. These clubs helped to facilitate learning at a community level. Farmers could come together to share their thoughts on FVR programs and their experiences implementing FVR practices in the field.

On the other end of the development process, FVR actively solicits farmer post-broadcast feedback for accountability and improvement. FVR's approach to receiving and acting on feedback to improve service delivery and increase learning revolves around the establishment of research desks at each of 36 participating radio stations. Their purpose is to systematically solicit, analyze, and respond to farmer feedback: to listen to farmers and act on their input. On a regular basis (daily, weekly, or biweekly, depending on the station's programming schedule), radio stations pose questions regarding the content, quality of programming, timing of programming, etc.—on the radio and/or via SMS text messages—and ask farmers to send in their feedback by SMS or other mechanisms. For areas with limited technology access, the radio itself is used as the primary mechanism for feedback via call-in and call-out shows.

Production teams meet weekly or biweekly to review feedback and decide how to respond. For example, if the majority of farmers are asking for more repetition of particular programs then the program schedule is adjusted accordingly. If the majority of farmers would like more information on a particular topic, the production team prepares additional content and amends the program schedule. Ideally, research desks aggregate feedback themes for distribution to the structures planning the L/NARAs. Research desks also collect demographic data from users so that feedback patterns can be disaggregated for reporting purposes.

This system did not work as effectively as hoped at all radio stations, however. We learned three important lessons when trying to implement research desks: that the technology selected is crucial to the success of the system (it needs to be relevant to the local context); that farmers will not provide feedback if it is too expensive or cumbersome to do so; and that production teams need to show farmers that they are listening and responding to feedback or else it will taper off over time. Running a successful research desk also requires sufficient resources—staff time, access to electricity, a strong mobile phone network—to operate. In response, we adapted our approach to the local context wherever possible—for example, by using simpler methods to solicit feedback where appropriate.

Some of our more successful feedback mechanisms came from low-tech and unsolicited approaches—for example, field reports from REOs based on their interactions with farmers. Others take advantage of mobile phones, but for telephony rather than texting, through call-in programs. This format, where extension experts interact with farmers live and on-air, remains a perennial favorite. What these two approaches have in common is a natural, conversational approach, which seems to offer the greatest potential for collective learning.

Figure 4.8 summarizes farmer-feedback mechanisms tested by FVR, and the lessons that we learned in return.[5]

As noted above, an effective, systematic feedback system proved difficult to operationalize. We initially relied on REOs and radio staff to collect data as part of their normal work, hypothesizing that this would lead to sustainable data collection in the long term. However, we quickly learned that these officers were unwilling to increase their workload to take on such a task. Subsequently, we separated feedback and data collection, making the former the responsibility of each production team and the latter the responsibility of the project implementers.

Another challenge arose from farmer expectations. Farmers often assume that feedback to radio stations represents the equivalent of contacting a call center. Understandably, they want answers to their individual questions. Station personnel, however, have neither the time nor the expertise to respond to each farmer. Since radio is a broadcast medium, we had to explain that the purpose of FVR feedback lies in trends based on aggregated data. Which topics garner the most, or least, interest? Which broadcasts and formats are most, and least, popular? Where do the greatest confusion or misunderstandings lie? The answers to such questions help production teams remain accountable to farmers and improve FVR services accordingly. We found that the power of learning from feedback in a meaningful way lies not in attending to individual needs (thereby providing an unsustainable, personalized extension service) but rather in understanding collective voice. On this basis, FVR production teams can make changes to programming that tend to the needs of the many, much as the broadcast medium of radio tends to the needs of large audiences rather than providing one-on-one service.

In exploring mobile phones as a feedback mechanism, we also discovered their potential for content delivery to niche audiences. In principle, different messages can be delivered by text (or even interactive voice response) to different categories of farmers—dairy versus cassava, for example. Radio, on the other hand, provides the same message to all listeners. In this regard we collaborated with Prof. Phil Parker of INSEAD University, whose content dashboard helped production teams to research topics and design SMS messages for different audiences. In future phases, we hope to develop complete taxonomies of support for all major crops and livestock with his assistance. His system can also help FVR provide support in many local languages, another aspect of our plans for the future once a cost-effective business model (possibly based on inexpensive smartphones) can be developed.

Unsolicited feedback		
	High technology	**Low technology**
Farmer call-in	FreedomFone - an open source Interactive Voice Response (IVR) system allowing for "leave-a-message" functions	Dedicated line (mobile phone) situated at the research desk
Lessons learned	FreedomFone is a useful tool, but requires continual financial inputs in order to be maintained. It also requires technological skill to install.	Easily implementable, well-understood technology, but tracking of feedback is difficult. Strong cultural barriers against leaving voice messages.
Farmer SMS-in	FrontlineSMS – open source bulk SMS management system.	Dedicated line (mobile phone) situated at the research desk.
Lessons learned	FrontlineSMS was unstable in areas of poor connectivity and not user-friendly.	More stable and applicable technology. However, it creates difficulties for SMS volume tracking and broad responses to feedback trends.
Feedback from the field	REOs used mobile phones or smartphones to liaise directly with radio stations (only applied in Uganda with CKWs who supplemented REOs)	REOs provide feedback on an ad hoc basis to the station, when they receive it from farmers while conducting their extension duties in the field.
Lessons learned	Smartphones worked well to facilitate regular communication between REOs and radio stations, but were expensive and reliant on good connectivity.	The system was cumbersome and increased REO and station workload. REOs were unwilling to submit feedback on a monthly basis.
Solicited Feedback		
	High technology	**Low technology**
Farmer surveys	Grameen Applab developed an application for data collection on smartphones. Data was collected quarterly and/or annually from the first year (only applied in Uganda).	Laminated (to avoid reprinting) paper-based surveys. Data was collected quarterly or annually, from the third year.
Lessons learned	Greater reporting compliance and higher data integrity, but required a strong technology backbone and ongoing funding, both for airtime and data collection costs.	Cost effective in areas of scarce resources, however larger margin of error in data capturing and sporadic reporting compliance.

FIGURE 4.8 Feedback

Collaboration at the implementation level

Although farmers can rightfully claim pride of place in FVR, as primary beneficiaries and important contributors, other actors assume responsibility for serving them. As noted above, FVR implementation takes place at three sub-levels: the core alliances in the field among REOs and radio station personnel; national consortia of implementing partners; and a Regional Office. Collaborative learning takes place between and within each of these levels. Without effective feedback and accountability across all levels, the entire process can fail.

At the *core alliance level*, FVR establishes a practical mechanism for institutionalizing collaboration: the production team. Just as radio stations create teams of studio producers, field reporters, and presenters, FVR creates teams of extension and radio experts who follow a systematic process of needs assessment (with farmer participation), production planning (to ensure that farmer input is captured as required for each topic), and program scheduling. Feedback and accountability loops develop naturally during regular meetings. The production team can also use these meetings to review farmer feedback for all stages of the process: needs, contributions to broadcasts, and feedback on programming. When budgetary or transport challenges make face-to-face consultations difficult, team members can consult by phone, although this is less satisfactory.

Turning to the country level, FVR establishes *national consortia* to inaugurate the model, support core alliances, and build local ownership. To date, these consortia have comprised agricultural universities or faculties (as knowledge partners) and civil society (NGOs working in fields such as media, community development, gender, and capacity building). Government participation has ranged from direct consortium membership to observation as a receiver of FVR services. Future consortia may also include other knowledge partners (such as agricultural research institutes) and private sector representatives.

These consortia served as our primary collaborators in developing, adjusting, and refining the model for each country. We worked hard not to present ourselves as outside experts. Rather, we explored every idea with the consortium and, in some cases, came up with new approaches to suit specific contexts. This became easier as consortium members acquired a better understanding of FVR's objectives and design hypotheses. We learned that, when establishing a shared perspective around an unfamiliar innovation, building local ownership takes time as colleagues acquire the knowledge and confidence to become active collaborators.

Each national consortium, with support from the Regional Office, collaborates directly with core alliances along multiple lines of action: establishing new partnerships with radio stations and extension services; building capacity in the field; providing technical support; and monitoring progress through regular field visits. In all of these areas, feedback and accountability flow both ways between the consortium and the alliance. For example, the consortium is accountable to production teams for providing the necessary training and technical support to implement and improve FVR programming. Production teams, in turn, are accountable to the consortium for implementing FVR in the field. Collective learning has perhaps been less effective here, however, since almost by definition consortium members take on an expert role in relation to local stations and REOs. As always, unequal power dynamics make true collaboration challenging.

The third level of FVR implementation lies at the Regional Office, to date based in South Africa. Originally the donor assumed that, in order to foster local ownership, each country would lead its own program, with only a small secretariat for coordination. This model, common for regional grants, may work well for loose networks. FVR, on the other hand, proved to require tighter, more formal collaboration in order to collectively develop and implement a brand new model for delivering agricultural extension. Eventually FVR took a "theme and variations" approach with a modest, but somewhat larger, Regional Office. We learned that a strong model requires accountability to core principles (the "theme"), but flexibility in adapting these to the unique circumstances in each country was based on local feedback (the "variations").

FVR's Regional Office works in six primary areas: consortium-building; strategic leadership; partnerships; coordination; capacity building; and MLE. All of these involve direct collaboration with national consortia, using two-way feedback and accountability systems (as limited by the power dynamics of contractual relationships noted above). It also supports core alliances in the field, occasionally through direct participation in training workshops and site visits but primarily through consortium members themselves. At the same time, the Regional Office serves as the primary point of contact with the funder, receiving donor feedback and reporting against measures of accountability set contractually. In many respects, therefore, this office represents the hub of all FVR feedback and accountability systems, as well as the primary mechanism for documenting the initiative's collective learning.

The chief difference between the ways in which national consortia work with core alliance members and the Regional Office derives directly from funding. As in almost all cases, external financial support creates both opportunities and obstacles. The funds that flowed from the donor to the consortia through the Regional Office facilitated vital research and development work, from inaugural visits to field monitoring, which could not have been accomplished without such support. At the same time, grantees and sub-grantees must account for the use and impact of donor funds in their roles as financial stewards. This requires formal reporting and accounting systems that proved challenging to many partners, unlike the informal feedback and collaboration between national and regional levels that generally operated effectively. Such formal systems, by their very nature, tend to work well only in one direction. It is difficult to "manage up," to speak truth to power, when you are trying to give feedback to someone who holds the purse strings, whether to a prime contractor (through the Regional Office) or to a donor (from the Regional Office).

On the one hand, it seems desirable to give consortium members as much latitude as possible—a grant model. On the other hand, each organization must contribute to implementing the FVR vision, not just to "do its own thing"—more of a contractual approach. The challenge here lies in the need to help members collaborate among themselves in reaching a common goal by employing a methodology initially unfamiliar to any of them. We found ourselves using the metaphor of a football (soccer) team. Each player (consortium member) brings his or her own skills to the field, but they must all play the same game as teammates.

In response we tried multiple reporting mechanisms, from broad scopes of work to very detailed deliverables. None worked well as either feedback or account-ability strategies. The broad approaches allowed too loose a focus on the basic FVR strategy versus normal institutional priorities. The latter created cumbersome administrative requirements.

Nevertheless, we did implement several practical mechanisms for fostering two-way feedback and accountability between the national and regional levels, such as the dual-workshop model mentioned above. Another example was the 2+2 evaluation methodology.[6] 2+2 follows well-researched principles of feedback that increase the likelihood of behavior change. The core techniques are balanced encouragement and suggestions, frequency of feedback, timeliness, focus, specific-ity, and follow-up. At the end of every day of every FVR workshop with national partners, each participant wrote down two compliments about the session and two suggestions for improvements, submitting them anonymously to encourage honest input. One group member analyzed the main trends for a report-back the following morning. Before then, the planning team met to consider any necessary changes based on that day's feedback, so that these could be included in the report. The power of immediate feedback and follow-up proved particularly exciting. When possible, facilitators made immediate changes in response to 2+2 comments, from adjusting tea breaks to speaking more slowly to spending more (or less) time on specific topics.

Accountability for learning was fostered among implementing partners in other ways. For example, the Regional Office conducted quarterly telephonic surveys with each radio station to gauge their performance. Instead of stopping there and simply sharing the results with national partners, we developed a comparative chart that showed them each radio station's previous performance against their current performance, indicating where performance had improved or declined. We took this to the next level by suggesting specific actions for our partners to implement in response, and met with them face-to-face in steering committee meetings to discuss both the review and the way forward. Often, plans were changed as we co-created solutions with each consortium.

In the final year of the project, the Regional Office implemented a data dash-board based on open-source software that utilizes a variety of ICTs, including smartphones and tablets, to collect, auto-analyze, and present data from the field. Besides its obvious utility for project management and MLE purposes, it provides near real-time feedback on outcomes to stakeholders at all three levels. In addition, the dashboard system is able to capture case studies and photographs to enhance qualitative learning. The system was used to strengthen evaluation of our perfor-mance, and can be used to enhance future learning in FVR.[7]

Collaboration at the donor level

In combined careers that comprise decades of work in service to rural develop-ment, the authors have found a collaborative-learning approach to be as important with donors as with any other stakeholders, perhaps even more so. Accountability and feedback are almost always present, at least in one direction: accountability from grantees to donors, feedback from donors to grantees. Yet the same power dynamics that challenged FVR's efforts to foster two-way feedback and account-ability between the Regional Office (representing the prime contractor) and national consortia (in their role as funded sub-grantees) also challenged reciprocal learning between the Regional Office and the donor.

In retrospect, the FVR team (under both prime contractors) could have done a better job of facilitating this collaboration in at least two important ways. First, we should have told our story more effectively, disseminating information earlier and more widely about the innovations being developed. Second, we should have implemented our MLE system sooner. Although we worked in a proof-of-concept mode, prior to scaling our innovations and evaluating their impact at the level of productivity and livelihoods, outcomes data were still available from the field and lessons learned could have been documented earlier. Had our execution of these two related areas been better, we would have provided more useful feedback to our donor that might have fostered more consistent collaboration.

From the donor side, we started with a level of cooperation unique in our expe-rience with other funders, whether bilateral, multilateral, or foundations. We found tangible demonstrations of our donor's stated commitment to taking risks, playing the long game, and making a difference. The Bill & Melinda Gates Foundation proved willing to fund FVR as a high-risk, high-potential endeavor. They contin-ued that funding for more than five years, longer than most projects. And in the initial stages of planning and executing FVR, they worked closely with us more in a collaborative than a supervisory mode. We believe that much of FVR's success can be traced back to this unusual type of donor–grantee relationship.

Over the final year or two of our work together this collaboration petered out. Communications dropped off, making it difficult for us to understand what was expected, to discuss what was being learned, or to jointly plan for the transition to a post-funding stage. In the end, the successes achieved in FVR's initial countries were somewhat offset by the withdrawal of support from newer countries before they were ready to cross the sustainability threshold. While we still expect FVR to con-tinue at current stations in Malawi and, perhaps, to expand modestly in Kenya, this loss of funding may jeopardize effective continuation of the system in Tanzania and Uganda. Furthermore, the termination of donor support calls into question prospects for scaling a proven model within current countries, or expanding it to new coun-tries, which means that its significant return on investment may remain unrealized.

Donor priorities do change. External funding can never be indefinite, nor should it be. However, building true collaboration takes time, more time than many funders generally are willing to offer. The World Bank has taken note of this problem specifically in the agricultural sector, pointing out that donor efforts to serve rural farmers terminate too quickly because donors often choose immediate impact over long-term institution building.[8] Without some way of completing the process of collective learning, investments may fail to achieve their full potential.

Therefore, a mechanism for grandfathering commitments to successful work, even when a donor's focus shifts over time, seems only logical. And whatever the circumstances, communication—frank, constructive, and ongoing—represents a key prerequisite for the kind of collaboration needed to help donors and their grantees achieve their goals together.

Conclusion

The roots of FVR lie in the reality of a broken agricultural extension system and the realization that effective extension can be, must be, a collaborative effort—with farmer participation at every stage of the process, continual feedback loops, and two-way accountability. Collective learning begins with, but is not limited to, interactions with farmers themselves. It includes all actors—implementing partners and donor representatives alike.

Beyond an extension model based on the reality of farmers as collaborators who generate knowledge as well as use it, we employed collective learning as our fundamental project-management strategy. From the very beginning, FVR used techniques of collaborative planning and in-flight corrections to translate principles into effective practice in cooperation with actors at the field, country, and regional levels. FVR's success demonstrates that collaborative learning represents more than a pious ideal. It offers a practical approach to finding creative solutions to evolving challenges.

As we noted at the beginning of this chapter, the FVR model continues to progress and develop. We have learned that it takes longer, with more support, than we originally anticipated to help a country reach the sustainability tipping point. We have also learned that this can be done, however, with some of our initial countries already operating on their own. Finally, we have seen outcomes that far exceeded our original expectations, whether measured in terms of farmers reached or changes in behavior.

Each of the authors feels that FVR represents the most significant development experience of his or her career. The power of collective learning has created a new, game-changing approach to helping smallholder farmers support themselves and their peers. As one such collaborator testified:

> Through FVR [I] am able to produce throughout the year, even during the dry season ... I am able to get income through the year through the sale of the agricultural produce ... Since I started listening to FVR programs on radio, my production has increased drastically and my finances too ... I managed to construct biogas that I now use as a source of energy on my farm ... My farm serves as a demonstration farm in the district. Many farmers come to get information on how to build a biogas and other practices on my farm. With improved varieties of tomato on my farm, more farmers come for the seeds and seedlings.
>
> (Agnes Wanda, subsistence and commercial tomato farmer)

Notes

1 The views expressed in this chapter are solely those of the authors, who do not speak for the American Institutes for Research, Khulisa Management Services, or the Bill & Melinda Gates Foundation.
2 Taken from the Overall Case Studies section of the FVR Dashboard: http://fvr.khulisa. com:8080 (accessed September 22, 2015. See also www.farmervoice.org).
3 For ease of reading, this chapter uses the terms "smallholder farmer" and "farmer" interchangeably. This book's theme, collective learning in rural development, implies a focus on the smallholder farmers who make up that vast majority of those in the global South with livelihoods depending on agriculture, including subsistence farmers.
4 Originally developed in China in the 1990s to improve feedback, promote greater accountability and enhance the overall outcomes of training.
5 Taken from an internal report prepared by Katharine Tjasink and Traceyleigh McLeod, entitled "Strengthening Research Desks and Feedback Systems," submitted to the Bill & Melinda Gates Foundation on December 28, 2012.
6 Originally developed in Namibia for teacher training purposes.
7 The data dashboard is available online at http://fvr.khulisa.com:8080 (accessed September 22, 2015). It is also linked to the FVR website (www.farmervoice.org).
8 World Bank Discussion Paper 45, 2010, http://siteresources.worldbank.org/INTARD/ Resources/Stren_combined_web.pdf (accessed September 22, 2015).

5

KEYSTONE ACCOUNTABILITY AND CONSTITUENT VOICE

Lessons from using feedback to manage and improve performance in agriculture extension, agro-forestry enterprises, producer cooperatives and coffee marketing

Andre Proctor and David Bonbright[1]

SUMMARY

Keystone Accountability explores and develops ways in which the views and experiences of those intended to benefit from development initiatives (the primary constituents) can meaningfully and systematically influence the way that programs undertaken in their name are designed, implemented, managed and evaluated. This chapter describes the emergence of 'Constituent Voice' (CV) as a cost-effective way of creating continuous systems of feedback and dialogue that turn farmer voices into real-time performance management data and reliable evidence on the performance, relationships and emerging outcomes of smallholder agriculture development projects.

The methods described here are being developed and adapted 'in the field' working with government extension systems, international NGOs and foundations, private companies and farmer organizations. The chapter explores successes and failures along this journey. Along the way Keystone discovered that feedback from frontline field staff provides valuable data on the performance of higher decision-making levels. Creative use of farmer and frontline staff feedback can do much to create a 'responsive performance culture' in otherwise top-down technocratic and bureaucratic initiatives.

CV is an evolving work in progress. Experience suggests that there can be real developmental value in 'imperfect data', and that data quality improves through using it for collective learning. But collecting feedback is the easy part. Keystone's latest and most interesting efforts are focused on affordable, practical and empowering ways to enable all constituents to access, analyse and engage with each other over the data and what it means: to use feedback to frame an inclusive process of listening, learning and improving. We call this the Feedback Commons.

Introduction

Keystone Accountability was launched in 2006 with a single purpose: to explore and develop ways in which the views and experiences of those intended to benefit from development initiatives (the primary constituents) can meaningfully and systematically influence the way that programs undertaken in their name are designed, implemented, managed and evaluated.

Keystone is rooted in the tradition of participatory development practice that began in farming systems research in the late 1950s. By the early 2000s it was clear that while participatory development may have transformed relationships and practice in individual development projects on the ground, it had not even begun to influence the development mainstream, which had grown into a multi-million dollar industry characterized in public and nonprofit sectors alike by top-down and bureaucratic management systems.

We realized that if you aim to change the way that a system behaves and learns, you need to confront that system on its own terms. This meant turning feedback from primary constituents into hard and robust *data* that could stand alongside the other performance and results data that programs routinely measure. In other words, we needed convincing metrics of key constituent perceptions and experience especially on the quality of services, the quality of relationships and the contribution of the programs to outcomes.

So from our comfort zone of participatory practice we started looking for potential models that we could learn from. We found some exciting relationship measurement practices in what was for us a surprising place, the customer satisfaction industry. This lost us many friends who rolled their eyes and accused us of reducing complex human processes to strings of numbers.

But soon it became clear that metrics alone were not enough to turn feedback into meaningful *voice*. Equally important was to ensure that the data is *used* in a public and transparent cycle of measuring, analysing and learning together – where constituents together make sense of the feedback, identify action points, re-frame expectations and agree to continue with ongoing feedback, dialogue and learning.

The really exciting discovery was that when all constituents can engage with data and focus dialogue on that data, and when the cycle is repeated as an integral part of how organizations learn and manage their performance, a new kind of conversation becomes possible – one that genuinely enables constituent voice.

This chapter describes Keystone's experiences in *introducing* the methodology that we call CV with a range of partners in the agriculture sector. In the almost three years that we have worked with the projects described in this chapter, we can say no more than that we have made a start to the longer journey that will be required to change systems.[2] Each context has had its own setbacks and successes and learnings for the practice of CV.

We use the word *introducing* to describe the initial process of shared action-learning with clients that arrives at a 'proof of concept' – or at least at a point where stakeholders speak with genuine appreciation of how useful CV has been and how they have learned through the process.

Our learning so far tells us that the first experience of collecting feedback and making sense of it in dialogue with constituents foretells for most organizations that a more committing process lies ahead. The next step, of *embedding* CV into how the entire organization or institution works, requires a different order of commitment and organizational change: the shift from an add-on 'useful activity' to a consistent practice that molds organizational culture and practice. One day we hope to write a sequel to this chapter that can tell the *embedding* story.

The process of *introducing* that we can describe now is a period of great experimentation and learning – and we try to bring out this 'learning journey' through the case stories presented in this chapter.

Six major themes emerge:

- How CV methods have evolved in response to the challenges faced.
- How 'imperfect data' can be profoundly useful – and how data quality improves through using it.
- How frontline staff must be seen as a core constituent in large-scale service delivery or program implementation.
- How we need to recognize that a feedback system is not just a technical process, but is deeply social and political. It needs to be designed and implemented sensitively to the fears and needs of all constituents.
- How a technological 'feedback infrastructure' that reduces the cost, lowers the skill levels required and improves the timeliness of data collection, analysis and use is the key to making feedback-based collective learning the new norm in development practice.
- How we need to understand the systemic challenges in the way of turning good intentions into consistent practice – why it is so difficult to move from a one-off 'useful activity' to a consistent practice that defines organizational culture and identity.

We hope that this chapter will inspire more to take this journey to new levels – from the exciting discovery of how useful good feedback-based learning can be to the deeper process of understanding how it can change organization systems, culture and practice.

CV in agriculture extension systems: an experiment in Ethiopia

What we set out to achieve and why

Over the last decade, the Ethiopian government has invested heavily in agriculture extension services and now has one of the highest ratios of extension worker to farmers in the world. However, a study conducted by the International Food Policy Research Institute (IFPRI) in 2010 showed that this had minimal effect on improving production or livelihoods in most areas.

The study identified a number of technical and capacity problems that could be addressed, but singled out two challenges:

1   How to overcome the top-down, bureaucratic management behaviour that seems to characterize government systems in general: how to turn the agriculture extension system into a much more 'farmer-driven' service that responds dynamically to farmer needs and that no longer treats farmers as passive recipients of services but rather activates their inherent individual and collective agency.
2   How to overcome the high levels of demoralization and frustration expressed by frontline extension staff and inculcate a responsive 'performance culture' in the extension system.

In 2010 a multi-pronged project to strengthen the extension system was launched, funded by the Bill & Melinda Gates Foundation and co-led by the Ministry of Agriculture, Oxfam and the Sasakawa Africa Association. In addition to a number of technical interventions, a small collaborative 'design team' was assembled consisting of staff from Oxfam and consultants from Keystone Accountability, the Agricultural Learning and Impacts Network (ALINe) and IFPRI. This team was tasked to design and pilot a new feedback-based approach to monitoring and evaluation (M&E) that would put the perceptions and experiences of farmers at the centre of how the extension system learns and manages its performance.

This pilot has involved a collaborative and iterative process of action learning involving farmers and extension agents as well as woreda and regional managers from the Ministry of Agriculture (a woreda is a local government district comprising a number of kebeles or village communities). It draws on a mixed methodological heritage: the long tradition of participatory development practice, conventional social research methods, tested customer relationship measurement techniques and Keystone's emerging CV method.

Part 1: the story of the pilot

It was clear from the start that this would be a major departure from mainstream agriculture M&E practice, which tends to rely on quantitative measures such as technology adoption rates, input and output analysis, levels of production and productivity, loss to pests/diseases and changes in household income and food security. These measures are clearly important for understanding the ultimate performance of the agricultural system as a whole. However, they are not so helpful for actors working in the extension system, and contribute little to a performance culture within the extension service that fosters responsiveness to the needs and insights of farmers and frontline extension staff.

The pilot would have an explicitly *management* rather than a *research* orientation with the primary purpose of measurement being to drive accountable learning and improvement at the level of the Farmer Training Centres (FTCs) in kebeles (villages). At the same time, this grassroots performance data needed to be aggregatable to enable comparative performance benchmarking and better management decision-making at all levels up the extension system.

The design team began by asking:

- Who are the main constituent groups in the extension system?
- What can farmers tell about their experience of the extension service and of the technologies and innovations being promoted that will explain the variable success of these inputs and suggest solutions?
- What can frontline extension workers (called Development Agents or DAs) tell about the conditions under which they work and suggest ways in which they can be enabled to work more effectively?
- What can woreda-level extension officials (Supervisors and Subject Matter Specialists) tell about the factors that enable or disable them from playing their part effectively?
- How can feedback from these distinct actors be organized, reported and used to hold managers and staff accountable to each other and to farmers for delivering the best services that will enable farmers to succeed and prosper?
- How can better performance management enable farmers to become active agents in their own development?

Then we asked some technical questions:

- How can we collect this information in an ongoing way – reliably but inexpensively?
- How can we analyse it so that it is timely and useful to extension workers, technical advisers, managers and farmers themselves who seek to understand the reasons behind success or failure and take actions to improve their performance?
- How can we present this information in simple, clear performance reports that can be understood and discussed by farmers, extension workers, advisers and backline managers?
- How can we store the information so that it is available quickly to support real-time learning, dialogue and decision-making at different levels in the system?
- How can we design the system so that most parts of it can be automated to make it even more cost-effective, accessible and useful?
- How can we make sure that the system really drives improved performance and accountability to farmers?

Over the past two years the design team has experimented with different tools and methods in four pilot woredas: Debre Libanos, Gumer, Shinile and Arsi Negele.

We started clumsily

Contracting took a long time and it was four months into the implementation period before we could really start work. The Gates Foundation needed a 'baseline' in a hurry, and Oxfam was under some pressure to contract a conventional research firm to conduct a classic baseline survey (even though the IFPRI study had already painted a detailed picture of the general health of the system).

Thus pressured, some creative thinking soon turned this into an opportunity for innovation and learning: why not use the 'baseline' to test some prototypes of the kind of farmer feedback survey tools and performance reports that we were considering for the Agriculture Extension Performance Management System (AEPMS)? And use this data as an indication of baseline perceptions?

Deadlines were tight, but we managed to design a short and reasonably comprehensive farmer feedback survey, using 12 multi-part questions and a Net Promoter System[3] rating scale of 0–10. IFPRI was hired to conduct the field work. We conducted a trial run in two FTCs before agreeing on a final prototype tool to conduct our modified baseline exercise.

To keep costs as low as possible we experimented with group interview methods that introduced each question and allowed for discussions to clarify the meaning of the questions, and identify the strengths and weaknesses of the extension service. Individuals then scored their answers privately. Each respondent had ten small stones in their hand and selected the number of stones corresponding to the score they wanted to give. They put their hands behind their backs and the facilitator went round entering each person's score onto a separate score sheet.

We were pleased to see that for most questions there was a wide range of responses suggesting that discussing the question beforehand did not make everyone score the same – though this remains controversial among the design team. We were also anxious that people might feel uncomfortable with this kind of secret rating of performance – but the feedback was overwhelmingly that men and women farmers alike appreciated the opportunity to score privately.

Within two weeks we had all the feedback data in hand and could produce FTC performance reports for the two pilot FTCs in each pilot woreda. We applied the simple Net Promoter Analysis (NPA) to the responses to each evaluative question. NPA is discussed more fully in Box 5.1.

Next we organized three reflective workshops – one in each of the three pilot woredas at which we presented and discussed the 'baseline' performance reports. Participants in the reflective workshops included farmers, extension staff from all pilot FTCs, woreda officials and a handful of more senior extension managers. It was very heartening to witness the animated and surprisingly frank discussion of the issues raised by the survey data between farmers, extension staff and officials. It demonstrated the potential of dialogue based on anonymous feedback in which participants could discuss very critical perceptions of the extension service without having to express personal views.

BOX 5.1 NET PROMOTER ANALYSIS AS ADAPTED FOR AGRICULTURAL EXTENSION

For certain questions the AEPMS uses a method for analysing and reporting perceptions that is used by many companies to understand and manage their relationship with their customers. It is called *Net Promoter Analysis* (NPA) (Figure 5.1). NPA gives us a very simple but powerful way of presenting feedback from farmers and frontline staff on the performance of the extension system.

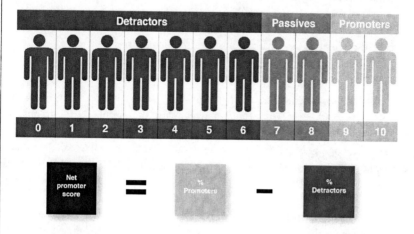

FIGURE 5.1 Net Promoter Analysis is a clear and simple way to show both the range of responses and calculate a single 'aspirational' score that can be used for benchmarking and to set performance targets together

In Net Promoter Analysis respondents are classified into three groups. This gives us a simple way of understanding the range of farmer or frontline staff views:

- The *promoters* or *positives* are people who give a satisfaction score of 9 and 10 on a 0–10 scale. These are the champions, those who feel that the FTC performs its work very well and that there is little improvement needed.
- The *passives* or *neutrals* are those who give scores of 7 and 8. These people feel mostly positive about the performance of the FTC. They do not have major concerns, but feel that there are aspects of the FTC's performance that can be improved.
- Those who provide scores from 1–6 are classified as *detractors* or *negatives*. They feel that the FTC does not really perform its work as well as it could. They have moderate to serious criticism of the extension service in their community.

In most of the AEPMS tools that have been developed to date, however, a scale of 1–5 has been used to simplify scoring and the classification into detractors, passives and promoters has been adjusted accordingly.

In addition to showing the percentage of promoters, passives and detractors, a single *Net Performance Score* (NP Score) can also be calculated. Having a single number score makes it easy to calculate Performance Indexes for a group of questions. It also makes it easy to compare changes in citizen performance ratings over time to track improvement or deterioration in performance.

Finally, it is easy to add the NP Scores together so that a woreda or zonal manager can see and compare the performance scores of all the FTCs in their area and calculate a Woreda or Zone Performance Score.

The workshops also demonstrated that even the least educated (functionally illiterate) farmers could understand and engage with the simple NPA graphs and understand the comparative performance benchmarking of one FTC against another. The openness with which the senior managers and woreda officials were willing to engage with critical feedback from farmers and frontline staff was encouraging. Indeed, the extension managers in the pilot woredas have become the project's staunchest champions.

The workshops affirmed one of Keystone's primary working hypotheses: that while independently collected and anonymous data is an essential vehicle for turning feedback into voice, simply generating the data is not sufficient. It is in completing the feedback loops by reporting the findings back to respondent communities and making sense of it together through open dialogue that feedback is transformed into voice and where mutual learning and accountability happens.

But the workshops also made us aware of shortcomings in the methodology, and prompted one technical modification and two significant design innovations.

Technical modification. A significant number of field workers reported that farmers were new to using a 0–10 rating scale. The field team argued that the data would be more reliable if in future we used a shorter 1–5 scale. The design team decided to try a shorter scale in the formal pilot. But the team remains divided on this point, critics pointing to the substantial survey literature (mainly from developed countries) plus Keystone's experience in using 0–10 scales in other similar settings that suggests that longer Likert scales still yield more accurate and nuanced data, and that we should concentrate rather on explaining better how to respond using the longer scale.

Design innovation 1. The experience of using a feedback survey to provide baseline data highlighted a number of sub-optimal features in conventional survey approaches such as this. Long surveys are *heavy*: they are burdensome to deliver, burdensome to respond to, demanding to analyse and cumbersome for organizations to translate into corrective actions.

Despite the fact that the early rounds of data collection and sense-making sessions were generating insights that everyone found useful and even exciting, we could see that farmer feedback of this type alone was not going to lead to sustained learning and improvement.

Our experience mirrored the experience of those working in the *customer satisfaction* field in the 1970s and 1980s. So we looked at where the customer service industry had moved to. We decided to abandon the large comprehensive 'baseline survey' approach and develop three much shorter tools that would be easier and cheaper to administer, quicker to analyse and easier to turn into short, accessible performance reports.

This suite of three tools (discussed in detail below) was applied in the first iteration of the pilot proper. And to reduce reliance on expensive research firms, two of the new tools were designed so that they could be applied, without compromising independence and respondent anonymity, by staff from other levels of the extension system or from other government departments in the same area.

Design innovation 2. From the engagement of frontline staff in the workshop dialogues, it became clear, as the IFPRI study noted, that frontline extension workers are often ill equipped, neglected, disempowered and demotivated. They are often unable to perform their work well because of management breakdowns higher up in the system and other factors that are outside their control.

We knew of studies from the customer satisfaction industry that demonstrated a direct correlation between satisfied frontline staff and satisfied customers. Good public service management practice knows this, and many public service reform initiatives in Africa seek to provide incentives and career paths for public servants. But without an effective metric, these reform initiatives often stagnate.

Could systematic feedback loops between frontline staff and their senior management generate the metrics to drive the extension system towards creating the conditions and incentives for more satisfied, motivated and effective frontline staff as well? Could the combination of farmer feedback loops and frontline extension worker feedback loops produce a tipping point to a larger transformation in the extension system? We set to work designing two new survey tools to measure the satisfaction and perceptions of extension staff at two levels: the Development Agents (DAs) in the FTCs, and the Subject Matter Specialists (SMSs) in the woreda offices.

A lightbulb moment

As we emerged from the 'baseline' exercise, we had one of those 'lightbulb moments' where suddenly things were much clearer.

Our experiential learning during the 'baseline' had generated three significant and distinct process innovations:

- First, we had an approach to performance improvement and learning based on collecting feedback and then closing the feedback loop with farmers.

- Second, we had discovered a model of light-touch, focused micro-surveys that could work like drip-feed irrigation – that could bring forth the specific data that was needed where and when it was needed
- Third, we had added a parallel feedback loop from frontline extension workers to complement farmer feedback.

This highlighted for us both the potential of the project to transform extension practice, and the difficulty in realizing this transformative potential. This was clearly more ambitious than traditional M&E. To emphasize this shift from traditional M&E to performance management we re-framed the project as a team effort to co-create an AEPMS. Since that time, this is how the project has been communicated to all stakeholders. The standard introduction states:

> The AEPMS generates empirically rigorous perceptual data on the performance of the extension system from the perspective of the most important constituents: the frontline staff and farmers. It provides constituents with a clear frame for engaging in dialogue on how the extension system is performing, where the problems are perceived to lie, and what the different constituents at different levels can do to improve performance – including farmers, frontline staff, extension managers and even project funders.

However, never far from our thinking is the key realization: feedback systems are not just technical processes! They are above all *deeply social and political processes*. They need to offer value to *all* the actors in the system. They need to be introduced and managed in ways that do not threaten stakeholders – at least not at first.

The AEPMS pilot enters its first full feedback cycle

With this re-framing and a suite of new tools, the design team set about planning the first full iteration of the pilot in the pilot woredas.

There were three revised tools to collect feedback from farmers on their perceptions on the performance of the extension system:

1 A 'technology tracker' to collect farmer experience on the performance of technologies promoted by the extension system.
2 Short micro-surveys to collect feedback after trainings and other services.
3 An annual diagnostic survey on the strengths and weaknesses of the extension service from a farmer perspective.

In addition, the perceptions of DAs and SMSs were collected using:

4 an annual 'satisfaction survey';
5 short micro-surveys after training.

Armed with the new tool suite, the next step in the pilot was a week-long reflection and training workshop at which DAs, SMSs and other woreda managers from all four pilot woredas were inducted as co-creators of the methodology. As co-creators, the DAs and SMSs were invited to reflect on and recommend ways to refine the tools and data collection methods. The process involved going out into the field and collecting data from farmers and others and reflecting together on the experience. Survey results were analysed and sample performance reports were generated overnight, and these were discussed and refined the next day.

Following this, the pilot then unfolded over the next six months. A further revision of tools was applied in 2015 (Box 5.2).

BOX 5.2 PRINCIPLES FOR AN EFFECTIVE CYCLE OF LEARNING AND IMPROVING

The AEPMS is based on a cyclical process based on Keystone's CV cycle (Figure 5.2).

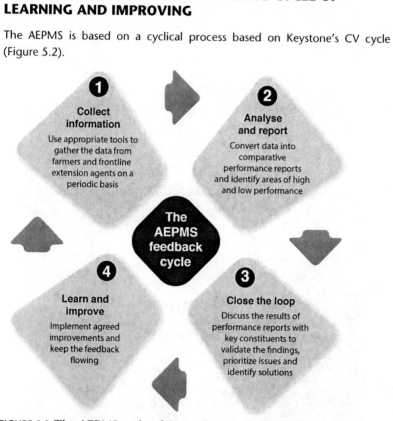

FIGURE 5.2 The AEPMS cycle of data collection, analysis, public performance reporting, dialogue and learning closely follows Keystone's CV cycle. It is essential to complete *all* steps in the cycle to move beyond 'research' and to a performance management system that turns feedback from farmers and frontline staff into meaningful voice in how the extension service is managed

Turning this idea into reality involves balancing a number of critical principles across these four stages.

Data quality

- Data quality must be credible, and every effort must be made to guarantee the quality of the data generated in the AEPMS. But conforming to strictly 'scientific' criteria for statistical validity would make it prohibitively expensive and impractical. Evidentiary rigour must be balanced against practicality and usefulness. For the AEPMS the most important principles are: (i) those collecting the data do not have an interest in manipulating the results; and (ii) farmers and frontline staff are able to give their feedback anonymously so that they feel completely free to express their honest views without fear of any negative consequences as a result.
- Data quality is strengthened through the refinements emerging from the public validation and sense-making dialogue where participants can question results; if they feel they are not representative. In such dialogue even imperfect data can be extremely useful.
- Even more importantly, as constituents over time become used to giving feedback and seeing how that feedback drives improvements, they are more likely to provide frank and considered opinions. This evolutionary approach to data quality is a core innovation of AEPMS and is illustrated in Figure 5.3.

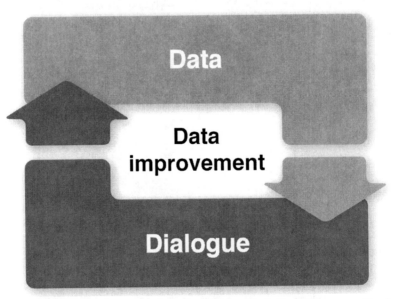

FIGURE 5.3 Discussing real data leads to a different kind of engagement, and leads to an improvement in data quality as farmers and frontline staff realize that it is in their interests to take the surveys seriously

Data quantity

Too much data creates noise. And it consumes time and money. The key is to collect just enough feedback data on just the right issues. Less in this context is definitely more. And we will leave it at that.

Cost

If collecting and reporting feedback data is too expensive it will not be sustained beyond the life of the pilot and will not be adopted across the entire extension system. The AEPMS cannot rely on expensive research methods using long surveys conducted by professional research firms. While respecting the need for independent data collection and anonymity for respondents (and until there are accessible automated mechanisms for farmers and frontline staff to give their feedback directly into the system) the AEPMS will rely on staff from other regions or departments to collect and enter the data.

Cost also requires short and relatively simple survey tools that can be applied frequently, with only limited training, to generate a continuous stream of feedback data without causing 'survey fatigue' in either collectors or respondents. And it also requires simple, easily automated statistical methods.

Timelines

Feedback needs to be collected regularly according to the rhythms of extension activities and the agricultural cycle. Some data should be collected at or close to key 'touch points' between the extension service and farmers, some at key moments in the agricultural cycle, and some can be collected annually. But time-sensitive data must be available quickly for prompt decision-making and corrective actions by managers and staff in the extension system.

In the introduction phase this can be done manually by a trained project team. But to become embedded, data must be able to be captured by non-expert staff and entered into a centralized, Internet-based database from anywhere in the country where there is an Internet connection.

Utility

To produce corrective action, the data must be useful, and those who give feedback must be able to see how it is being used to improve the way in which the extension system supports them. Feedback data must be analysed and converted into simple but credible performance reports that even poorly educated farmers can engage with.

- The purpose of the AEPMS is not just to create knowledge, but to use it in a way that drives improvement. One way of doing that is to produce performance reports that enable organizations to benchmark their performance ratings. In the AEPMS, performance reports enable an FTC or woreda office to see their performance scores compared, not against some abstract and often unachievable performance standard, but against the ratings of other facilities in the same woreda or region.

- Finally, if the AEPMS is to avoid the accusation that it is simply another extractive, top-down data extraction process, performance reports must be reported back to the constituents who gave the feedback, and management needs to respond to the feedback contained in the reports in a way that allow respondents to 'connect the dots' between their feedback and the changes they are observing. We call this 'closing the feedback loop'.
- Closing the loop is a critical part of the cycle of learning and improving that makes up the AEPMS. It is important as a public validation of the feedback data collected. But it is the key mechanism that ensures that the extension system places farmers' needs at the centre of its practice, and that its performance is assessed by how well it does this.

Farmer feedback on quality and relevance of training and demonstration events

The main instrument for collecting farmer feedback on the quality and relevance of training and demonstration events is a short, one-page micro-survey that should be administered at or soon after an event or 'touch point' by someone independent of the service provider.

A micro-survey can consist of between two and five questions. One or more closed rating questions for quantifiable and comparative feedback, and one open question to enable farmers to explain their scores or add any other feedback.

Farmer assessments of the quality and relevance of services provided by the FTC are communicated using NP analysis in short, comparative performance reports for discussion between FTC management and farmers as well as higher up the system.

FTCs can compare their ratings with those of others in their woreda and develop strategies to improve. Woreda management can use the data to reward FTCs that perform well in the eyes of farmers. The reports can be discussed internally with senior management as well as publicly in communities to identify what can be improved and to make commitments to improve.

Farmer feedback on the performance of specific technologies

The design team developed a special survey tool called a 'Technology Tracker' to collect farmer feedback on their experience of applying new technologies promoted by the extension system.

This tool requires neither independent data collection nor anonymity as it is the performance of the technology that is being measured, not the performance of the DA. The Tech Tracker has gone through a few revisions since it was first tried, and no doubt will benefit from further experimentation.

Typically, DAs will randomly select a representative group of farmers that have been trained in a given technology. They will visit these farmers twice – once during the early phase of adoption and once towards the end of the cycle. They will collect feedback from the farmers on their stage of adoption, the challenges they face, how they rate the technology in terms of key performance dimensions (ease of understanding, ease of getting required inputs, labour requirements, quantity produced, quality of produce, amount sold, price obtained and overall profitability). There is space for open feedback as well. Results are captured into a database.

In 2015 a new online performance dashboard was developed by Andre Ling to enable real-time online performance reporting. The dashboard is updated constantly as new data is generated and can be accessed by anyone with the necessary authority.

The dashboard enables a user to select what data to represent, to select comparative benchmarks and to disaggregate the feedback by any demographic category. Through the Feedback Commons, Keystone offers a similar 'performance dashboard' for performance analysis and reporting.

The NP graphs in Figure 5.4 show farmer perceptions on their experience of introducing modern beehives. Satisfaction varies considerably indicating where the extension system needs to focus its attention. When operative, senior managers could have an instant picture of where this technology is being applied successfully and the main problems faced by farmers. Discussing these results with farmers will reveal the reasons for the ratings and help identify and share solutions.

Farmer feedback on the performance of the extension system as a whole

There are many performance dimensions of the extension system beyond the quality and relevance of specific services or the performance of individual technologies. To collect farmer feedback on these aspects, such as the relationships between farmers and officials, a diagnostic feedback tool has been developed that asks farmers to assess the performance of the service across a range of dimensions. This is referred to it as the Farmer Voice Diagnostic Tool.

The tool is divided into the following sections:

• Part 1: *Services* – measures farmer perceptions of the range of technologies promoted, overall quality of key services provided, the functionality of the FTC and the inclusiveness of the extensions services.
• Part 2: *Relationships* – assesses the quality of relationships with DAs, FTC Management Committees, Development Units, networks and kebele officials.

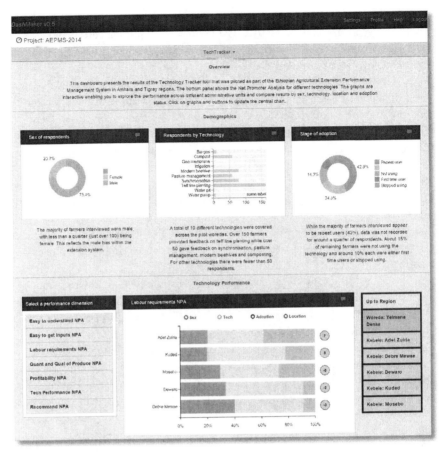

FIGURE 5.4 AEPMS feedback data can be uploaded into an online database and used to generate close to real-time performance dashboards. Managers can access up-to-date, feedback-based performance reports of local FTCs, upstream managers and new technologies at the click of a button. Feedback from one kebele, woreda or zone can be benchmarked against other similar areas or against any demographic category. Feedback from young and old, male and female, wealthy or poor farmers can be compared

- Part 3: *Challenges* – farmers prioritize challenges, identify long-standing problems and unwanted extension activities (if any).

The Farmer Voice diagnostic survey can be carried out periodically – usually annually – by other agriculture department staff that are independent of the extension system at the local level. The current questionnaire consists of a mix of rating questions and open feedback.

Frontline staff feedback on service quality and relevance

The main instruments for collecting feedback from DAs and SMSs on the specific training and other management support that they receive is also a set of micro-surveys very similar to the farmer micro-surveys, but tailored to the specific services in question.

Because most extension staff are literate, micro-surveys can be distributed and self-completed anonymously after each event. We know that training evaluation surveys are often not taken seriously, but we hypothesize that once staff realize that their feedback will be reported back and discussed with them, and used in performance management of the FTC, they will take these micro-surveys more seriously. Reports look very similar to the farmer service quality and relevance reports – and so are not discussed separately here.

Frontline staff feedback on their experience of working in the extension system

The most important feedback from DAs and SMSs focuses on their experience of working in the extension system. As noted earlier, a motivated and equipped frontline worker is key to the success of any service enterprise. While mindful of the realities in rural Ethiopia, by systematically measuring staff satisfaction the design team intends that supply-side management will improve, bottlenecks and breakdowns will be more easily identified and resolved, and staff will be motivated and enabled to perform their work better. The two main tools tested so far are:

* a DA satisfaction survey;
* an SMS satisfaction survey.

Both tools are self-completed once every six months or annually. Questions address:

* Do they have the facilities, equipment, seed and other requirements to do their work well?
* Do they get the support they need from managers and other actors to play their role?
* Are their living conditions bearable?
* Are the production targets achievable? Why? Why not?
* Are they feeling motivated to do their job well? What would make them feel more motivated?
* Is the training they receive useful and relevant?
* Do they have enough time to perform their work well?
* Do they feel confident in their own knowledge and abilities to help farmers address most of the problems that they face?
* How well are the higher management levels of the extension system performing their supervisory and support roles?

Closing the loop

This is the next great frontier of learning in feedback-based collective learning methodologies!

Survey data creates that safe space where a collective set of experiences and perceptions can be engaged with by power holders and the powerless in any institutional relationship.

But it is equally important that the way data is presented and handled in dialogue is sensitive to the fears of those who hold power. In other words, if power holders are to remain party to the process, the focus of dialogues should be emphatically on collectively learning and improving rather than blaming and shaming. At least at first, until confrontation becomes the only strategic option.

Closing the loop is a vital phase in the AEPMS cycle. It involves two main steps, the first being 'internal' (involving key decision-makers and managers) and the second 'external' (involving those who provided the feedback as well).

The 'internal' step involves those who receive the various performance reports in discussing the results internally, analysing the findings, preparing their response and planning for the external, public step.

The 'external' step takes the performance reports along with the management response back to those who provided the feedback. The purpose of this is to validate the results with those who provided the feedback, to identify priority performance issues from their perspective, to explore the reasons for these performance issues, to jointly identify the solutions to address these issues and to identify the responsible bodies.

Once completed, the results of the closing the loop process are documented and then communicated to the concerned authorities for follow-up and action. Guidelines for the closing the loop process have been developed for farmer-level and extension agent-level performance reports.

At the time of going to press, the project team in Ethiopia had only managed to conduct two 'closing the loop' sessions in one woreda – one with farmers and one with frontline staff and woreda officials.

Key components of an AEPMS have now been designed and tested in these early pilots. The initial results have been encouraging and those involved in the pilot process have given positive feedback on its usefulness and relevance. The AEPMS is now ready for larger-scale piloting and integration into mainstream performance management and M&E of the extension system.

FOSCA and the Banana Growers Association of Kenya

Since 2014 Keystone has been able to take this work a little further as part of a Grand Challenge grant by the Bill & Melinda Gates Foundation. In early 2015 it began work with the Farmer Organization Support Centre in Africa (FOSCA – a project of the Alliance for a Green Revolution in Africa [AGRA]) and the Banana Growers Association of Kenya (BGAK) to pilot a similar feedback-based performance management system for the member cooperatives of the BGAK.

This partnership is still in its early days. It aims to pilot simple and affordable ways to convert farmer perceptions and experience into reliable performance data in a form that can be integrated into existing performance management and M&E systems, and then to find ways of using this data to drive improvement and empower farmers.

The idea is that data will not be collected through expensive independent surveys, but as part of routine everyday activity. Farmers and local independent feedback coordinators will be trained to collect feedback using short targeted micro-surveys at selected 'touch points' such as market days, seedling nurseries, input suppliers' training events, field days, AGMs, etc.

Methods will include simple paper questionnaires and toll-free polling via mobile phones. It will involve asking a few questions frequently and as widely as possible, then using the 'headline' data to frame inclusive learning dialogues with stakeholders where the details can be explored and addressed.

Questions for farmers (the cooperative members) cover four main performance dimensions:

- the quality and value of cooperative services (e.g. how strongly would you recommend this service to other farmers?);
- the quality of relationships (e.g. how much do you trust the advice and support you receive from the cooperative?);
- the agency and commitment of members (e.g. to what extent do you believe that you can achieve your goals?);
- emerging outcomes (e.g. have you been able to get a better price for your bananas because of the cooperative?).

Farmer feedback on seedling nurseries and market mechanisms such as market service centres will be supplemented with feedback from the commercial banana buyers. We will also track the performance of technologies promoted by the BGAK and the Ministry of Agriculture. Finally, we will be collecting feedback from the cooperative leadership on the support and funding provided by FOSCA.

The feedback data is being entered into the Feedback Commons and will be accessible to constituents of the project through a real-time online performance dashboard. Figure 5.5 is a screenshot from one of the early steps in the creation of this dashboard. It shows the NPA of farmer responses to the question: How strongly would you recommend this market service centre to other farmers?

Users can select one or more cooperative market centres (selected in the box in the upper left corner) and see farmer responses alongside one another for easy comparison. They can then disaggregate the feedback by locality, a wealth proxy (in this case the number of dairy cows in the household), sex or any other demographic category. In Figure 5.6, the feedback is disaggregated into male and female. This chapter describes a learning process in its very early stages. Keystone and

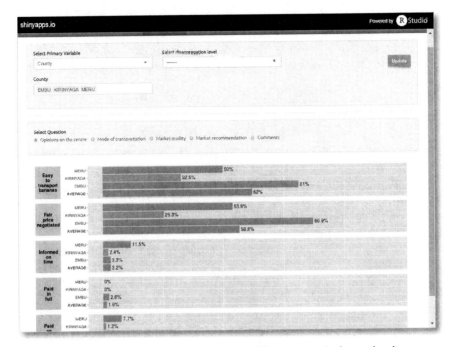

FIGURE 5.5 Keystone's Feedback Commons enables any agriculture development project to upload their data into the Commons database and generate benchmarkable, feedback-based performance dashboards and reports on project offices, farmer associations, upstream managers and even project funders against a range of identified performance dimensions. All this at a fraction of how much it would cost them to do it themselves, and in association with other projects and organizations similar to themselves. This screenshot compares farmer responses in three counties in Kenya to five common questions about their local market service centre. The graph shows the percentage of 'yes' responses to a simple yes/no question. The dashboard allows a manager to select and compare performance of any specific service centres and also compare responses over time

its partners have adopted the 'lean start-up' approach that recommends an agile learning approach in which you learn by doing in a rapid cycle of 'build, measure, learn, repeat'. What we describe here are the earliest 'minimum viable products'. They are presented here as such: undeveloped and imperfect. We invite feedback on these and later iterations as we and others grow this field.

FIGURE 5.6 Net Promoter Analyses disaggregated by any demographic category, or over time. Open comments are accessible and categorized for easier analysis by searching for common words or phrases. Here we compare the NPA and NP scores of men and women farmers in three different counties on their perception of their local banana market service centres. At a glance we can see that satisfaction is much lower in Embu than in the other counties – a clear guide to action

Part 2: some other case examples of constituent voice

BOX 5.3 CONSTITUENT VOICE IN PRIVATE AGRO-FORESTRY COMPANIES IN AFRICA

Since 2012, Keystone has been contracted by the Global Environment Fund (GEF; the investor), a private equity fund invested in sustainable forestry projects internationally, to design and conduct surveys among the three key constituencies that are most directly affected by the operations of two of its companies, the Kilombero Valley Teak Company (KVTC) in Tanzania and Peak Timbers in Swaziland. The investor had learned that cooperation and goodwill with core constituents were essential to the success of the companies as the existing poor worker and community relations had resulted in signficant harm to the companies, including arson, illegal woodcutting, poaching and labor disruptions. The subsequent Keystone surveys included:

1   A *community survey* of a representative sample of households in selected communities living adjacent to the timber plantations.
2   A survey of *contract workers* that are employed by contracted service providers and are often drawn from neighbouring communities.
3   A survey of local *contractors* from whom the companies source most of their forestry, transport and other services.

The surveys were based on Keystone's CV methodology, and sought to generate accurate perceptual data on each constituent's experience and perceptions of the company, its labour and land use policies, its operations, its community development initiatives and its impacts.

The survey results confirmed management's sense that community and contract worker perceptions were generally low, but it also discovered a strong residual vein of goodwill towards the companies across all stakeholder groups: few would like to see the companies close down. In particular, surveys revealed a high level of misperception and misunderstanding among the three stakeholder groups towards each other and towards the company. Clearly, current practices of engagement and dialogue were not working very well.

The results provided the companies with a baseline set of perceptual data to share with constituents and were used to develop new communication and relationship management strategies that could be managed through ongoing feedback metrics.

In addition, by incorporating a simple but reliable, asset-based *poverty scorecard* the surveys offered a way of tracking improvement in household poverty in communities over time. When correlated with data on destructive community behaviour such as poaching and arson, the survey data provided a way of predicting and minimizing future harm.

The data generated by these surveys prompted the companies to develop new and systematic communication and engagement strategies with their key stakeholders that are based on solid measurement. These include dialogue forums and a variety of communication media.

The GEF believes that these metrics will make the companies more profitable – and better at managing major operational risks – through improved understanding of, relationships with and accountability to their key constituents. It will also help them understand and measure the social value generated by their investments.

The experience of the companies since the surveys has borne out many of the expectations, but also shown that using feedback effectively is an art, and that there are many lessons still to be learned.

4   The contractor survey highlighted perceived delays in paying contractors as a big issue – so we made sure that our frontline forest managers were

able to explain the process of approving and making payments – and what contractors can do to help expedite payment. We have definitely had fewer complaints since.

BOX 5.4 THE KILOMBERO VALLEY TEAK COMPANY (KVTC) IN SWAZILAND

Hans Lemm, Managing Director of the KVTC, said of the survey reports: 'They provided useful management data that gave us a kick in the butt to address issues that we were already aware of but had not given full attention to.

'It gave us a concrete sense of the extent of some of the problems and motivated us to:

1   Improve our communications with communities, in particular to work more with radio. We have not consciously measured it, but general feedback suggests that community awareness of company services has improved. We have had more applications for our teak out-growers pro-gram since we have done this.
2   Correlate community feedback with other data we collect on poaching and arson to give us a better understanding of the threats to the company posed by community misunderstanding of our land management prac-tices. We are more consciously focusing on this in our communications.
3   Step up our compliance audits of labour contractors following complaints made in the worker survey.
4   Highlight perceived delays in paying contractors as a big issue – so we made sure that our frontline forest managers were able to explain the process of approving and making payments – and what contractors can do to help expedite payment. We have definitely had fewer complaints since.'

KVTC was less successful in using the community feedback report to frame a dialogue with the community leaders. The company presented extracts of the reports at its annual village seminar, but they were not really engaged with. Lemm thinks that rural community leaders do not immediately understand how data can be useful to them in their negotiating with the company. There is not a direct service provider–recipient relationship between the company and the community, nor really a sense of how to improve the partnership for shared development objectives. Lemm thinks that the survey findings needed to be introduced in a larger conversation about the relationship between

KVTC and the community. The approach they took to community dialogue was, in his view now, too academic.

Lemm said it was good for management to have this data but institutionalizing it into KVTC's management practice has been difficult. KVTC is a large company in terms of the people they employ, but he believes they lack the internal management capacity or the resources to do regular feedback collection, or to use the data systematically in performance management. The KVTC community liaison officer is over-stretched, and does not have the bandwidth to design micro-surveys, collect the data, analyse it and generate feedback reports on top of what he does already.

Lemm said, 'The survey that Keystone conducted remains a very useful reference document, and we may well do it again in a few years. But right now I don't have the staff that I would need to drive it in the company, and cannot justify the cost of employing and training them.'

BOX 5.5 PEAK TIMBERS, SWAZILAND

The experience of Peak Timbers, a gum plantation in the highlands of Swaziland, is similar. The survey data provided useful management information and a spur to action. Management has responded to the most urgent issues raised, but integrating feedback into ongoing management practice is happening slowly and faces many challenges.

Spurred by the findings of the survey of workers employed by sub-contractors, management engaged with contractors on the data and used it to justify more regular compliance audits of wages and working conditions. One contractor has been dismissed for repeated non-compliance and his workforce absorbed by the company itself.

The findings of the sub-contractors' survey were discussed with sub-contractors. One sore point emerging from the survey was addressed immediately. The company found ways to expedite payments to contractors so that they in turn can pay workers on time.

Some of the findings of the community survey have been shared with chiefs and village elders and a number of agreed actions are being implemented.

- Meetings are being held more frequently in the villages.
- The company has decentralized its system of issuing permits for the use of timber, honey and other resources on plantation land to village level, making these much easier to get and resulting in reduced illegal activity in the plantations.

- In a win–win for all, the company has appointed local licensed contractors to extract honey for community members more safely and with less risk of fire. The contractor also makes it easier to market honey and community members get paid more quickly.
- A new communications strategy has been developed focusing on youth and schools with environmental knowledge competitions and employment opportunities.
- A toll-free number was installed so that community members can phone with any queries or to provide information on things like the location of beehives and to warn of fires. This is increasingly being used. According to Nhlanhla Nxumalo, the Community Liaison Manager, the toll-free number is helping clear up misunderstandings about land use policies.

General feedback suggests that community leaders and ordinary members feel heard and taken seriously and there has been a visible improvement in community relations. However, capacity and resource challenges mean that embedding feedback in ongoing management practice is slow.

Major learnings

CV has delivered considerable value for management of both companies in managing and improving relationships with workers, contractors and surrounding communities. However, in the form of externally conducted comprehensive surveys, it has not yet found a way to really empower community leaders. The important lessons from this experience include:

- CV needs to become cheaper and easier for busy managers and community liaison officers to apply. Light, short-cycle feedback loops are one part of the solution. The Feedback Commons offers one solution to cost-effective support for tool development, automated analysis of results and generation of usable feedback reports. But most important is the need to embed the practice in the company by building the capacity, working with and supporting the relevant staff to do it themselves.
- CV must deliver continuing value for both management and communities to make it worth the effort. Management found the feedback data very useful – but lack the capacity and resources to institutionalize it in its current form. As for communities where there is a direct service provider–recipient relationship this is easier, but the relationship between communities and the forestry company is not as direct. The challenge remains how to render data in ways that poor rural communities can understand and want to use themselves.
- A particular challenge facing any private company is that the employer–worker relationship is often conflictual, highly regulated and subject to agreements

with trade unions. In situations like this, employers seeking feedback directly from workers can potentially threaten both contractors and labour unions. Feedback data can also be abused by individuals and groups for their own agendas with potentially damaging effects on the company and all stakeholders. It is important therefore to understand the risks involved in such situations and manage them very carefully to avoid a raft of unintended consequences.

CV in cooperative development and program evaluation

CV began to take shape as a coherent methodology from about 2010, and one of the first opportunities to put its ideas into practice was through a short, mid-term evaluation commissioned by United States Agency for International Development's (USAID) Cooperative Development Program (CDP) and three of their grantees working on cooperative development programs in Kenya.

The CDP was interested in exploring the potential of CV and, for the projects, pooling their evaluation budgets for a comparative feedback survey was a cost-effective way to meet their M&E obligations. For Keystone it was an opportunity to explore the value of CV as a component of M&E.

Our efforts initiated two important feedback loops:

- one between the implementing agency and the cooperative management in which cooperative leaders give feedback on the performance of the agency;
- another between the cooperative management and the ordinary members of the cooperatives in which the members give anonymous feedback on the performance of the management.

Both surveys sought feedback on three key enablers of developmental impact: the relevance and quality of services; the quality of relationships; and the perceived contribution to intended outcomes.

The surveys were conducted in 17 cooperatives over two weeks in December 2012 by a Kenyan research firm supported by Keystone. The questionnaires were developed in close consultation with implementing organizations. They were fairly long (30 questions) in order to cover the full range of evaluation indicators, but were structured in such a way that they could be broken down into three or four micro-surveys for subsequent use on an ongoing basis. Each contained a mix of quantified rating questions and open questions.

Our hope that the implementing agencies, co-op boards and co-op members would (1) engage each other on the data and (2) integrate CV metrics into their ongoing M&E and performance management systems was only partially realized. When co-ops are presented with data findings they can use them very effectively. But developing a culture of feedback data collection, analysis and use is beyond their current culture and capacity. Here are some responses and findings from the cooperative development agencies that reinforce the general conclusions of this chapter.

Greg Grothe of Land O'Lakes (an implementing agency working with larger cooperatives) wrote:

> We have shared the results of the work with each of our cooperative partners in Kenya. The data and information was received with great interest and we had significant dialogue on a number of areas that were highlighted in the survey results. Of particular interest was where management and members had differing perceptions about the co-op. These were obvious places where the co-ops chose to probe and better understand the root causes. However, the co-ops' ability to execute actionable plans in response has been a more difficult matter.

The co-ops really like the NP methodology and intuitively this was easy to understand. I know the results have been discussed with the respective boards of each co-op. But I don't think this has been discussed with membership at AGMs or other means. The co-ops themselves have shown little ownership and intent to use this type of information on a regular basis.

Matt Rhody of Cooperative Resources International wrote:

> When presented with the findings from the performance reports carried out by Keystone in South Africa, the most valuable information for the cooperatives was the evaluation of the board's performance. As a one-time tool its value was limited, but we have adapted it into a short self-evaluation tool that can be used annually ... by boards to track member satisfaction and focus their management strategies. However, this loses the independence and anonymity of the Keystone survey which has definitely protected some individuals from being targeted by threatened board members.

By way of contrast, Emily Varga of NCBA/CLUSA (a USAID development project), working among very small-scale farmers in remote rural areas, said co-op members were uncertain about giving anonymous, independently collected feedback as this is culturally foreign and implies distrust, suggesting that there would be a considerable *courtesy bias*. She felt that that the effort it would take to properly introduce this practice was not practical given the small size of co-op groups and the large distances between them. It was also too costly.

Farmer voice and smallholder coffee in Nicaragua

Between August 2011 and January 2012, Keystone Accountability conducted three surveys of Nicaraguan coffee farmers, beginning with the Ramacafé trade fair in late August 2011 and concluding with interviews at harvest sales in January 2012 at ECOM *acopios* (coffee harvest collection points).

The Farmer Voice project, commissioned by coffee buyer ECOM and its investor the International Finance Corporation, had two purposes. The first was to understand how to improve ECOM's services to its supplier farmers and thereby to optimize its social and financial impact. The second and more ambitious objective was to create and test the tools and practices that would enable ECOM to embed effective accountability to farmer experience at the heart of its business model. We described this in the project as a system for collective learning across all of ECOM's constituents, from its investors to its smallholder farmer suppliers.

The final report of March 2012 included a great deal of data about farmer preferences and experiences with ECOM. There were two main recommendations. First, ECOM should act on the farmer feedback insights in the report to improve its performance as well as evolve its business model. The most actionable farmer feedback detailed how farmers experienced and valued ECOM's different services. Second, to embed the 'Farmer Voice' tool that Keystone had developed at the heart of the ECOM performance management system.

In July 2014, we interviewed Tomás Gutiérrez Acuña, ECOM's sustainability manager for Nicaragua and Costa Rica, to learn what, if anything, had resulted from the Farmer Voice project.

With respect to the first recommendation, Gutiérrez noted significant results at two levels. At the highest level, the survey report

> convinced us that we should invest in improved, two-way communications with farmers. We have adapted and repeated the Farmer Voice survey each year for the past two years, developed related Key Performance Indicators, and significantly increased our communications back to farmers about what we are hearing from them, and what we have on offer.

The report suggested that ECOM move beyond a large annual survey to a system of continuous micro-surveys delivered at touch points with farmers. Where is ECOM on that recommendation? Gutiérrez smiles:

> Well, I guess that is still a 'next step' for us. We see its value, and as a step towards it we have put much more emphasis on the short evaluations that we collect from farmers after the training course – which is the one touch point where we do seek immediate feedback. But you have to understand how large a step we have already taken.

> Alongside the introduction of supplier feedback, we have significantly improved our data collection regarding our farmers' farms and farming practices. Before the Farmer Voice project we did not segment our suppliers, nor tailor services to different farmer types. We used the data from your survey to identify different farmer segments and to provide more tailored services to small farmers. The number one demand from the smallest farmers was for credit. So we revised our credit policy and put in place a special credit line

for small farmers. It has proven to be a great success, and, in the spirit of the Farmer Voice project, we have used the credit relationship to greatly expand our data collection with those farmers. We are using these strengthened relationships to develop more services specifically suited to small farmers.

Further expanding on this second level of results – at the level of services and new ways of working with farmers – Gutiérrez noted that the report had highlighted a large variation in the capabilities of ECOM technicians:

We have significantly tightened our assessment of technicians. Assessments now include farmer feedback. We are now able to deploy our best technicians to the farmers having the most difficulties. The overall increase in productivity for farmers, and for ECOM, is evident.

When asked what was the main constraint now on Farmer Voice work, Gutiérrez answered rapidly:

We get it now, there is no question. Farmer feedback is an important part now of our quality management process. We are improving, and the main constraint is capacity. For example, there is no one here at ECOM who regularly does the kind of data analysis used in your report. But at least now we know that this feedback data is valuable. We need to work more on getting to this value.

SIX MAJOR LESSONS LEARNED

1   CV methods must evolve in response to the potentials and challenges faced in any context. We are witnessing the birth of a new field in development practice.
2   Used in the right way, there is real developmental value in 'imperfect data'; data quality improves through using it for collective learning.
3   We must recognize frontline staff as a key constituent in large-scale service delivery or program implementation.
4   A feedback system is not just a technical process, but is deeply social and political – and needs to be designed and implemented sensitively to the fears and needs of all constituents.
5   An online 'feedback infrastructure' like the Feedback Commons that reduces the cost, lowers the skill levels required, and improves the timeliness of data collection, analysis and use is catalytic to making feedback-based collective learning the new norm in development practice.
6   A deep and nuanced understanding of the systemic challenges to turning good intentions into consistent practice is essential. Which helps explain why it is so difficult to move from a one-off 'pilot' or 'useful activity' to a consistent practice that defines organizational culture.

Notes

1 The section on the Ethiopian Agriculture Extension Performance Management System is a truly collaborative effort of the core AEPMS design team: Andre Ling of ALINe, Andre Proctor of Keystone Accountability, Elias Zerfu of IFPRI, and Berhanu Dirirsa and Adil Yassin of Oxfam in Ethiopia.
2 The projects are: Agriculture Extension Service in Ethiopia; producer cooperatives in Kenya; investors and coffee buyers in Nicaragua; and investors and agro-forestry plantations in Tanzania and Swaziland.
3 Net Promoter Systems is a leading relationship management methodology from the world of customer satisfaction. Keystone has adapted many of its principles and ideas into the CV method, and they are an important component of the AEPMS as well.

6

TRANSFORMATIVE POWER OF DREAMS

A PRADAN case study

Anirban Ghose

SUMMARY

PRADAN is one of India's most experienced community development organizations and is one of the pioneers of self-help groups (SHGs). These SHGs
are a simple yet effective way of reaching out to and connecting with rural
poor, particularly women. In this case study PRADAN reflects on its experience, specifically its approaches that focus on building a 'sense of agency'
that have proved to be transformative in multiple environments. PRADAN
sees success or failure as a trigger for introspection and reflection both for
itself and the SHGs it promotes. PRADAN is learning about the importance
of creating enabling conditions where young initiatives ('green shoots') take
root, and communities emerge as active agents of change fulfilling new and
quite transformative roles. Among the many challenges PRADAN faces is how
to maintain the balance between evidence-based success (tangible gains
that require technology, discipline and a degree of regimentation) and the
ability to not be prescriptive. Constituents need to learn to read their own
reality accurately, and to avoid implementing the best practices of others
blindly. Approaches and practices need to emerge organically, and not follow blueprints or templates. Otherwise, they will not be capable of capturing
the creativity, or catalysing and mobilizing the energies of the participating
communities, let alone see them take the initiative to widen their circle to
gradually benefit more and more communities and women.

Drivers of poverty in India: PRADAN's understanding

India is the world's third-largest[1] and one of the fastest-growing[2] economies, with the fastest-growing number of dollar billionaires.[3] Paradoxically this home to one-fifth of humanity hosts the largest concentration of global poor – over 40 per cent of the world's $1 poor. Despite spectacular growth of the Indian economy over the past decade (7+ per cent per annum) having enabled poverty reduction in many regions, particularly in the southern and western states, large portions of India are still being left behind.

There are multiple perspectives on poverty and its drivers. The classical view is that poverty is essentially a material or economic condition, caused by past economic circumstance – lack of assets, income sources, access to services, infrastructure, access to technology, etc. This leads to the *trickle down* formulation, i.e. if the economy grows fast enough through investments, induction of technology and expansion of markets, everyone will eventually get out of poverty. This model assumes that growth, with a bit of policy tweaking by the state, will in due course change everyone's circumstances. An alternative perspective draws on the notion of power asymmetry as a key driver of poverty and deplorable human conditions. This view holds the distribution of power in society as the key driver of poverty and deficient material conditions as its manifestation. In this schema, the majority of the economically poor and socially marginalized have a lower *sense of agency*[4] and are consequently unable to access entitlements or respond to market signals, much less to influence either. Consequently, the poor may continue to remain so in the midst of a growing, bustling economy and in spite of state interventions to create a level playing field for them.

In PRADAN's understanding, the latter perspective seems to better describe the stubborn nature of poverty in India perhaps even globally. The poor increasingly are those who are *disconnected* from the mainstream due to historical phenomena, such as geographical isolation, social exclusion, occupational segregation, resource appropriation by more powerful groups and changes in the nature of the economy and resource ownership that leave certain groups *stranded*. In the Indian context the tribes and Dalits bear a disproportionate burden of poverty in India,[5] with nearly 190 million of them nationally, including about 160 million in villages, below the government-defined austere poverty line. Age-old and globally applicable gender inequities persist and, among the marginalized, women are the more marginalized and bear a greater physical and emotional burden at home of coping with social and economic marginalization. In a primarily patriarchal and feudal society it is difficult for women to engage in any discourse on development unless they are included proactively, systematically and strategically.

Sense of agency: a key driver

A person's sense of agency includes the notion of *self-efficacy*, which helps explain what either constrains or supports people's ability to seize opportunities. Self-efficacy is the belief about one's own capability. It is the belief, whether or not accurate, that one has the potential power to produce that effect. Self-efficacy motivates a person to persist in the face of setbacks and to acquire the necessary competence[6] to succeed. By the same token, a person with low self-efficacy would harbour feelings of hopelessness as one often encounters among members of the poorest social groups in India. It follows then that enhancing the sense of agency of poor people must be a necessary and key element of strategies to remove poverty. This can only be done by engaging directly with them focusing on her sense of *being*, i.e. her aspirations, her dreams, her dilemmas and internal blocks rather than the set of tasks or the specific technical aspects of 'project' at hand. This kind of 'person focus' is best done with each other in support groups.[7] And to succeed, such engagement must be rooted in the belief, a priori, that *poor people have capability*, that they are worthy and can be the *drivers of change for themselves and their communities*. This belief is the foundation of PRADAN's theory of change and thus all human processes and technical interventions on the ground.

Self-efficacy, though central, is not the sole driver of the human condition; there are other supporting factors that matter, too. Poverty is also a function of the physical location a person finds themself in. A vast majority of poor people in villages typically inhabit regions with complex and vulnerable ecologies – the undulating, hilly and mountainous regions, often with modest and variable rainfall. Many others have no material assets whatsoever and have no experience of any venture except selling their unskilled labour in hostile markets without much choice. It is necessary therefore to stimulate human intervention in ecologies that result in higher productivity and carrying capacity of natural resources, and those without assets must be helped to adopt ventures yet unknown to them. This calls for scientific knowledge of natural and other material resources, their potential and limits, and both an ability and a willingness to innovate, to think on one's feet, to spawn new ventures, to learn from and with others.

Finally, the institutional environment poor people inhabit clearly fosters and sustains poverty as the social and political geography of poverty in India clearly brings out. A vast majority of poor people live in regions with the weakest institutions, including poorly developed markets, weak governance and unequal relationships historically embedded in the social structure. In PRADAN's understanding the deplorable human conditions of millions of disadvantaged people is systematically perpetuated by societal structures and institutionalized processes that ensure that power inequities around class, caste and gender remain though generations. These processes can be challenged only when alternative institutions of the most marginalized come up and challenge these notions. As stated above enhancement of the sense of agency of these communities is a key process in aiding them to take a fresh look at the inequities being perpetuated by social structures.

Thus PRADAN triggers processes for the powerless to come together to create a counterbalance. Women from disadvantaged communities are helped to come together and to spearhead the change process and support each other at times of need. These grassroots groups engage in a wide range of activities starting from economic leveraging economies of scale around input–output market linkages, to helping women access their rights and entitlements vis-à-vis the state, to looking at intra-community and intra-family inequities perpetuated by social norms and gender-related practices. Groups also provide a safe space for women to dream of a better future, make concrete plans to actualize these dreams and take small incremental steps towards their goals.

The current focus of state agencies and the donor community – and the alternative approach

State policies and programmes have over the years come to acknowledge the need for poverty 'targeting', tacitly accepting the limits of 'trickle down' and treating the poor as a 'special category' needing focused attention.[8] However, poverty continues to be treated essentially as an economic condition in targeted programming too; the failure of trickle down is ascribed to market failure. Targeting therefore mainly addresses economic symptoms, such as access to finance and, to a limited extent, lack of occupational skills; the human or psycho-social dimensions of poverty are not even acknowledged let alone attended to. Interventions are essentially transactional, meant to make up for the failure of the market to reach out to the poor. Provisioning of assets and skills is the only offering of targeted programmes; nothing is done to develop their sense of agency and to change the institutional landscape inhabited by poor people. Not surprisingly, targeting has fared no better than trickle down in lessening poverty in a sustained way. With significant financial resources at the disposal of the government of India, and civil strife across states, *the idea of dealing with poverty separately from economic growth, though controversial, is a political reality,*[9] and there is a sense of urgency to remove poverty, but the focus of policy and action continues to be 'transactional' rather than 'transformational'. PRADAN closely working with the government and the donor community has over the years attempted to demonstrate an alternative model at scale based on 'transformational approaches'. These approaches focus on empowering poor women to build their voice, claim assets, and influence decisions, procedures and the formal and informal rules of the game. They also foster capabilities among poor women to be able to effectively deal with key social institutions, including the state by way participation and influencing formal governance spaces for improvement of public systems and the market.

PRADAN's development engagement

Flowing from the above-mentioned context of understanding the drivers of poverty, PRADAN aims at altering the lives of the most vulnerable and disadvantaged people at the cross-section of gender, caste and class, i.e. the focus is on poor, Dalit/tribal women. PRADAN believes that women in whatever situation they find themselves have potential to change their own life and influence change in the lives of others,[10] a potential that can be realized by altering one's self-view and building networks of such enlightened women. PRADAN facilitates women to organize themselves into grassroots-level groups and creates a critical-sized nucleus of growth. PRADAN works extensively with these groups to engage on tangible goals around livelihoods and other important issues affecting their lives (access to basic services, etc.). At a later stage PRADAN facilitates these matured grassroots groups to network among themselves to self-replicate the process and take on larger local societal issues and challenge discriminatory community customs.

To summarize PRADAN simultaneously works on:

- *Creating sustainable enabling conditions*: For example, building linkages for accessing relevant livelihood services to access quality production inputs (e.g. seeds, fertilizers, credit, production knowledge and skills, etc.), marketing links, support services (around technical knowledge and skills) for production, etc. PRADAN works with women's collectives to develop enabling support systems at the level of individual women, their villages and at a cluster of villages level (local economy).
- *Facilitating women's collectives to trigger and aid reflective processes*: These processes are aimed at bringing the *person* in focus, to help her identify and deal with internal blocks, attitudes, behaviour, etc. Thus, after each successful cropping season women who had started with a self-assumption of being *incompetent* farm labourers are forced to re-evaluate their assumptions about themselves. This action–reflection process spearheaded by support groups[11] at the grassroots and their associated tiers leading to individual and collective action is based on Kolb's learning cycle approach. This simultaneous focus on both support environment to get tangible success and on the personal blocks of the person leads to an altered sense of agency which we have discussed at length in the earlier section.

In PRADAN's theory of change, strong livelihoods, sustainable economic gains and other successes of collective action are critical steps in the process of empowerment. PRADAN also realizes that sustainable change can happen only when the action is at a very large scale, otherwise the gains will roll back in short periods of time due to larger societal forces. This requires PRADAN to work in partnership with a large number of community collectives, other civil society actors, government institutions and private bodies to trigger a large-scale change in the norms of society, whereby every human being is valued equally and with dignity.

Three cases of transformative change from three different poverty regions

First case: transforming a 'backward' tribal-dominated district (Gumla, Jharkhand, India) into a horticulture production cluster.

Gumla is home to about 153,000 households,[12] predominantly rural (95 per cent) with almost 70 per cent of these households belonging to the three predominant tribal communities, i.e. Oraon, Munda and Kharia. These communities are first- or second-generation settled agriculturists, having a history of being hunter-gathers till about the mid-1900s. The population densities are sparse by Indian standards at 193 persons per sq km and large tracts of land are still under forest cover (25 per cent) or wastelands (13 per cent). The net cultivable land is about 62 per cent, of which irrigated land is only 6 per cent.[13]

When PRADAN started intervention in four selected backward sub-districts within Gumla, availability of food for the entire family was a critical issue, and in every village all able-bodied men and women migrated for wages to distant parts of the country from November to May each year. The community had lost hope in agriculture as a primary source of livelihood. PRADAN initially started promoting micro-lift and flow irrigation schemes (each scheme irrigating ~15 ha of land benefiting ~35 households). PRADAN assumed that the key missing link was water in the farmland and when water was supplied to even a small portion of farmland the rest would be taken care of, by the community. However, over time when PRADAN formed grassroots groups of women and started a process of livelihood planning with these groups we realized that people needed grain stocks at home to stay back in the village to invest more in agriculture. By 2004 PRADAN responded by working strongly with the communities to enhance production of paddy which is a staple food crop in these areas. The interventions were not limited to improvement of the production technology but also entailed working on the agri-input supply chain. Responding to community issues and working closely with women's groups, within a period of 4–5 years the impact on the food scenario and migration was very powerful.

A study[14] done in 2007 by the CiNI Cell of the Sir Rattan Tata Trust in the project villages shows that over 90 per cent of the participating families achieved significant enhancement in paddy production. The average productivity increase reported was 82.3 per cent. The study also captures the impact of productivity enhancement on food security and reduction in distress migration. Table 6.1 summarizes the findings.

It is clear from Table 6.1 that the food security status of the project villages has undergone dramatic change. The change is from about 70 per cent of families with

TABLE 6.1 Impact on food security from crop productivity enhancement

Food security status	% families	
	Pre-project*	Post-project
Less than 6 months	46	9
6–9 months	22	17
9–12 months	31	57
More than 12 months	0	17

*Percentages do not add to 100 due to rounding error.

less than nine months' food security to almost 75 per cent of families with more than nine months' food security from their own production. Over one-sixth of the families now have reserves to tide them over in the event of future drought or other unexpected expenses in the future.

The improvement in food security reduces distress migration and brings stability in the family, allowing it to take up other livelihood initiatives. The study found that *long-distance, long-period* distress migration has stopped in the sampled project villages and local wage labour has replaced long-distance migration. Even the pattern of families' dependence on wage labour has undergone change, from 66 per cent of families being engaged in wage labour to only 36 per cent.

On the whole the impact on the families of various initiatives can be summarized as:

- significant improvement in food security for a large number of participating families;
- reduction in distress migration;
- redemption of old mortgages (mainly land) and reduced dependence on loans for basic needs; and
- positive impact on agriculture stimulated others to take up similar livelihood activities, creating a huge demand for scale-out to adjoining villages.

The next phase of work started[15] with women's groups as partners of the change process. They now were interested in investing themselves in intensive agriculture and diversifying to cash crops. PRADAN worked closely with the groups and helped them access finances from mainline government programmes both locally and centrally sponsored. This phase, which was part-supported by the Gates Foundation, focused on developing commercial agriculture production clusters. The planning process with the women's groups involved matching family aspirations, production resources, skill-sets and market demand. Over the next four years a large poultry, vegetable and horticulture (mainly mango) production cluster grew in this area. Gumla, which was a food-importing district, in a short span of time has become a major exporter of live chickens (4,300 Mt annually), fresh vegetables (35,000 Mt annually) and mangos (500 Mt annually). Local youth from the participating families have taken up new service sector roles as marketing support agents, production support experts,[16] etc. The impact in one village (Kurag) in the district is provided in Figure 6.1.

The change in the economic vibrancy of the area is visible. The women have found self-belief and a confidence to take on larger challenges. They are now taking up issues beyond livelihoods and seeking to change access to basic services like health care, education, safe drinking water, electricity, etc. They are now wanting to play a larger role in fostering the development process in adjoining areas. Now the 15,000-woman SHG federation promoted by PRADAN has entered into a tripartite agreement with the NRLM[17] and PRADAN to mobilize about 80,000 new women in the SHG movement and start the change process with those women

Creating a Ripple Effect of Transformation

The Change Process – Kurag Village, Gumla district, Jharkhand

Before

- 91 tribal families were food secure for only 6–8 months – distress migration was the main survival mechanism
- No family had any savings and none of the children went to school

PRADAN's Intervention

- Social mobilization through women-led SHGs covering 85% of families
- Introduced irrigation systems and agriculture best practices to improve land productivity
  - Stabilisation of paddy yields
  - Diversification into seasonal vegetable cultivation
  - Horticulture in the uplands

After

- All families are food secure throughout the year
- Each family earns an additional annual income of INR 35,000
- All children attend school in a nearby village

The Ripple Effects

- Seeing the progress, government has established a 20-bed hospital in the village
- A sorting, grading and storage centre for vegetable and fruits has also been set up
- Government officials visited Kurag to assimilate learning and replicate the approach with other communities in the region

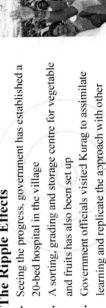

FIGURE 6.1 Impact on the village of Kurag

Seeding and Scaling Change: Gumla

Today

- 15,000 families, 52% Panchayats and 45% villages in five poorest blocks of the district
- 4,460 Women Leaders and 480 Community Resource Persons
- Sustainable Community Collectives – Poultry Cooperative largest in Jharkhand, five SHG federations, largest organized vegetable production cluster, large mango cluster in eastern India

Multiplying Impact

- NRLM has entered in partnership with PRADAN and SHG collectives to reach 60,000 families building on the success nuclei
- Partnership with two local NGOs for wider replication

Annual livelihood output: $6.3 million

$6.3 million	Incremental output from all livelihood interventions introduced by project in FY 2012

Resource Deployed 2004–2012

	Investment in building assets and capabilities of the poor
Community Investment: **$3.5 M**	$1.5 million
	$2 million
PRADAN's DSC: $0.57 M	**$0.15 million**
	$0.17 million
	$0.25 million

Team staff salaries, travel, overheads, etc.

BMGF	Government	SRTT & Others

FIGURE 6.2 Summary of investments made and future directions of Gumla

too. Figure 6.2 summarizes the investments made and future directions of Gumla. Our estimates show that an investment of about $4.1 million, of which investment to PRADAN is $0.57 million, has now created annual production flows in the order of $6.3 million and the social capital to self-replicate.

Second case:[18] women's groups led alliances with local panchayat leaders and district administration to leverage finances from government schemes at significant scale.

This next case is from the adjoining state of Chattisgarh, again a state that is home to a large number of tribal communities. PRADAN's focus for intervention was Nargi sub-district of Dhamtari district where tribal communities (predominantly Gond community) form about 80 per cent of the population. Over 61 per cent are below the very austere official poverty line, which is just about a dollar a day for the entire household (typically five members).

PRADAN's work started with mobilizing women from poor households into SHGs. Initially when PRADAN staff talked about improving the quality of agriculture-based livelihoods women were not able to see a potential and there was very tepid response. PRADAN sought support from the Tata Trust to demonstrate the potential to revive and make agriculture resilient. There, PRADAN demonstrated in-situ water harvesting and land development work in a contiguous patch of 17 ha belonging to 32 families. It turned out well during the monsoon. Whereas crops were struggling to survive in other patches of land for want of water, there was sufficient water in these farm ponds to save the crop. PRADAN organized large-scale exposure visits to this village and the community became enthusiastic about planning for the development of land and water resources. When the issue of raising finances at a large scale for implementation of these plans was discussed in village groups PRADAN pointed at the possibility of engaging with the gram sabha, to get the plans sanctioned under MGNREGS (the Mahatma Gandhi National Rural Employment Guarantee Scheme, India's flagship rural development programme guaranteeing 100 days of unskilled labour to every willing adult. This program has an annual national outlay of ~$60 billion).

This demonstration of possibilities caught the imagination of women in the adjoining villages and they enthusiastically started participating in local-level planning for improvement of farmlands, and developing water resources for strengthening monsoon agriculture and taking a second crop. This led to great efforts by the PRADAN team to trigger local-level planning and then women's groups linking with the local panchayat system to access finances from multiple government departments. PRADAN too played a facilitative

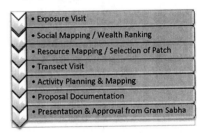

FIGURE 6.3 Process to engage with the gram sabha to get plans sanctioned under India's flagship rural development programme MGNREGS

role in helping align staff in various government departments to converge their programmes to implement the micro-plans developed by the community. The typical process is depicted in Figure 6.3.

Planning is a three-day exercise, in which the present status and use of resources, and the potential of using these resources more effectively and sustainably, is discussed. The process, typically lasting three days, is facilitated by PRADAN with the active participation of the SHG members and the panchayat members. The planning process involves the following.

Social mapping: All the households of the hamlet and the facilities available in the hamlet are depicted in this map. The mapping helps identify the missing basic facilities such as a hand pump, an *anganwadi* centre, toilets, etc. Plans are then made to create these facilities (see Figure 6.4).

Resource mapping: Different types of land (upland, medium land, lowland and homestead), available water bodies and vegetation are depicted on the revenue map of the village. The present status of these resources, their use and the returns earned are discussed with the community. The alternative and potential uses of these resources are also discussed, as are the expected returns from them, which help the community in developing a vision. Based on considerations such as patches on the ridge, the relative status of the family, etc., the community selects a patch for the annual plan.

Transect visit: Representatives from all the households who own land in that patch, SHG members, panchayat members, Community Service Providers and PRADAN professionals visit each plot of the patch. The land-use options and the work required to be done, based on the location of the land and the other resources available, are discussed.

Finalization of the plan and activity mapping: After the transect visit, a meeting is organized at the hamlet or the village level, to finalize the options discussed during the transect visit. The community depicts the final plan on the revenue map of the village. During the planning exercise, staff from different government departments such as Agriculture, Horticulture and Fisheries are involved. Later on, as the existing schemes of the district are mapped in the planning format, this includes plans from the MGNREGS and other government schemes (see Figure 6.5).

Thereafter PRADAN supports the SHG member to pursue the plan and get it approved in the village council under the panchayat system. At the time of implementation PRADAN provides technical support to the groups to implement the civil structures or other interventions.

This process is being expanded and taken up in over 50 villages in the area. The impact of this effort on one village is depicted in Figure 6.6:

> Sushila Bai is a member of an SHG in village Chhindbharri. She has one-and-a-half acres of land. Of that, one acre is upland and the rest is a paddy field. The returns from farming were not sufficient to meet the basic requirements of the family. Her husband, Kisun Netam, was primarily an agricultural labourer. He used to migrate to the plains of Chhattisgarh for 45–60 days a year to harvest paddy.

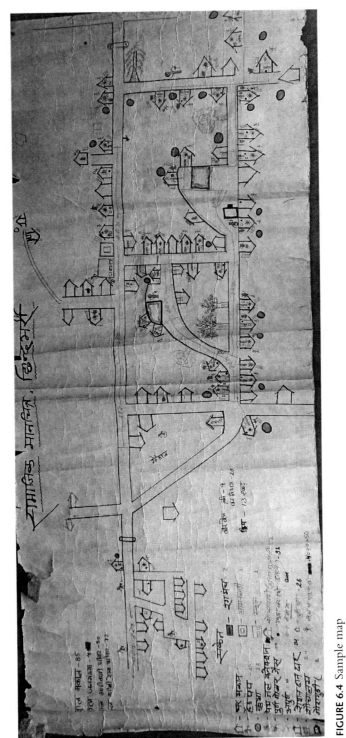

FIGURE 6.4 Sample map

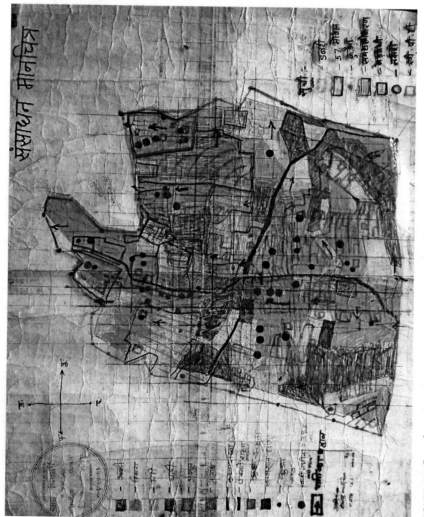

FIGURE 6.5 Sample activity map

Creating a Ripple Effect of Transformation

The Change Process – Chhindbharri Village, Dhamtari district, Chhattisgarh

Before (2009)

- 71 tribal families (85% among them BPL) were food secure for only 6–8 months – distress migration was the main survival mechanism
- No family had any savings

PRADAN's Intervention

- Social mobilization through women-led SHGs covering 85% of families.
- Introduced alternate land use, development of land and water resources and improved agriculture practices to improve land productivity
  - Horticulture in the uplands
  - Integrated Natural Resource Management-based resource development and utilization planning
  - Helping community to establish linkages with different department-convergence
  - Stabilization of paddy yields
  - Diversification into seasonal vegetable cultivation

After (2012)

- All families are food secure throughout the year
- Each family earns an average additional annual income of INR 25,400 from farming
- All children attend school
- No distress migration

The Ripple Effects

- Community has provided tap water facilities to all the households through their contribution.
- SHG members influenced administration to sanction and construct a heath centre in the Gram Panchayat.
- Community has mobilized support from Chhattisgarh State Renewable Energy Development Agency for bio gas and 56% of families started using it.
- Government officials visited Chhindbharri to assimilate learning and replicate the approach with other communities in the region.

FIGURE 6.6 Creating a ripple effect of transformation

Fruit plantation in the adjoining land and the development of irrigation infrastructure motivated Sushila Bai to experiment with fruit and vegetable cultivation in her one acre of upland. She planted 25 mango and 30 cashew plants on her land in 2010 and also undertook vegetable cultivation. She developed her land and constructed a small vegetable polyhouse with support from the MGNREGS and got a sprinkler pipe from the Department of Horticulture. She cultivated potato, brinjal, tomato, chilli, bottle gourd and sponge gourd on her land and earned about INR 33,000 ($550) from the land, from which earlier she got less than INR 1,000 ($17) a year by cultivating black gram. Last year, her husband did not migrate for paddy harvesting. He stayed in the village and worked for 100 days under the MGNREGS earning ~INR 12,000 ($200).

This experiment has drawn attention from policy-makers both at the state and national level. Convergence of government departments and schemes existing in silos has been India's biggest challenge. This effort has shown a way forward where communities make a comprehensive plan and different departments and programmes are converged to fulfil financial needs for implementation. This programme created a host of new jobs on the ground for implementing programmes, providing technical support in crop production, marketing support, etc. The challenge for us is to convert this pioneering effort into a large-scale movement.

The third case involves women's groups going beyond livelihoods to challenge gender-based discrimination, engaging the political processes: this case focuses on an area (Hazaribagh) where caste dynamics are powerful and the norms and practices of society are deeply patriarchal. Women face deep-seated, gender-based discrimination and have little say in household and community affairs. This is a predominantly non-tribal area with Dalits and Other Backward Classes being the focus poor communities PRADAN works with. As PRADAN started forming women's groups in the area the deep-rooted, caste-based and gender-based discrimination came to light. These were the key issues these women faced, in addition to the universal issue of poverty and lack of sustainable livelihoods. For many years PRADAN struggled to align the interventions with the aspirations and critical issues women wanted to work with. For many years the staff placed in the local team made several pleas to the internal management of the organization to allow extensive work on issues beyond livelihoods. It was only much later, when the extent of the discriminatory practices came to light and an internal strategic re-think looked at broader outcomes well beyond livelihoods, that the PRADAN team started systematic engagement around issues of domestic violence, class- and caste-based denial of access to social welfare programmes, gender-based violence generally in the area, etc. PRADAN sought support from a reputed feminist organization Jagori to help perspective and capacity building of both PRADAN staff and leaders of the women's groups. Thousands of SHG members have now undergone various events and exercises to understand the concept of patriarchy and how it plays out in their lives. Groups have spent a very long time reflecting on these issues and thinking of what changes they can bring. Typically women start with small steps, first deciding that they will not perpetuate patriarchal practices, e.g. at least not discriminate between their own sons and daughters, give both equal shares of food, not drill in gender segregated roles, encourage their girls to go out and get higher education, etc.

Many women facing severe domestic violence take support from their groups to resist and then confront the perpetrator. In many cases women have found courage to move out of the family and seek justice under the legal framework from relevant courts. Many others have mustered courage to challenge discriminatory practices against widows, especially young widows. These have successfully challenged official practices that automatically change the names of widows for quick recognition, normative requirements to wear no jewellery and wear only white saris, etc. Selected women have been trained on legal literacy by another expert organization, Marg. These women act as paralegals and support other women who need to take their disputes to formal courts of law.

These issues apart, women are taking an interest in claiming their rightful place in public spaces. In village meetings (panchayat meetings) women typically are not expected to attend. Now there are thousands of women who are attending panchayat meetings. They are demanding more devolution of power to the panchayats as elections to these local bodies happened after a gap of 30 years. They are taking an active interest in school management bodies, ensuring teacher/student attendance and effective implementation of feeding programmes in schools, etc. Women (15,000 from ~1,000 SHGs, which are federated into clusters and block-level federations) are working on streaming the Public Distribution System, which provides subsidized food grains.

This deeper engagement with understanding gender and gender-based discriminatory practices plays out as a question of space in decision-making and access-control of productive assets and income. These questions lead to issues of land rights, space for women to engage not only as silent agricultural labourers in the production system, etc. As the women say, I think the journey on this path has just begun over the last two or three years.

Women in Mayurbhanj state of Odisha have taken this effort further and made bold steps towards political empowerment. In the local body elections 30–50 per cent of the seats are reserved for women candidates. There are numerous cases where women getting elected on reserved seats are then controlled by their husbands or fathers-in-law to take official decisions at their behest. 'Sarpanch-Pati', i.e. husband of the village-head, has become a near-official designation and the husband happily takes all decisions in the name of his wife.

In this kind of context women from the SHGs in Karanjia sub-district filed nominations for contesting seats in the panchayat election well beyond what was reserved for women, which is unheard of. With deft pre-election planning women from these groups were able to get stunning results winning roughly 70 per cent of the basic representation seats. Table 6.2 summarizes the effort and its result.

TABLE 6.2 Participation of women from SHGs in local governance in Mayurbhanj, Odisha

Nature of seats in the panchayat	Total number of seats	Seats reserved for women	SHG leaders filing nomination	No. winning elections	% of seats held by SHG leaders
Ward member	127	75	137	88	69
Sarpanch	13	7	29	7	54
Panchayat Samiti member	13	7	33	8	61
Zilla parishad member	56	2	8	2	1.3

This is in fact a new trend where women from SHGs are not only engaging in influencing local governance issues but now they are starting to aspire to and attain leadership roles in statutory bodies like the panchayat. In this case the efforts of women went far beyond what PRADAN had facilitated and they took giant steps under their own steam. These new leaders are now actively engaging themselves in effective implementation of public works in their area. In the context of widespread disenchantment with political processes and public office around widespread corruption at various levels of governance, this new brand of grassroots leaders hold a hope for a better future.

Learning–feedback loops in these cases: Each success or failure is a trigger for introspection and reflection both by PRADAN and the SHGs at different levels. For PRADAN this journey creates hope for triggering a much larger social transformative engagement well beyond the initial focus of additional incomes. This hope comes from the 'green shoots', as we call it, where communities being active agents of change take on transformative roles far beyond what the intervener had ever imagined. The challenge that PRADAN faces today is to maintain the balance between concrete, tangible gains (which require technology, discipline and a degree of regimentation) and the ability to have a non-blueprinted approach that is able to fire creativity and mobilize the energies of the participating communities to rapidly deepen the programme and reach out to larger and larger numbers.

Notes

1 Behind the USA and the People's Republic of China, in terms of purchasing power parity.
2 The current and projected growth rate is between 7 and 8 per cent.
3 Forbes 2011, List of Billionaires (www.forbes.com/billionaires).
4 Belief in one's own capability to change things around oneself (e.g. having the perception of being tossed around by 'fate' helplessly).
5 About 48 per cent Scheduled Tribe (ST) and 38 per cent Scheduled Caste (SC) were Below Poverty Line (BPL) as per the old method. The new method puts rural poverty at 50 per cent higher. Four of the five poorest states have the highest ST and SC percentages outside the Northeast and three are the most rural. Mean incomes of

the ST and SC groups are lower than for the entire population. It is reasonable then to assume that their share of poverty is likely to be higher by more than 50 per cent in the new method, i.e. almost 75 per cent of the ST and 60 per cent of the SC populations may be BPL.

6 'If I have the belief that I can do it, I shall surely acquire the capacity to do it even if I may not have it at the beginning' – Mahatma Gandhi.

7 The efficacy of support groups was established a long time ago by the German–American psychologist Kurt Lewin while working on the promotion of breastfeeding practices in the 1940s.

8 Targeting has been a part of state policy since independence but the scale, importance and specificity has grown since 1980 when the Integrated Rural Development Plan and the National Rural Employment Program were introduced, specifically to reduce the BPL numbers.

9 The changing landscape of constitutional guarantees is an example.

10 'People have it in them' (see www.impatientoptimists.org/Posts/2013/06/An-Indian-Mothers-Call-for-Change-For-Us-All#.Vn23d5MrLCU).

11 The SHGs, in this instance.

12 Population of about 1 million persons.

13 About 4 per cent of total land (~5,300 sq km). Source: Gumla Admin official website: www.jharkhand.gov.in/web/gumla/facts-figures.

14 A. Petwal and G. Neelam (2007), 'Kharif Paddy Stabilization: Proven Strategy to Enhance Paddy Production in Tribal Regions of Jharkhand', internal publication, unpublished.

15 Around 2008–9.

16 Called Community Resource Persons or Community Service Providers depending on the service provided.

17 National Rural Livelihood Mission.

18 Adapted from an article published in *NewsReach*, Sept–Oct 2012 issue.

7

THEORIZING WOMEN'S EMPOWERMENT IN AGRICULTURE

Progression of learning in CARE

Maureen Miruka and Emily Hillenbrand

SUMMARY

CARE's journey toward a central focus on women's empowerment and gender equality as pillars of poverty reduction has involved decades of systematic
learning and ongoing refinement of its guiding frameworks and tools for
conceptualizing empowerment and promoting gender equality both in its
organizational practices and in its sectoral programming. This chapter turns
a spotlight on CARE's journey toward that organizational focus on women's
empowerment and details the learning and research processes that went into
developing this approach with the consent and input from the "ground" as
well as from the academic and policy worlds. We trace the development of
CARE's Women's Empowerment Framework and gender analysis guidelines,
showing how resources and time were dedicated to theoretical as well as practical research, with the participation of the communities.

We then illustrate the implications of CARE's shift to a focus on women and
girls by following the application of these key frameworks through to its work
in the agriculture sector. We describe the collective learning processes that
defined what it means to empower women in an agricultural context. Using
the case study of CARE's Pathways to Secure Livelihoods program, we go on
to illustrate how CARE's guiding frameworks and practices of learning and
personal reflection are embedded in the Pathways model, which in itself has
become a field-tested framework for flexible, gender-responsive agriculture
programming across diverse contexts.

In sum, this chapter examines how an institutional learning culture
that prioritizes gender equality, values collective learning, and invests in

"ground-truthing" robust theories of change has led to programming models and theoretical frameworks that (a) are grounded in programmatic experience and that (b) provide a common language for diverse country programs to be accountable to gender outcomes in their respective sectors. This collective learning approach enables CARE to contribute effectively to the global discourse, ensure institutional accountability to gender equality, and continually enhance the quality and suitability of gender-responsive programming.

Introduction

CARE is one of the largest international NGOs, with over a half-century history of rural development (including agriculture), and a current presence in 90 countries around the world. Programmatically, CARE has been involved in emergency response, maternal and child health, sexual and reproductive health, food and nutrition security, and natural resource management. As well as its sectoral approaches, CARE prides itself in its strengths in community-grounded and participatory implementation approaches, and in its respect for local innovation and local knowledge of the context. Starting in the 1990s, CARE started a deliberate journey from a broad-focused, multi-sectoral NGO to a rights-based one that places a particular organizational focus on gender equality. In recognition that gender inequality is an assault on human rights and a root cause of poverty in particular through its impact on women, CARE decided to make women's and girls' empowerment a core focus of their programmatic work.

Naturally, sharing learning and developing a cohesive, organizational stance across such a diverse and widespread organization can be a challenging enterprise. In the feminist literature, empowerment is variously conceptualized as a process, an end-state, and a capacity (Kabeer 2001; Malhotra et al. 2002; Alsop et al. 2006). It is generally accepted that efforts to measure women's empowerment need to consider different levels (micro/macro, individual/collective), different spheres (economic, political, social), different temporal scales (often beyond the lifetime of a single program), and must be sensitive to social context. Such approaches generally involve defining what is meant by empowerment and identifying the different elements that make up this definition. These elements of empowerment are variously defined as: resources, agency and achievements (Kabeer 2001); control over resources and agency (Malhotra et al. 2002); and agency and opportunity structure (Alsop et al. 2006). In most cases, these elements are then broken down into sub-dimensions with associated indicators and sources of measurement.

These complexities of empowerment and the nuances of gender relations are challenging concepts for development organizations to tackle and apply in programming—leaving many to apply limited or oversimplified approaches that do little to fundamentally change gender inequalities. Often, the programmatic focus is on tracking the gender of program participants, or delivering "empowering" tools to women, in the form of self-confidence-boosting skills, training, and access to micro-loans and economic activities. To synthesize the evidence base and agree on suitable theoretical structures to make an effective shift toward a rights-based approach in a rigorous way, CARE began by commissioning an organization-wide Strategic Impact Inquiry (SII) to assess how its programming had contributed (to date) to women's empowerment and gender equity and what "empowerment" in fact meant in the context of CARE's programming (CARE 2006).

CARE's Strategic Impact Inquiry: ground-truthing a theoretical framework of empowerment

Building on an extensive review of the feminist literature led by gender specialists, this SII process engaged country offices from across the CARE world in a systematic review of their own programming experiences, to identify how participants around the CARE world define and understand "empowerment," and to classify the types and packages of interventions that seem to foster women's empowerment and gender equality. By committing its own core resources and over 300 members of staff over a period of three years, the SII was an expression of CARE's commitment to promote internal learning and to value the voices of those to whom it seeks to be accountable: its program constituents and implementers. The SII used a mixed-methods approach that emphasized reflection, rigor, empowerment and participation of institutions, experts and women themselves in key steps of research to lead to programmatic and institutional recommendations to ensure that CARE's work impacts on the underlying causes of poverty. Specifically, the SII explored the following questions: What contributions have CARE programs made, if any, to the empowerment of women and the advancement of gender equity? What evidence (pro and con) exists regarding the link between (a) CARE's program approaches and principles, (b) CARE's internal gender equity and diversity practices, and (c) the advancement of gender equity and empowerment?

The SII—substantiating the feminist literature—revealed that empowerment is about much more than women doing more "productive" work or having more assets, being smarter or more confident. It also requires change in the institutional structures and relations that shape women's strategic life choices and aspirations. It also illustrated that women's empowerment is complex, nonlinear, and multi-dimensional. It is beyond the scope of one organization, let alone one time-/resource-bound project; contributing to longer-term change requires a fundamental shift from the artificially resourced "project laboratory" to the dynamic world of society and social change. This led to the development of CARE's simple, organization-wide Women's Empowerment Framework, which defines women's empowerment as the sum total of changes needed for a woman to realize her full human rights—that is, the interplay of changes in the dimensions of agency, relations, and structures (Figure 7.1). In this framework, *agency* is defined as the skills, capacities, and confidence to act in one's own interest and meet one's own aspirations. *Relations* refers to the gender rules that govern the interpersonal relationships

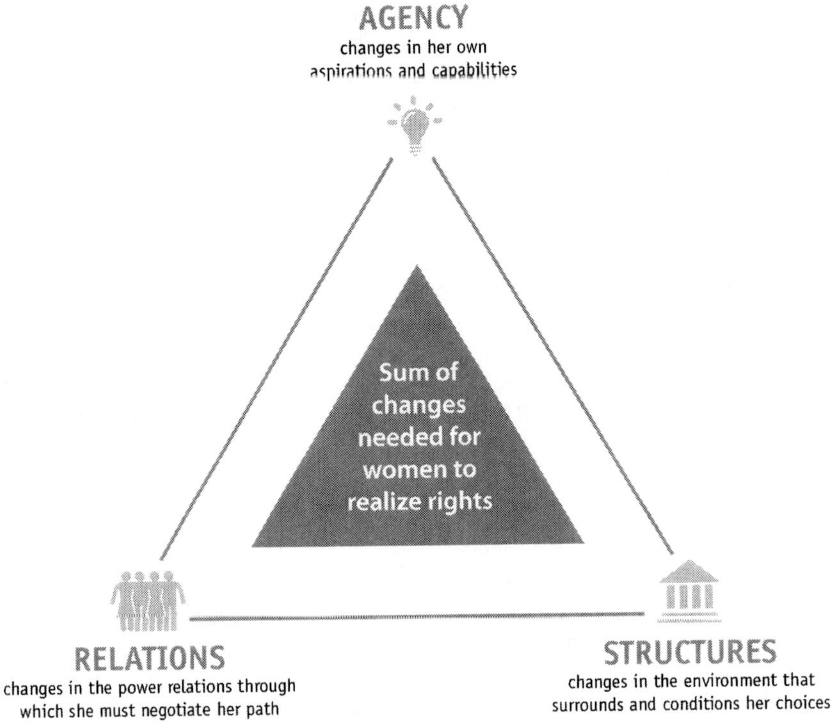

AGENCY
changes in her own
aspirations and capabilities

Sum of
changes
needed for
women to
realize rights

RELATIONS
changes in the power relations through
which she must negotiate her path

STRUCTURES
changes in the environment that
surrounds and conditions her choices

FIGURE 7.1 CARE Women's Empowerment Framework

(within and without the household) that mediate women's ability to make choices, access resources, and take advantage of opportunities. *Structures* refers to the institutional rules—including the informal social norms as well as formal rules of institutions (such as land laws, lending institutions, or extension systems)—that condition women's choices (CARE 2006).

In sum, CARE's framework is thus grounded both in the relevant literature and in programmers' experience; and it synthesizes this richness of data into a model that implementers without an academic background in feminist theory can easily grasp and use. And it is a simple prism for making sure that implementers don't just focus on the individual-/agency-level interventions, which tend to focus solely on building women's skills, capacities, or economic potential.

To ensure that sectoral programming focuses on a holistic expansion of women's strategic life choices and not just their sector-specific needs (Kabeer 2001), CARE's SII also synthesized a framework for Good Practices in Gender Analysis, which identified eight core "areas of inquiry" that reflect critical areas in women's lives where gender rules and norms disfavor and limit women's choices, capacities, and rights (Figure 7.2). At the base of this model is a thorough contextual analysis, and, at the peak, a reminder to focus on women's strategic needs—that is, the changes that fundamentally reshape power inequalities. These core areas of

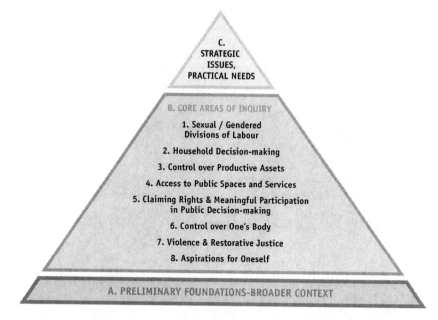

FIGURE 7.2 CARE gender analysis core areas of inquiry

inquiry, in turn, become the indicators by which empowerment outcomes can be measured. Following this guidance, as each program is designed, a gender analysis is carried out across these core areas of inquiry (viewed through the three dimensions of agency/relations/structures) to conceptualize how programmatic models could bring about outcomes in these critical core areas and, conversely, how gender challenges related to the core areas might affect other program outcomes.

This model of social change retains a political focus on shifting power, not only in the individual's ability to make (autonomous) choices, but in challenging and changing the institutional context that restricts women's opportunities and underpins their social subordination. On organizational alignment, the SII recommended that CARE support advocacy be led by women's own movements, while grounding global advocacy efforts in their broader vision and theories of change. It suggested that global indicators of key change domains should be grounded in local realities, and that CARE engage partners in shared analysis, hypothesis generation/ testing, and critical reflection, as CARE completes this strategic shift. This commitment would only be possible if staff are supported through training, accountability, and organizational structures that emphasize gender equity and expand space to question who we are and what we are doing—ensuring consistent action-learning on what constitutes good empowerment work. Eventually, a Gender Equity and Diversity (GED) curriculum was institutionalized throughout CARE, providing a common language and shared processes for staff at all levels of the organization to reflect inwardly on their own gender norms, beliefs, and practices, and to reflect critically on power. Reflective spaces and participatory tools for self-reflection are a core part of the continual-learning values of the organizational culture.

A place to grow: applying the evolving framework to the agriculture sector

CARE has a long history of supporting agricultural productivity and food security in development. The shift to a rights-based approach and a women's empowerment focus entailed a rethinking and restructuring of CARE's agriculture programs to carry these women's empowerment principles across this sector. Following on both the programmatic and organizational recommendations from the SII, CARE commissioned an extensive study, "A Place to Grow," which sought to reflect on gender and women's empowerment in agricultural and value chain-based programs and how to measure it (CARE 2009).

Like the SII process, "A Place to Grow" drew on evidence in the literature about the key factors that disadvantage women in the agriculture sector. For example, there is well-documented evidence that gender inequalities in access to and control over resources, which are defined by culturally specific roles, continue to undermine a sustainable and inclusive development of the agriculture sector (World Bank et al. 2009; Meizen-Dick et al. 2011). The limitations women face in turn impose huge social, economic, and environmental costs on society as a whole and rural development in particular, including lags in agricultural productivity. It has been demonstrated that giving women the same access to productive resources, technologies, and services as men could increase agricultural productivity and, ultimately, household food security and general welfare (Quisumbing and McClafferty 2006). Worldwide data further indicate that if women had the same access to productive resources as men, they could increase yields on their farms by 20–30 percent and that alone could raise total agricultural output in developing countries by 2.5–4 percent and reduce the number of hungry people in the world by 100 million to 150 million people (FAO 2011).

Similar to the SII process, "A Place to Grow" paired a thorough review of the literature with a systematic scan of program experience into what approaches seem to lead to greater equality, empowerment, and productivity in the agriculture sector. Funded by the Howard Buffet Foundation, an overview of CARE's agriculture projects in sub-Saharan Africa, Central America, and Asia was undertaken, followed by country-specific case studies in Mozambique, Ghana, Uganda, and Honduras to reflect upon project planning and impact assessments. The "A Place to Grow" process also assessed CARE's staff gender capacity and experience in gender work through "Circles of Learning," a participatory adult learning-based approach with a focus for building practical skills for analysis and action using participants' own work experiences. The Circles of Learning were the beginning of a continual process of capacity building through sharing of knowledge, skills, and innovation among CARE colleagues who are committed to empower women and reduce gender inequality in the context of agriculture. Building on the agency, relations, and structures framework, these exercises led to the development of a specific Women's Empowerment in Agriculture framework and to the definition of illustrative indicators for measuring success in agriculture.

CARE Pathways to secure livelihoods: a programming approach to empowering women in agriculture

These key lessons from "A Place to Grow" heavily informed a subsequent learning and proposal-development process that took place in six CARE countries in Africa (Tanzania, Mali, Malawi, and Ghana) and South Asia (India and Bangladesh), with the aim of designing a women-centered agriculture program. Funded by an 18-month development grant from the Bill & Melinda Gates Foundation, CARE engaged these six country office partners to co-develop a rigorous theory of change that would address the underlying causes of poverty and women's exclusion from agriculture and create a common, robust intervention model that could be tested in several diverse contexts.

The overarching goal of the resultant program model, called "Pathways to Secure Livelihoods" (Pathways), is to increase productivity and empowerment of women farmers and create more equitable agricultural systems at scale. Based on theories of change from each of the implementing countries, CARE identified five common and closely interelated change levers that together can create more equitable agriculture systems (for women farmers), leading to more secure and resilient livelihoods. These critical change levers are: (1) increased capacity and skills; (2) expanded access to services, assets, and inputs; (3) increased productivity and profitability; (4) greater influence of women over household decisions; and (5) a more enabling environment for gender equity (Figure 7.3). The theory of change contends that changes in all the five levers are essential in order to realize sustainable and systemic change for women farmers, and meet what are seen as indivisible goals of productivity/equity/empowerment.

Pathways places women's empowerment at the center of the program, believing that women's empowerment, equity, and productivity are mutually reinforcing forces. Through processes of empowerment and greater household influence, women can gain greater control over the essential resources and decisions that affect yields and incomes, and food and nutrition security. In turn, by building women's productivity and market access, women's incomes can improve their agency, household influence, and community representation. The basic core dimensions of CARE's women's empowerment framework (agency, relations, and structures) are reflected in the change levers of the Pathways theory of change (Figure 7.4). In change levers 1 and 3, Pathways builds women's *individual agency* (skills and capacities as farmers and businesspeople and their self-confidence in their rights). In change levers 2 and 5, the Pathways program challenges inequalities in the *institutions*, including discriminatory policies but also traditional beliefs about men's and women's roles, rights, and abilities. Critically, Pathways also works for greater equity in women's *relationships*, including within the household, in business negotiations, and in community structures, particularly through change lever 4.

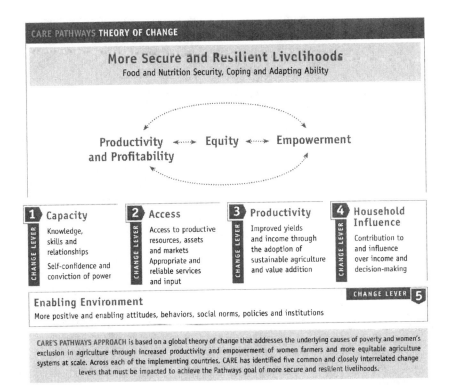

FIGURE 7.3 Pathways theory of change

The program applies the push–pull operational framework (CARE 2013a) to enhance women's individual and collective agency (push interventions) and engage other direct stakeholders, including men and boys, in the change process (pull interventions). "Push" activities are carried out directly with the producer groups through a decentralized service delivery capacity strengthening model, the Farmer Field and Business School (FFBS), developed by the program as a platform for building producer capacity on sustainable agriculture, market engagement, nutrition, gender equity, and participatory monitoring and evaluation (Miruka et al. 2015). The FFBS is developed on the model of the traditional Farmer Field School approach, which places emphasis on hands-on management skills based on adult learning principles (CARE 2013b). The FFBS engages local thought leaders, youth as well as men and boys around women's empowerment. Spouses are invited early, to secure support for the activities and to introduce them to the goals of the program. "Pull" interventions are conducted at the community or institutional level, targeting systemic changes—negotiations with market actors, with extension services, input systems, with community leaders for collective access to productive resources such as land, input and output markets, information, and financial services.

AGENCY:
A woman's own aspirations and capabilities

- Improved agriculture, market, communication, planning skills
- Equitable control over productive assets and income
- Mobility and access to information and services
- Knowledge of laws and opportunities; confidence to claim rights
- Bodily integrity, self-efficacy, and self-confidence
- Positive images of women as farmers, entrepreneurs, leaders

STRUCTURES:
The environment that surrounds and conditions her choices

- Equitable land, property, resource laws, and practices
- Extension services; market structures address women's needs and interests
- Accessible legal support and GBV services
- Transformation of inequitable social norms
- Community authorities respond to women's interests

RELATIONS:
The power relations through which she must negotiate her path

- Equitable workload-sharing and caregiving practices
- Equitable power relations in household, marketplace, collectives
- Fair and non-threatening decision-making and negotiation processes
- Ability to lead, influence, participate meaningfully in groups
- Engagement of male change agents and collectives to challenge social norms

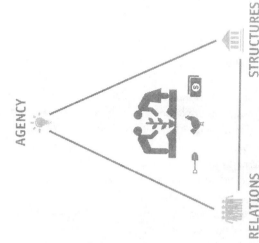

AGENCY

STRUCTURES

RELATIONS

Greater gender equity
Productivity
Empowerment

FIGURE 7.4 CARE Pathways Women's Empowerment in Agriculture Framework

A 2014 World Bank report reinforces the role of collective action in enhancing women's voice and agency and reducing gender disparities (World Bank 2014). Pathways builds on this very concept of collective agency to engage women through Village Savings and Loan Associations, self-help, and producer groups as the main entry points to facilitate women's capacity building, access to and control over resources, and inclusion in financial and agricultural markets while tackling barriers to empowerment. Serving as a livelihoods platform, Pathways enable women farmers to access markets, pool produce, and purchase bulk inputs in order to gain power and secure larger buyers. Pathways plays a key role in establishing these linkages, building market skills (through committees) and building up networks among producer groups. As a social platform, working with existing groups creates a safe space to discuss norms and challenges and to identify potential solutions to lead to the social transformation that the program strives for. Having had a chance to reflect on the topics among themselves, they can have greater confidence and voice in public dialogues. With support from Pathways, groups have applied their collective voice to advocate for livelihoods needs—in particular, access to land, control over land, and equal wages in the day-labor sector.

Feedback loops: structures and processes for learning through the Pathways program

While the main objective of the Pathways model was to increase the productive engagement of poor women in sustainable agriculture and contribute to their empowerment, CARE's institutional cultural focus on continual learning to improve performance was also reflected in the design, which built in two sub-objectives that focus on influencing other programs across CARE's country and global networks and contributing to the global discourse on women in agriculture via a robust learning and advocacy agenda. The Pathways measurement, learning, and evaluation (MLE) system was therefore designed to ensure that the implementing partners as well as beneficiaries take an active role in designing what gets measured, how it is measured, and that their feedback and perceptions are taken into account throughout program implementation. Thanks to strong feedback loops and a robust MLE system design, knowledge from the ongoing Pathways program is already being utilized to influence the quality of other programs implemented by CARE, while data from the program is contributing to improvements in programming practice and discourse related to food security, agriculture, and the empowerment of women more broadly.

One of the key debates that puzzle policy-makers and program implementers alike is how best to measure empowerment in agriculture systems. As hinted at the outset of the chapter, measuring women's empowerment is complex, due to the multi-dimensional nature of empowerment, the multiplicity of indicators that can be used as proxies, and balancing contextualization with the need to standardize indicators (Narayan 2005; Ibrahim and Alkire 2007; Kabeer 1999). CARE

Pathways sought to face this complexity through a mixed-methods approach that combines both qualitative and quantitative approaches to measurement, learning, and evaluation, and that facilitates programmatic and organizational learning processes to ensure that the program is in line with the target groups' own aspirations and goals. The key outcome and impact areas and change levers outlined in the Pathways theory of change are measured by assessing improvements in productivity, equity in agricultural systems, empowerment, and progress toward secure and resilient livelihoods for poor women smallholder farmers, with additional direct impacts on their household members using a mixed-methods approach that combines both quantitative and qualitative tools. The expected result of these interrelated MLE elements is the ability to course-correct during implementation, and ultimately to articulate specific pathways toward the empowerment of prioritized segments of women smallholder farmers and toward more secure and resilient livelihoods for their households.

To measure women's empowerment at baseline and endline, CARE in collaboration with TANGO International in 2012 combined the Women's Empowerment in Agriculture Index (WEAI)[1] and CARE's own women's empowerment frameworks and core areas of inquiry to develop an adapted index (the Women's Empowerment Index) that aligns with the CARE Pathways' theory of change. This index does not focus only on women's achievements as producers but captures key individual, relational, and social dimensions of women's empowerment—including autonomy, self-confidence, mobility, and gender-equitable attitudes—which reflects the holistic approach to empowerment incorporated in CARE's frameworks. This index was validated for each country and has country-specific thresholds for empowerment, providing a quantifiable measure that allows comparison across contexts.

Along with the baseline and endline surveys, quantitative annual review studies are designed to generate an overall snapshot of program progress toward target outcomes every 12 months and to enable course correction and learning from year to year of implementation. The program also applies a Participatory Performance Tracker (PPT) tool to monitor data on: (a) individual farmer adoption of targeted practices in domains related to sustainable agriculture, marketing, gender, and nutrition; and (b) producer group maturity. Maturity is assessed using a common set of factors such as group governance, leadership, transparency, group marketing, and group input purchasing. Lastly, Pathways adopted key concepts from the qualitative Outcome Mapping approach to evaluation to undertake a mid-term review to enable CARE to understand what intra-household and community-level changes are being produced in the direction of empowerment, equity, and productivity for female producers by the Pathways Program. Outcome Mapping was selected because it is a methodology

> oriented toward organizational learning and adaptive management and is considered
> appropriate when an intervention is focused on changed behaviors or relationships,
> which may evolve or emerge unevenly and in a non-linear way; and when the
> intervention wants to focus on results as defined by local actors or beneficiaries.
>
> (Earl et al. 2001)

The mid-term review (MTR) evaluation addressed an important dimension of empowerment measurement through its focus on "ground-truthing" and contextualizing the definition of key terms (decision-making control, women's empowerment/men's engagement, and equitable relationships) from the perspective of the participants. The approach captured the unexpected and unanticipated results (both positive and negative) that can emerge in programs that aim for social change. The MTR was designed deliberately to be carried out with the involvement of staff as data collectors and analysts, with the objectives of building qualitative analysis skills across the Pathways teams, enabling teams to better understand the nature of gender dynamics, and giving them the tools and information to course-correct their gender and empowerment approach as needed.

Reflective practice: institutionalizing internal capacity for gender transformative change

CARE's vision makes fighting discrimination, promoting empowerment and dignity, and respecting human rights central to its work of eliminating poverty. CARE's global strategy on gender equality, its Women's Empowerment Framework, and Good Practices in Gender Analysis framework give staff a common language and set of guidelines for designing gender-aware and gender-sensitive programming. This set of common guidelines has made CARE a credible and authoritative voice on gender equality in the development space. However, taking gender equality guidelines from theory to practice remains an ongoing challenge for countries in diverse contexts, where implementing staff approach these models from their own culturally specific lens and their own internalized set of beliefs around gender norms and the possibilities of social change. Particularly in "hard" and technically oriented sectors such as agriculture and food security, implementing actors and local partners may be uncomfortable with the idea of challenging social norms, which is central to CARE's position on engagement for women's empowerment. Without truly believing in these gender-equality values themselves, implementers cannot expect to achieve transformative outcomes.

In recognition of these challenges, CARE has also developed systematic processes and approaches for internal reflection and personal discovery about one's own beliefs, power positions, and gender identity. One such process is the GED training curriculum that helps ensure that all personnel uphold these principles both within the organization and within programs as a measure of accountability to those that we serve. CARE's diversity training curriculum therefore aims to build skills within staff and within the organization, to deepen our sensitivity to power dynamics, to value differences, and to learn how to utilize the rich diversity within CARE. The ultimate goal is to enhance effectiveness as a development organization and ensure that the skills and competencies required to meet our commitment to this work are present. This curriculum is integrated into the onboarding process for all new staff, in all country offices. GED was integrated into human resources processes for Pathways as a key entry point for ensuring uniformity in integrating these practices into our programming—and also continuing to refine our ideas about how to ensure that GED is at the heart of all aspects of our work. Second, GED training is undertaken for staff and partners on orientation and on a continuous basis to ensure they acquire a strong understanding of gender implications in the work they are doing in the sector (agriculture, market engagement and value chains, food security, and nutrition) so that they can better integrate gender into their work.

The Pathways program teams were oriented on GED and engaged in the initial gender analysis. This basic gender training supports them to carry out one of the integral and transformative components of the program model—the facilitation of participatory "gender dialogues" with the communities. These dialogues themselves are a process of creating safe spaces where men and women can reflect on and discuss prevailing gender norms and practices from another perspective, and to propose their own solutions and action plans for correcting perceived inequalities.

It has been one of the key lessons of the program that GED capacity, internal reflection processes, and facilitation skills (to lead gender dialogues) require continuous capacity building throughout the course of the program, to maintain the skills and competencies required to meet our commitment to this work. Following the principle that transformative social change starts from within, the Pathways teams developed another self-monitoring tool for helping program staff hold themselves accountable as role models. The "Personal PPT" is a set of behavioral indicators related to the gender practices that the team is encouraging among the target group (such as equitable workload-sharing and decision-making). The staff themselves define the progressive indicators and, on a monthly or quarterly basis, use this tool as a catalyst for discussion of progress and struggles to change social norms and practices in their own lives. This helps them to apply the personal to the professional (and vice versa). Engaging Pathways teams in the Personal PPT, and in the overall MLE data collection and analysis processes, complements the personal GED reflection processes, enabling staff to continue to build their analytical skills and to continually deepen their understanding of how gender and social inequality transverses their sectoral and technical work.

What have we learned so far?

Developing scalable programs that can address the contextual complexities of reality on the ground demands a rigorous theory of change as well as systematic learning and feedback processes that enable teams to interpret and apply learning as they innovate. The path that CARE has taken from the initiation of the SII process to the current lessons being drawn from Pathways illustrates that, for CARE, learning together with our diverse constituents in 90 countries worldwide entails an investment of both time and resources. Specific, dedicated learning grants have enabled CARE to bridge the divides between the best thinking from the policy and academic worlds, the interests of diverse donors, and the grounded experience and understandings from our partners and impact groups on the ground. The result of these learning investments are simple (but theoretically grounded) guiding frameworks (such as the Women's Empowerment Framework) and theories of change that provide a structure within which programs can innovate, scale, and adapt to new poverty challenges while holding firm to the organization's core beliefs and mission.

Note

1 IFPRI's Women's Empowerment in Agriculture Index (WEAI) was developed for the Feed the Future program (Alkire et al. 2012). It provides a quantifiable index to measure women's empowerment in agriculture programs. The WEAI measures the empowerment, agency, and inclusion of women in the agriculture sector in five key domains, reflecting gender inequalities related to productivity, resource control, and time use.

References

Alkire, S., Hazel, M., Meinzen-Dick, R., Peterman, A., Quisumbing, A., Seymour, G., and Vaz, A. (2012). *The Women's Empowerment in Agriculture Index.* IFPRI Discussion Paper 1240. Washington, DC: International Food Policy Research Institute (IFPRI).

Alsop, R., Bertelsen, M. F., and Holland, J. (2006). "Empowerment in Practice from Analysis to Implementation." Washington, DC: World Bank.

CARE (2006). "The Courage to Change: Confronting the Limits and Unleashing the Potential of CARE's Programming for Women." *Synthesis Report: Phase 2. CARE International Strategic Impact Inquiry on Women's Empowerment.* Atlanta, GA: CARE.

CARE (2009). "A Place to Grow." Empowering Women in CARE's Agriculture Programming. Atlanta, GA: CARE.

CARE (2013a). "CARE Pathways Push–Pull Operational Framework." Atlanta, GA: CARE. Available online at: www.care.org/sites/default/files/documents/AG-2013-Innovation-Brief-Operational-Framework-Pathways.pdf (accessed July 13, 2015).

CARE (2013b). "CARE Pathways Farmer Field and Business School." Innovation Brief. Atlanta, GA: CARE. Available online at: www.care.org/sites/default/files/documents/AG-2013-FFBS-Pathways-Innovation-Brief.pdf (accessed July 13, 2015).

Earl, S., Carden, F., and Smutylo, T. (2001). *Outcome Mapping: Building Learning and Reflection into Development Programs.* Ottawa: IDRC.

FAO (2011). "State of Food and Agriculture Report." *Women in Agriculture: Closing the Gender Gap for Development.* Rome: FAO.

Ibrahim, S. and Alkire, S. (2007). *Agency and Empowerment: A Proposal for Internationally Comparable Indicators.* Oxford: OPHI.

Kabeer, N. (1999). "Resources, Agency, Achievements: Reflections on the Measurement of Women's Empowerment." *Development and Change 30:* 435–64.

Kabeer, N. (2001). "Conflicts over Credit." *World Development 29* (1): 63–84.

Malhotra, A., Sidney, S. R., and Boender, C. (2002). "Measuring Women's Empowerment as a Variable in International Development." Washington, DC: World Bank.

Meizen-Dick, R., Quisumbing, A., Behrman, J., Biermayr-Jenzano, P., Wilde, V., and Noordeloos, M. (2011). "Engendering Agricultural Research, Development and Extension." Washington, DC: IFPRI.

Miruka, M., Hillenbrand, E., Kaganzi, E., Newman, C., Cottrell, B., Njuki, J., Kruger, E., Mohanraj, P., and Nurul Amin, S. (2015). "The Farmer Field and Business School Toolkit." Atlanta, GA: CARE. Available online at: www.care.org/ffbs (accessed July 13, 2015).

Narayan, D. (2005). "Measuring Empowerment." Cross-Disciplinary Perspectives. Washington, DC: World Bank.

Quisumbing, A. R. and McClafferty, B. (2006). "Food Security in Practice: Using Gender Research in Development." Washington, DC: IFPRI.

World Bank, FAO, and IFAD (2009). *Gender in Agriculture Sourcebook*. Washington, DC: World Bank.

World Bank (2014). "Voice and Agency." Empowering Women and Girls for Shared Prosperity. Washington, DC: World Bank.

8

LISTENING TO FARMERS AT ONE ACRE FUND

Andrew Youn and Matthew Forti

SUMMARY

One Acre Fund builds highly efficient and effective agricultural input supply chains in East Africa. This case study examines how One Acre Fund adopts and innovates user-centric approaches to research and product development—starting with surveys, but moving rapidly into immediate "market testing" that creates products and services that meet the real needs of smallholder farmers. The organization explores how its own success can be measured by the degree to which it elevates the perspectives of farmers above others. This relates to its motto of "Farmers First," and it is simply a common-sense approach that sees farmers as the best authorities on technologies or services that purport to help them. One Acre Fund believes that the idea of farmer "perspective" goes well beyond what they literally share via surveys and focus groups. Rather, One Acre is exploring how it is possible to more deeply foster Constituent Voice by making it a part of the organizational culture and structure, through making sure its leadership lives and works alongside farmers. This proximity lets them learn from and with them. By embedding constituent participation and voice into its service delivery and the structure of its field units, by asking for payment from farmers to strengthen the incentives for One Acre Fund to learn from them, and lastly by asking farmers to interactively experience product innovations alongside One Acre Fund, new relationships are forged and mutual accountability structures assured.

One Acre Fund does not only practice Constituent Voice because it is the "right" thing to do. While there is intrinsic good in listening to farmers, true learning is also about driving impact and scale. Deeply embedding farmer voice in all of its operations is the major driver of the results achieved, both in terms of helping farmers to improve their productivity and growing to serve a meaningful population of farmers in East Africa.

One Acre Fund is exploring how Constituent Voice can be strengthened when married with other sources of data (quantitative, private sector, etc.), questioning the assumption that they are somehow mutually exclusive. Collective learning is strengthened when farmers take a direct role in service delivery, via their roles as group leaders and group members. Among the most important discoveries is that trust is essential to a collective process of learning, and comes most readily when farmers can easily recognize themselves in the organization's staff. Lastly, co-creating technologies with constituents starts by talking with them at the outset, but goes well beyond that once experience with a product has been gained and feedback on its use incorporated into next-generation technologies.

Introduction

One Acre Fund is a social enterprise dedicated to serving smallholder farmers to help them raise their farm profitability. We work together with farmers in rural parts of East Africa to deliver simple and proven farm technologies to their doorsteps. We offer farmers in Kenya, Rwanda, Burundi, and Tanzania a four-part "market bundle" that includes delivery of farm inputs (such as seed and fertilizer), financing (so that farmers can afford to repay for our services), training, and postharvest market facilitation. At the conclusion of 2014, we served 280,000 farm families through our core model, and are poised to grow to serve over 305,000 farm families by the conclusion of 2015. We are increasingly leveraging this growing farmer network to introduce new technologies that farmers have asked for, and that extend our impact, including agro-forestry, solar lights, and livestock kits. On average, farmers who enroll with One Acre Fund increase their incomes by between 50 and 100 percent on every planted acre.

We are inspired by the work of Professor Robert Chambers, who has made important contributions to the intellectual foundation of the Constituent Voice movement. The theme of his work, putting the *farmer first* in agricultural development, resonates with our motto of "Farmers First." We share Professor Chambers' principles of respecting the voices of the rural poor, listening to their own definitions of a better life, and, when in doubt about how a program may affect them, to take the most logical step and *ask them.*

We are deeply committed to putting "Farmers First" in everything we do. In the nearly ten years since our founding, we have come to believe that a mix of philosophies and tools—some borrowed from the private sector, many borrowed from the concepts of Constituent Voice—are the best way to prioritize the actual needs of farmers while creating a program model that can scale to sustainably serve thousands. We try to weave Constituent Voice into the very fabric of our work. This chapter details the tactics we have found most useful in transforming the ideal of Constituent Voice into a reality:

- ensuring that organization leadership live and work alongside farmers in rural Africa;
- staffing our organization with constituents, and empowering a volunteer network of farmers to deliver many of our services;
- using the feedback loop generated by (partially) charging for our services to strengthen our learning from farmers; and
- conducting R&D with constituents in the field.

This chapter discusses how these key aspects of our approach foster Constituent Voice at all levels of our program. Along the way, we present concrete examples of what this means for the farmers we serve, what we are learning from them, and how we see Constituent Voice interacting with other tools and processes to best enable a collective process of learning in rural development.

One Acre Fund does not just practice Constituent Voice because it is the "right" thing to do. Rather, we fundamentally believe that listening to farmers drives greater impact and scale on their behalf. We believe this has been the single most important factor in our ability to scale from 40 farmers to 280,000 since 2006.

Leadership living in the field

Constituent Voice is often necessitated by the fact that the key leaders of development organizations live and work at great distance from their end customers. Constituent Voice is a proven means of mitigating this structural challenge but, at One Acre Fund, we have found that nothing can substitute for simply eliminating the root problem and living among our clients. This is why roughly 97 percent of One Acre Fund's staff—including our executive director, every one of our country directors, and all of our field directors—live in rural parts of East Africa, typically within walking distance of the farmers we serve. It is impossible to overstate the importance of the lessons we have learned from farmers through simple osmosis.

It is likely that few decisions we have made as an organization have been as important as the simple, structural one of insisting that key leaders live in rural parts of East Africa, alongside farmers. It would be very difficult indeed to co-create a project or movement with others who are located halfway around the world. By living near our clients, we are able to build common ground with them, share (to the best of our ability) their perspective, understand the peculiar and unpredictable constraints that they live under, and try to serve them with the humility and respect that come from shared experience.

Involving constituents in service delivery

We have found that one of the best ways to promote farmer voice within One Acre Fund's operations is to directly involve constituents in the delivery of our services, in two primary ways:

1   Our organization is staffed with former and current constituents.
2   We empower a volunteer network of farmer "group leaders" to deliver many of our services.

The daily engine for promoting farmer voice within One Acre Fund's operations is our basic "field unit" (Figure 8.1). One Acre Fund farmers organize themselves into groups, which are led by a volunteer group leader, and served by a full-time, paid One Acre Fund field officer. Our field unit creates a practical management structure that is intentionally designed to maximize the quantity and quality of our interactions with farmers, the speed and degree to which lessons from farmers make their way to our leaders, and, most importantly, the number of farmers who permeate our staff ranks.

We believe that staffing these field units with former constituents is a powerful way to strengthen Constituent Voice throughout One Acre Fund. When hiring field officers, we often hire One Acre Fund farmers. Field officers are thus identical to our constituents—they live in deeply rural parts of East Africa and farm small plots of land. Once they begin working for One Acre Fund, field officers spend much of their time walking and biking amongst the fields of the farmers they serve. In addition to being former constituents, field officers are uniquely positioned to fulfill the more standard functions of Constituent Voice. One example of this is the way in which field officers serve as a daily and continuous feedback loop. This loop is closed every time a field officer returns to a farmer to inform her of how One Acre Fund is responding to her feedback, what the organization is up to, and to learn more about her needs.

One Acre Fund's farmer group leaders complement the role of the field officer, serving as another vehicle for increasing farmer participation in our programming. At the beginning of each season, farmers form groups of eight to ten, with whom they will spend the season conducting all One Acre Fund-related activities. They also select a group leader, a volunteer who takes a very active role in helping to deliver our service by arranging meetings, mobilizing members, and leading her fellow farmers in difficult tasks like meticulous weeding or the push to repay One Acre Fund loans. Particularly active group leaders are prime candidates to become full-time One Acre Fund field officers in future seasons. Similarly, active farmers in the group are well-positioned to become future group leaders. We believe that calling on constituents to participate in service delivery and then promoting from within their ranks is a powerful way to embed Constituent Voice into our program.

One Acre Fund is more receptive to constituent voices because it heavily relies on former and current constituents for service delivery. It also works in the other

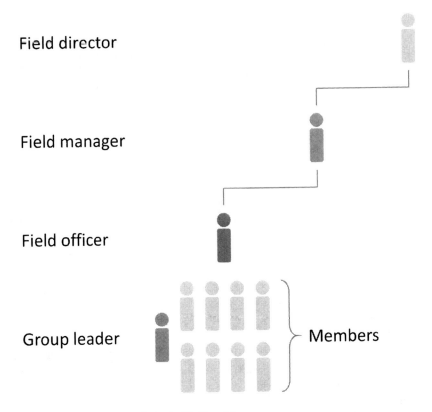

Field director

Field manager

Field officer

Group leader

Members

FIGURE 8.1 One Acre Fund's basic "field unit"

direction—farmers are more trusting of One Acre Fund because we listen to them and live among them. We have observed that the farmers we work with rely on peer credibility as a check on the validity of the information they receive. They justifiably believe that those proffering information on agriculture techniques should share their language, share their home turf, and share their profession. Farmers also know their group leaders intimately, and generally know their field officers on a personal level as well. They can (and routinely do) walk by their field officers' land to visit and say hello, but also to check whether our field agents actually practice what they preach.

In its ideal form, the field officer–farmer relationship is one of peers, with the field officer's primary role being little more than that of a facilitator for collective learning. A standard meeting between a field officer and her clients takes the form of a small village gathering, often under a large tree at a local schoolyard or farmer's house. As is customary in meetings such as these, farmers greet each other, greet their field officers, and participate actively. They laugh and joke, and are not afraid to press a field officer when they disagree with what he or she has to say. Field officers always speak the same language as the farmers they serve. Generally, field officers engage in dialogue with farmers—reminding them when inputs will be delivered, or asking how their crops are doing, for example—before conducting farming demonstrations in the actual fields of farmers. Farmers take turns practicing techniques and routinely step in to teach each other.

We invest significant organizational resources in the leadership, communication, and technical skills of our field officers so that we can promote from within. Our goal is for field officers to become field managers and then field directors, rather than reserving these management roles for more formally educated outside hires. By doing this, we ensure that farmers are represented amongst the highest ranks of leaders in our organization, and that they have a seat at the table when One Acre Fund is making decisions that affect them.

Customer is king: using payment for services to strengthen farmer voice

In the development field, the people who pay for services or programs are sometimes different from those who consume these services. Development organizations have multiple stakeholders (donors, board members, government officials, staff) in addition to beneficiaries, and the leaders of these organizations are often inclined (or even incentivized) to respond to the perspectives of these stakeholders before the perspectives of beneficiaries. Constituent Voice is an important solution to this structural imbalance, which demands that organizations ask and report what beneficiaries think of the programs that affect them.

Although we recognize that it is by no means an appropriate solution for every organization, One Acre Fund believes that a potential method for further strengthening Constituent Voice is to ask for partial payment for services from those constituents. This ensures that those who pay for development programs are the same as those who consume them, at least to some extent. Since we began operations, we have asked farmers to repay for the services we provide them. Although this decision comes from a number of goals—including extending the efficiency of donor dollars and serving as a proof-of-concept for the private sector—the most important is the fact that repayment empowers farmers to provide immediately tangible feedback on the quality of our programs. Instead of beneficiaries complaining about free programs, farmers are paying clients empowered to influence the services rendered. This gives them the leverage to provide powerful feedback.

Repayment gives us a useful barometer on how we are performing as an organization. The rate at which farmers repay their loans to One Acre Fund is based on both their satisfaction with the service we are providing them as well as their farm productivity. When our service at a particular field site falters, we immediately start to see repayment drop. This allows us to quickly direct resources to fix the problem. Payment (or lack of payment) for services rendered does not substitute for seeking constituent input on our operations, but it is an additional ingredient with the added benefit of a very rapid feedback loop.

Seeking repayment further helps to align our incentives with those of small-holder farmers because they choose to enroll with us each growing season. If they do not like our offerings, they will "vote with their feet" and choose not to enroll. The farmer's commitment to repay a loan makes this a more weighty decision: instead of being passively enrolled with little at stake, farmers make an informed, voluntary judgment about whether our services are worth their cost. Conversely, farmers know that if they fail to repay their loan, they will not be invited to re-enroll in subsequent seasons. This mutually reinforcing relationship between how farmers enroll in our services and how they repay creates a clear customer service metric and ensures real farmer autonomy and choice.

We are thoroughly aware of the dangers of putting too great an emphasis on the market mechanism to ensure the responsiveness of One Acre Fund to its clients. Seeking revenue from clients, when taken to an extreme, can lead to perverse incentives for an organization's staff. One need only examine the crisis of over-indebtedness and farmer suicides in India's state of Andhra Pradesh to understand that seeking repayment for supposedly beneficial services can backfire terribly. Thus, repayment is only one of One Acre Fund's tools for understanding farmer perspectives, and we *never* undertake an initiative for the sake of revenue alone. Furthermore, it goes without saying that certain aspects of rural development that are hugely beneficial—more secure land tenure, or the global public good of smallholder-friendly innovations—cannot and should not be paid for by the world's poorest farmers. Asking clients to pay is not necessarily appropriate for all or even most social organizations.

A common theme of our work is that impact and sustainability are not mutually exclusive. We believe that tools and inspirations of the private sector can go hand-in-hand with the qualitative and empathetic approach of Constituent Voice. In this case, by relying on farmers for repayment, we have more to lose from being deaf to their voices. We think this hybrid approach helps to deeply embed Constituent Voice practices into our organizational culture.

Better together: co-creating innovations with farmers

We often think of One Acre Fund as a delivery platform for technologies that can help smallholder farmers become more successful. Which technologies to deliver, and in what configurations, are questions that we increasingly seek to answer together with the farmers we serve. Our preferred method for discovering whether an innovation will be successful is to let farmers express their preferences through rapid, iterative, and interactive trialing of new products. We combine a questioning, collaborative method with techniques borrowed from A/B testing and the traditional R&D practiced by the corporate world. We think that lessons from farmers come in many forms, from what they tell us directly to how success-ful they are at using technologies we trial.

Admittedly, One Acre Fund was not always good at incorporating farmer per-spectives into our innovations work. In our early years, we experimented with a variety of high-value or "export-grade" offerings, including passion fruit and mushrooms, which ended up not being a good fit for our particular target population of subsistence farmers. The ideas for these innovations, crucially, came not from farmers, but rather from recent agronomic research reports touting their income-generating possibilities. Had farmers been participating more actively in our project design at the time, we would likely have learned from them that passion fruit was unfamiliar, very difficult to grow, prone to diseases, and very difficult to sell—in other words, the sort of product most smallholders would struggle to make use of. We plowed valiantly ahead and with the best of intentions, but eventually realized that to be successful, we needed to be laser-focused on the needs of our customers.

With a goal of avoiding similar mistakes, we created a systematic innovations process that tries to incorporate farmer perspective at every stage of a product's development. The process is in some ways inspired by the data-driven experimentation of the corporate world, but it is applied in a manner that is much more collaborative with farmers. Most importantly, farmers are the ones who actually test new products, in their own fields and with their own labor. We ask farmers at each stage of the process for their feedback on what worked and what failed. We then combine the valuable insights produced by farmers' experiences with the precision of hard numbers like input usage, yields, and farmer profitability, which we measure in a randomized control trial when possible. We think this combination of tactics produces richer insights than either would on its own.

Our innovations process is designed to ensure that any product we develop meets the following key criteria:

- *Impact*: What is the average incremental income for farmers generated by the product?
- *Adoptability*: Are farmers interested in the product? How many will use it?
- *Simplicity*: Is the product straightforward enough that *all* farmers can use it successfully?
- *Operability*: How much complexity is required to deliver the product at scale?

We have realized that it is impossible to answer any of these questions without the input of farmers. Farmers have preferences about any given innovation—whether it is desirable, if it is configured properly—and our innovations process is only successful to the extent that it allows farmers to express those preferences. For example, we cannot make any reasonable test of "simplicity" without giving products to farmers for them to experience directly. Our farmers routinely uncover all sorts of problems with the way a product is designed that we could never have discovered in even the most rigorous laboratory testing. Individual farmers are the end-users of these innovations, so they are the best authority on whether they will work for them.

That said, we have found that new technology may still be worth our attention even if farmers are not initially banging down our doors to get it. To assess adoptability, we start with focus groups and surveys of our farmers. But farmers, like all humans, sometimes need a more thorough understanding of a product or service before they can assess whether it would actually be useful to them. To account for this, we do not stop at asking farmers questions. Instead, we increasingly are relying on rapid prototyping of product ideas and interactive sessions, in which farmers test the usage of products in real-life scenarios. For example, we recently conducted a series of cookstove "demo days," which gave farmers in Kenya the chance to cook their favorite staple, *ugali*, on a variety of different stoves (Figure 8.2, and available as a video online at http://vimeo.com/100406859, accessed September 25, 2015). Farmers taught us more—and learned more themselves—from actually using these stoves together than they would have with a traditional focus group. We plan to make greater use of live demonstrations like this in the future.

We believe that fostering real Constituent Voice, in the context of disseminating technology for rural agriculture, must go beyond asking questions, recording answers, and reporting results. Had we asked the farmers we served in 2008 whether they were interested in solar lamps, many would have said "no," because they had little familiarity with solar lamps. It was through an iterative and interactive process of product discovery, exploration, testing, and early adoption that our farmers, with the gentle facilitation of One Acre Fund, gradually learned about solar lamps, expressed their interest in them, and eventually adopted them. As of this writing, tens of thousands of farmers have purchased solar lamps from us.

To formally test the criteria of *impact*, *adoptability*, *simplicity*, and *operability*, we have created a four-phase innovations process which incorporates farmer participation in different forms at each stage. Generally, the phased innovations approach is intended to ensure that actual farmer experiences with new technologies occur and are taken into account *very early* in the process. When an innovation fails, we

FIGURE 8.2 One Acre Fund farmers demo various cookstoves in Kenya

Source: photo by Hailey Tucker/One Acre Fund.

want it to fail early, and at a small scale, so that risk for farmers is minimized. The phased innovations process is as follows:

- (Phase 0: Desk research)
- Phase 1: Nursery/research station trials
- Phase 2: Small-scale farmer trials (N < 1,000)
- Phase 3: Large-scale farmer trials (N ≈ 10,000)
- Phase 4: Full-program roll-out (N > 10,000).

Even in the early stages of the process, direct farmer voices are important. For example, although desk research answers certain necessary questions (e.g. "what brands of portable solar lamps exist?"), the initial idea for a product is often generated through the capacity of our field unit to listen to the needs of farmers, and to identify promising technologies by observing them. Every field officer at One Acre Fund serves roughly 150 farmers, each of whom is a potential innovator-in-waiting.

Similarly, we strive to make our research stations miniature, field-based laboratories for the co-development of products by and with farmers. To facilitate this, we staff our nurseries largely with experienced farmers, as opposed to university-educated agronomists. Furthermore, when we test a new crop variety or method at our nurseries, we invite One Acre Fund farmers to perform the actual planting, as opposed to permanent, trained nursery workers. While this is happening, we observe and ask farmers about their experience. Occasionally, we receive feedback along the lines of "this planting method might improve yields, but it is extremely complicated and way too hard!" This is a great signal that we will have adoption problems down the road unless we change course. Thus, we strive to ensure that even our nurseries—typically the domain of top-down R&D—serve as incubators for farmer ideas and scenes of dialogue between farmers and the organization.

As candidate innovations move further through the pipeline, they are tested and experienced by more farmers. In Phase 2 of our innovations process, we perform side-by-side trials in farmers' fields comparing existing techniques with potential variations, seeking both quantitative and qualitative information on the results. In Phase 3, a sufficient number of farmers participate that we can perform randomized control trials of new interventions. These later stages of our innovations process have the benefit of being employed in the actual fields of farmers—conditions that even the most farmer-centric nursery plots cannot entirely mimic. These larger-scale trials give us the opportunity to learn from more farmers simultaneously, and to introduce statistically valid comparisons of product configurations.

We think it is critical to marry the scientific discipline of hypothesis testing, rooted in the social sciences concept of the randomized control trial, and the business concept of A/B testing, with a more qualitative, farmer-centric approach to innovations. This approach triangulates a variety of information streams, all of which have important things to teach us about what works for farmers. We learn more when we join these tools. For example, a randomized trial of different sweet potato varieties might suggest that a particular variety produces the highest yields, but our qualitative work with farmers might tell us that it is their least favorite, due to its poor taste. In this case, we would tell farmers about the high yields and seek to understand from them how important taste is, before moving forward. To reiterate, we are inspired by a variety of performance management and evaluation traditions, many coming from the private sector, but we believe in pairing these tools with the rich learning that comes from more qualitative methods of Constituent Voice.

Sample innovation: grevillea trees

It is helpful to understand how the innovations process described in theoretical terms above actually plays out in practice. The introduction of grevillea trees by One Acre Fund, and their subsequent high rates of adoption amongst our farmer network in Kenya, is a good example of how we attempt to ensure that farmers participate actively in our product innovations.

Since One Acre Fund's founding, we have noticed that a portion of our farmers have diversified their income through modest amounts of sustainable agro-forestry. This is how many of our innovations ideas begin: by observing the farmers we work with, or how their non-One Acre Fund neighbors are investing, in order to gauge whether a particular innovation might be viable. With this foundation in place, it becomes One Acre Fund's job to create the facilitating environment such that *all farmers we serve*, not just the richest or most risk-tolerant, have the opportunity to succeed with a given product.

We started asking farmers what they wanted in a tree product as we were conducting background desk research. We surveyed farmers, both formally and informally, about whether they would plant trees on small portions of their land, what types or species of trees they thought were most suitable, and what concerned them most about the possibility of a tree product offering. Most farmers were enthusiastic about both the financial and non-financial benefits of trees. On the financial side, farmers told us (and our field research confirmed) that timber for construction was highly sought-after and thus fetched a high price in local markets. On the non-financial side, farmers explained to us that they appreciated the ability of trees to prevent soil erosion on their fields, provide shade and privacy, and help give soil depleted by years of intensive monoculture a rest. Farmers were concerned, however, that trees might leach excessive moisture from soil.

The most crucial lesson we learned from the farmers was that it was highly uncommon for them to plant tree seeds directly—if farmers grew any trees on their land, they transplanted expensive seedlings from a nursery. This cut into the value of tree investments for farmers and was not scalable—there just were not enough nurseries to generate seedlings for all our farmers. We wanted to find a more democratic method than forcing farmers to go to nurseries that are traditionally the realm of skilled specialists. We wanted to make *every* farmer into someone who could create a tree nursery.

With this in mind, we decided to begin trials of a product that would allow farmers to plant a tree species, called *Grevillea robusta,* directly from seed. The grevillea tree product entered our standard innovations process, beginning in 2010 with Phase 0 research. Our innovations process ensured that grevillea trees passed a battery of tests around *impact, adoptability, simplicity,* and *operability* before being rolled out as a product offering. We also continue to further refine the grevillea tree product in our research stations and small-N farmer trials to this day, despite simultaneously offering it to our farmer network.

Through the course of this product development, two fundamental challenges emerged:

- *Difficulty of planting directly from seed*: As discussed above, we wanted to find a method that would allow any farmer to create her own tree nursery. Farmers told us, and testing confirmed, that it was hard to find a planting method that achieved consistently high rates of tree seed germination and survival.
- *Allowing trees to mature*: Many of our farmers wanted to sell saplings for quick profit, rather than waiting for the large income increases that would come from selling trees at maturity.

We used farmer participation and feedback in trial phases 1 through 3 to address the crucial challenge of helping farmers plant directly from grevillea seed. With our facilitation, farmers experimented with a variety of different methods for planting grevillea seeds. These methods included using "germination bags" and "seedling sockets," along with variations in the soil composition of each (Figure 8.3). Throughout this process, we solicited farmer feedback on which planting method they found most successful and easiest. We supplemented this feedback by looking at the quantitative germination results. Somewhat surprisingly, farmers expressed a preference for the "socketing" method. Even though it requires some more steps, it improves seedling survival rates and helps farmers to give each individual seedling the care it needs to thrive. We continue to set up experiments for farmers to find optimal methods of planting tree seeds.

Next, farmers had no trouble understanding that the trees became more valuable the longer they waited to sell them, but wanted a way to avoid the temptation to sell early (Figure 8.4). They routinely needed cash to pay their children's school fees or respond to health emergencies, and selling immature tree saplings was a good way to accomplish this—even if it meant forgoing larger income streams in the future. With this in mind, we are currently testing a variety of commitment devices with our farmers. In one case, we are inviting them to make specific pledges, in the presence of their farming groups, about what the tree income will be used for in the future, like college tuition fees for children who are currently in secondary school.

Participation by farmers was critical in the development of the tree product. Farmer practice and feedback showed us that methods for planting trees in nurseries would not translate well to their fields—they needed a method of planting directly

FIGURE 8.3 Grevillea seedlings in "tree bags" (above) and "sockets" (below)

Source: photos by Joseph Scarpelli/One Acre Fund.

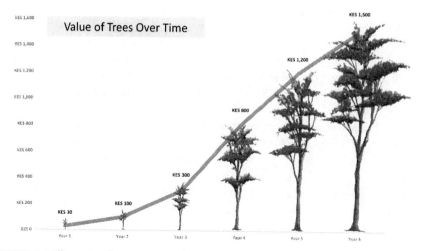

FIGURE 8.4 Illustration from a training showing how grevillea trees increase exponentially in value over time

Source: graphic credit One Acre Fund.

from seed that *every* farmer could use. Similarly, it was only through listening to farmers that we understood how difficult it would be for them to avoid cashing in on a ready source of income in their fields. Focus groups and questionnaires were certainly a part of this learning process, but, as we have suggested earlier in this chapter, the richest lessons came from a combination of quantitative data, randomized trials, and qualitative feedback from farmers actually experiencing and reacting to the tree product in practice. Asking people what they want is of course crucial, and served as the starting point for all of our work with grevillea trees. From there, we began to experiment *with* our constituents, to discover insights and methods that neither One Acre Fund nor farmers could have predicted in advance. As of now, grevillea trees have been rolled out across our 136,000-strong farmer network in Kenya, resulting in millions of trees planted.

Everyday innovations in the field

We believe that the co-creation of innovations with farmers need not be limited to those products or services that pass through our standard, rigorous innovations pipeline. In fact, we have repeatedly found that farmers hold the collective wisdom to solve their most difficult challenges, and are merely in need of a facilitating mechanism to share their solutions. One Acre Fund still has more work to do to ensure that every farmer we work with has the chance to contribute actively to the design of new technologies; but so far we have been fortunate to see many major and minor improvements percolate from the voices of the farmers we serve throughout our entire operation.

Some telling examples come from the manner in which One Acre Fund's farmers helped us arrive at elegant technologies for improving the precision and consistency of planting and top-dress fertilizer "micro-dosing" for maize. In One Acre Fund's early years, we struggled to find a way for farmers to apply top-dress fertilizer at a consistent and proper spacing from an individual maize plant (approximately ten centimeters). Simply instructing farmers was not sufficient; farmers had different mental conceptions of what ten centimeters looked like. The solution, eventually, came from one of our clients in Kakamega, a town in Kenya's Western Province. This farmer had realized that a four-inch nail, hammered perpendicularly into a sturdy stick, provided the desired spacing (Figure 8.5). This insight may have stayed with just him and a handful of close peers, but the knowledge-spreading power of our field network (and, if we are being honest, a bit of luck) saw his clever idea gain traction. He first told his field officer, who told his field

FIGURE 8.5 Illustration from a training showing the maize top-dress stick designed by a One Acre Fund farmer

Source: graphic credit One Acre Fund.

manager, who told her field director. At this point, the solution made its way into our R&D pipeline, and, within a few years, is now standard operating procedure for 136,000 farmers in Kenya.

Similarly, we have learned from farmers over the course of many years about how to design a functional "fertilizer scoop" for both planting and top-dress fertilizer. The goal of delivering an accurate micro-dose of both planting and top-dress fertilizer to each maize seed and plant is surprisingly elusive. It took us many years to learn from farmers how they actually applied fertilizer in the field. Our field staff gradually understood that farmers wanted to apply fertilizer quickly, without stopping to level each scoop of fertilizer before applying it. But farmers also cared about ensuring that the proper dosage was applied. This suggested that we needed to design a scoop that was deliberately slightly lower in volume than the actual dosage, since farmers would be quickly applying rounded spoonfuls in the field. We worked together with farmers on everything from the ergonomics of the scooping motion to observations on the perceived heft and weight of the plastic, involving at least 100 different farmers over 40 different co-creation days. The result is the custom fertilizer scoop pictured in Figure 8.6.

Conclusion

One Acre Fund's fundamental goal as an organization is to create as much positive impact (defined as incremental income generated per farmer) for as many

FIGURE 8.6 Double-sided fertilizer scoop for planting fertilizer and top-dress fertilizer

Source: photo by Hailey Tucker/One Acre Fund.

smallholder farmers as possible. This is why we are happy to make use of any and all tools that will help us toward this goal, including Constituent Voice, but also the more quantitative tools and experimentation of the private sector and behavioral economics—they all have important things to tell us, and they need not be mutually exclusive.

That said, as One Acre Fund has grown, we have realized that we are most successful when we elevate the perspectives of farmers above others. This relates to our motto of "Farmers First," and it is simply common sense that farmers are the best authorities on technologies or services that purport to help them.

Crucially, we believe that the idea of farmer "perspective" needs to go beyond what they literally tell us, via surveys and focus groups. As this chapter has argued, we think it is possible to more deeply foster Constituent Voice by making it a part of our organizational culture and structure, in the following ways:

- making sure that our leadership live alongside farmers and are therefore better able to learn from them;
- embedding constituent participation and voice into our service delivery and the structure of our field units;
- asking for payment from farmers to strengthen the incentives for One Acre Fund to learn from them; and
- asking farmers to interactively experience product innovations alongside One Acre Fund.

Finally, it bears repeating that we do not want to learn from the farmers we serve simply because it is the "correct" thing to do. While there is certainly an intrinsic good in listening to farmers, we increasingly find that *learning drives impact and scale.* Deeply embedding farmer voice in our operations is the major driver of the results we have been able to achieve, both in terms of helping farmers to improve their productivity, and scaling to serve a meaningful population of farmers in East Africa. It is at the heart of what it means to put Farmers First (see Box 8.1).

BOX 8.1 ONE ACRE FUND AT A GLANCE

- *Organization description*: One Acre Fund delivers a complete value chain of services, including delivery of farm inputs, financing, training, and post-harvest facilitation to rural smallholders in East Africa.
- *Time frame/founding date*: 2006–present.
- *Latest annual budget*: $41.2 million (2014).
- *Countries of operation*: Kenya, Rwanda, Burundi, Tanzania.
- *Current number of staff*: ~3,500 (2015).
- *Key statistics*:
  – Average $ income increase per farmer per year: $128 (2014).
  – Farmers served: 307,700 (2015).

CHAPTER SUMMARY

Type and frequency of key feedback tools:

- ongoing (formal and informal) reports from field officers across the program;
- weekly review of Key Performance Indicators such as repayment, plant germination, harvest sizes, etc.

Building an organizational culture that fosters collective learning:

- farmers take active role in creating program;
- organization leadership lives in the field;
- field staff is largely composed of constituents;
- repayment reinforces collective learning by enhancing farmers' voices;
- new innovations are co-created with farmers.

Key lessons learned:

- Constituent Voice can be strengthened when married with other sources of data (quantitative, private sector, etc.). There is no need for them to be mutually exclusive.
- A collective process of learning is strengthened when farmer voice is embedded into the program structure itself, for example by hiring constituents into the organization staff.
- Collective learning is strengthened when farmers take a direct role in service delivery, via their roles as group leaders and group members.
- Trust is essential to a collective process of learning, and comes most readily when farmers can easily recognize themselves as key protagonists in the organization.
- Co-creating technologies with constituents should start with asking them, but then go beyond that, with the recognition that farmers will often best express themselves through their experience of a product.

9

IDEO.ORG AND DESIGNING WITH FARMERS

Jocelyn Wyatt

SUMMARY

IDEO.org is a non-profit design organization that works to improve the lives of low-income communities around the world. The case study examines IDEO.org's experience of using human-centered design to understand and work alongside those in the greatest need. By co-designing solutions to development challenges, they're building problem-solving capacity and designing a path to prosperity. Design Kit, a teaching platform aimed at spreading human-centered design, assists other development actors to more effectively listen to and co-design with the constituents they seek to serve. The journey explores how IDEO.org continuously seeks input and feedback not only from constituents, but from experts as well. IDEO.org shares design solutions and gets feedback based on what people have seen works (or not) in other contexts. Just as it learns from its partners, it seeks to inspire a more human-centered approach in them. And the uptake of human-centered design amongst its partners (other non-profits, social enterprises, and foundations) is inspiring. The solutions, systems, and social innovation that arise from truly understanding and designing alongside low-income communities are the most likely to offer hope and improve lives. And for IDEO.org, if it can't see real impact, it hasn't done its job.

Learning to learn from farmers

IDEO, a global design firm with roots in product design, has been a true innovator for decades. But despite the success of the company's human-centered approach to design, one rooted in truly hearing and understanding the needs and desires of the people it's designing for, poverty alleviation work is still a relatively new pursuit. To build out its portfolio of social sector work, and to have as much impact as possible, IDEO took the bold step of launching IDEO.org in 2011. Since then, we've been able to bring IDEO's deep experience in hearing the voices of people and understanding their deep-seated needs and desires to design solutions squarely aimed at alleviating poverty.

Our human-centered design methodology was born out of IDEO's history of designing products, services, and experiences with private sector companies (Figure 9.1). For the past three years, we at IDEO.org have been on a path of understanding and adapting this approach to working with low-income communities, many of whom are farmers.

I trace the seeds of IDEO.org and its approach to agricultural work back to 2001, when IDEO was approached by Kickstart International to design the Deep Lift MoneyMaker pump, a human-powered treadle pump used for irrigation. The designers and engineers who worked on the project took it on as a volunteer opportunity, which meant they were unable to travel to East Africa to speak with farmers and prototype irrigation solutions in context. Because the designers never got to see how this pump would work in person, or talk with the people who would ultimately use it, the design focused more on the engineering elements and less on the context in which it would be used. As a result, the product didn't ultimately make it to market. Despite being a fine piece of design, it just wasn't affordable to smallholder farmers. But in failure comes learning, and though IDEO didn't have the direct impact on the lives of the poor that it wanted, the Kickstart project helped the designers who touched it see that they could use their talents in service of those who most need great design.

In 2005, IDEO's CEO, Tim Brown, took a trip to India with Jacqueline Novogratz, the founder and CEO of Acumen, to try to understand where design

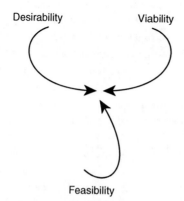

FIGURE 9.1 Innovation comes from the intersection of these three lenses, with desirability being IDEO.org's point of departure

could have the most impact on the lives of the poor. It was a galvanizing experience, one in which Tim came to understand that so many of the challenges he saw organizations facing could be addressed through a human-centered approach. Tim was inspired by how Aravind Eye Clinic treated its customers with such dignity and how they developed a business model that allowed them to serve both the poor and the rich with high-quality health care while differentiating the offer on the surrounding services and hospital experience. Tim saw both examples of great design and not-so-great design and was motivated to make a commitment at IDEO to build a portfolio of this type of work. "I wanted to see new ideas implemented in the world that are having a measurable effect on the world's poorest and underserved communities," he said.

A couple of years later, Tim and Roy Steiner of the Bill & Melinda Gates Foundation found themselves at a convening in Seattle talking about how IDEO could transform agricultural organizations through human-centered design without the Bill & Melinda Gates Foundation or other funders paying for long, expensive design projects with each of their grantees. A central tenet of human-centered design is that everyone has the power to come up with innovative solutions, often they just need a little guidance. What if we could set the power of human-centered design loose in the social sector? What would an army of human-centered designers be able to accomplish on behalf of the poor? By the end of the heady, exciting evening, Roy agreed that the Bill & Melinda Gates Foundation would be willing to fund the creation of a human-centered design toolkit that would share IDEO's approach and benefit many organizations around the world.

IDEO had developed toolkits in the past, codifying the human-centered design approach for its clients. Oftentimes, after working with IDEO designers, companies saw the value in the human-centered design approach and asked IDEO to teach them how to bring this methodology in-house. Companies hired IDEO to train their employees on human-centered design and, in so doing, IDEO would create a toolkit that could serve as the teaching materials and the leave-behind for future reference. The challenge with some of these toolkits, however, was that to truly grasp the key concepts you'd need to participate in a design project or a series of workshops for it all to add up. In addition, these toolkits tended to be proprietary, confidential, and focused on doing research and design for the American market.

So we set out to create a toolkit for non-profits and social enterprises working in the developing world with rural communities and smallholder farmers. Building on what we'd learned from making toolkits in the past, and the Kickstart treadle pump project, we knew we needed to get out to the field, work with farmers, and learn from the organizations that had been doing this work for decades. The idea wasn't to start from scratch, but to fold the wisdom of others into our approach, to adapt our methodology to a new context.

The toolkit team worked with IDE, Heifer International, and the International Center for Research on Women (ICRW) to test IDEO's approach with field teams in Ethiopia and Cambodia and to incorporate these NGOs' methodologies into our own. IDE's programs with smallholder farmers included the development of tools and technologies such as drip irrigation and treadle pumps and capacity-building support for farmers to better understand how to increase their yields. Heifer's program in Kenya provided livestock inputs to farmers and taught them how to effectively raise animals. And ICRW's role was to support other organizations in how they were designed for women farmers.

As Tatyana Mamut and Jessica Hastings, two IDEO designers, prepared to travel to Ethiopia and Nepal to meet with farmers, they considered which design methods would be appropriate in a developing-world context. The human-centered design approach always starts with listening to people so we needed to figure out how to best learn from farmers and community members about their contexts and desires.

The first challenge was recruiting people to talk to. IDEO typically recruits interview participants by sending out emails to the IDEO network or posting ads on Craigslist. And when the IDEO team visits someone in their home, they encouraged the clients to stay back, thinking the client could make the interviewee more reluctant to be open and honest. However, in this context, it was critical to rely on our partners, in this case, IDE, to introduce us to community members and accompany our designers. Because the local organizations have built a level of trust in the local community, we needed them to introduce us and participate deeply in the research.

Once Tatyana and Jessica arrived in Ethiopia, they saw that even when they tried to interview a single woman in her home, within ten minutes, other family members had entered the house to listen in on the conversation and local children would surround the house, peering in every window and door, curious to see what was happening. In essence, no conversation was ever truly private. This made talking about things like money and community relations very challenging. Tatyana and Jessica quickly developed worksheets that allowed them to ask questions in a way that wasn't so direct. Instead of asking "Who makes decisions within this community?" they could point to the head of a sketch of a figure and ask "Who is the head of the community? Who is the heart of the community, the hands, the feet, etc.?"

At IDEO.org and IDEO, we have a strong bias toward visualization. We sketch, sculpt, make charts and graphs, and generally try to render our ideas visually. And when we go out into the field to learn from others, we encourage them to do the same. Turns out, this approach makes even more sense when interviewing people with varying levels of literacy. We found it highly effective to keep things visual. Pictures generally trumped the written word. Of course there are times when people are better verbal learners and times when a verbal explanation must accompany the visualization. But great researchers are adept at adjusting their methods to various learning styles and language abilities, and figure out the best way to ask questions and get great answers in response.

I've participated in many interviews in which a designer will ask a farmer "What is your annual income?" The farmer will appear confused and really struggle to answer the question. She doesn't consider her income on an annual basis because it is generally earned seasonally. However, if we were to ask her how much land she has, what crops she grows on the land and in what quantities, and how much those crops sell for, we can get a picture of her income.

The same applies when asking about monthly expenses. For many farmers, expenses aren't static from month to month, so answering that question is very challenging. Instead, we've found it useful to present cards with images of major expenses—seeds, fertilizers, school fees, rent, water, health care, food, mobile phone credit—and ask people to rank which expenses are most significant and estimate how much each costs. With this information, we're able to construct a rough profit and loss statement for a family. This activity also helps us understand how people prioritize their purchases and how they make decisions about what they spend. We quickly learned that asking villagers in Ethiopia hypothetical questions about community leadership, family decision-making, or inflows and outflows of money was futile. However, if we could present them with diagrams and visual worksheets, they could sketch with us and show us how decisions got made and when it made sense to make particular investments.

We also experienced the challenge of conducting interviews through translators. Often, our partners will suggest that one of their staff play this role. And though our preference is to hire a professional interpreter, we frequently run up against budgetary constraints or are working in an area where it can be very challenging to find a trained professional. We try to orient the interpreter to our project as best we can so that he or she understands what we're aiming to learn. Frequently, though, we will ask a question like, "Who manages the money in your household?" and the woman will respond for three or four minutes, clearly articulating many nuances of what decisions are made, by whom, and how. And the interpreter will provide us with the one-sentence summary, "She says that she and her husband make the decisions." We often have to remind our interpreters several times that we want the direct translation rather than his or her spin on it.

Getting to the nuance of what a farmer is saying is critical, as it's often in the details, rather than the generalities, that we find insight that leads to design solutions. For example, on a project in Kenya, we were interviewing farmers who were part of a banana-growing cooperative. When asked about their personal consumption of bananas, one woman told us that she had learned how to make cassava flour using a combination of two parts maize flour and one part banana flour. And another woman told us she had baked a cake for her husband's birthday using banana flour. These stories helped us understand that people were willing to try new recipes and cooking techniques if they had the information to do so. However, if we had heard from a translator, "They say they use the bananas in their cooking," we would have understood something entirely different and it would not have led us to a concept about the introduction of cooking classes, new recipes, and advertising campaigns about how to cook and eat fruit and vegetables in new ways.

We also make sure to interview our interpreter and driver as well. During a project in Senegal, our driver Jean told us that his parents actually run a peanut farm not far from Dakar. We organized a visit and benefitted tremendously seeing a small-scale peanut operation. Even more so, the connection we already had with Jean and his familiarity with our methods helped us ask more probing and engaging questions of his parents.

We found that the longer we spend with people, the richer the stories we got from local community members. Tatyana and Jessica did homestays with families, finding that by the second or third day the personal narratives and local commentary would be flowing, whereas on the first day people would oftentimes be quite shy. Connecting with teenage and young women tended to be easiest for women on our teams. They were often much more open and enthusiastic to spend time with our teams than their mothers.

Once back in San Francisco, Tatyana and Jessica set to work writing a first draft of what would become the HCD Toolkit. After sharing it internally at IDEO and with our partners, we published an agriculture-only edition online.

After devising this first iteration of our toolkit, we continued to prototype with IDE in Vietnam and Zambia. In 2008, after incorporating more learnings from a variety of sectors, we put the HCD Toolkit online and also offered a print edition. Not long after posting the HCD Toolkit on the IDEO website, we were stunned to watch the downloads rise week after week. We heard from people around the world using the HCD Toolkit and what was most interesting was how it gave students, interns, and young professionals a sense of credibility when they joined an organization. They were extremely enthusiastic to employ design thinking and now they suddenly had a place to learn more about it. Best of all, they could suddenly back up their approach with a toolkit authored by IDEO and supported by the Bill & Melinda Gates Foundation.

Now, seven years later, the HCD Toolkit has been downloaded 155,000 times and has been translated by users into Portuguese, Spanish, Korean, Czech, and Japanese. It evolved into HCD Connect, an online community platform with over 55,000 users around the world practicing human-centered design and sharing their stories. We've also turned the core of the HCD Toolkit into the Course for Human-Centered Design, a free online course that has been taken by 82,000 people.

Taking everything that we've learned in the last six years, in 2014 we launched Design Kit, a suite of tools teaching human-centered design to the social sector. In 2015 we updated the HCD Toolkit and launched it as the Field Guide to Human-Centered Design. In the first three months we've had over 68,000 downloads.

We believe that Design Kit amplifies the voices and capacity of social sector practitioners. It allows those who are working around the world to share their stories about how they are applying human-centered design, and we love seeing their work mingle with stories from the IDEO.org team as well. The site is all about getting under the hood of our design methodology and sharing what we've picked up in the field. This culture of talking, listening, thinking, sharing, and storytelling is native to human-centered design and part of what helps us not just learn from farmers, but also from each other (Figure 9.2).

This design approach articulated in Design Kit remains central to how we work today.

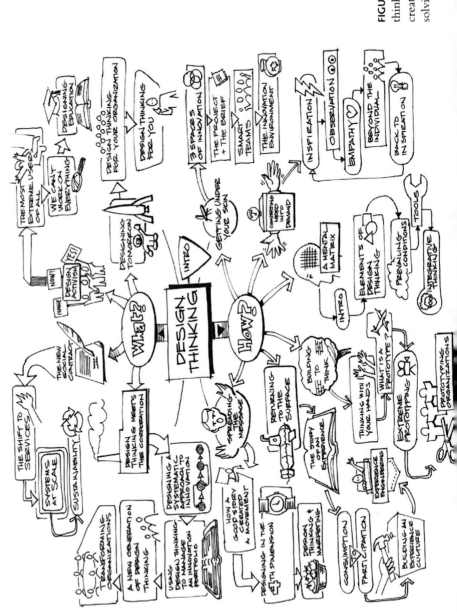

FIGURE 9.2 Design thinking is an iterative, creative approach to solving problems

HCD in action

In 2014, we completed a project with Rockefeller Foundation to understand post-harvest loss for smallholder farmers and recommend solutions to decrease it. When our team spent time in Kenya and Senegal, they conducted interviews with and observed more than a hundred farmers, middlemen, traders, wholesalers, and retailers. When conducting interviews was difficult due to language barriers, they showed farmers cards with sketches of tractors, dryers, fertilizers, water pumps, and more and asked them to prioritize the items and describe what would be most valuable to them and why.

Though our interest was in post-harvest loss solutions, farmers almost never addressed ideas like grain storage containers or product dryers as high-priority items. Instead, they focused on investing in inputs, believing that it was most important to increase crop output rather than care for its quality once it has left the vine. By practicing human-centered design, and being led by what we heard from farmers, we came to realize that part of solving post-harvest loss is understanding how farmers actually see their problems.

Learning from farmers isn't just about interviewing them and asking them to talk to us, it's also about experiencing what they do, seeing how they live, and visiting their farms. When my colleagues were designing a teff row planter with farmers in Ethiopia, they asked many questions about whether farmers preferred an oxen-drawn machine or a hand-pulled option. They didn't get a strong preference for one over the other from the farmers in interviews. However, when they tried to drive an oxen cart themselves, they saw how challenging it was to keep the oxen on track and get them to pull the cart in a straight line. When planting seeds in rows, it's critical to pull the cart in a straight line and oxen just weren't going to cut it. So, they decided to design the cart so that farmers could push it by hand.

As is typical on an IDEO.org project, we use a combination of proven human-centered design methods as well as new ones we're experimenting with. We start with the questions that we need to answer through our design research and then develop a plan with the appropriate set of methods that will help us gain the understanding we need. Sometimes the new methods flop—they can be too difficult to explain or too complicated, they may not deliver us any helpful information, or they may prove to be too logistically challenging to be worthwhile.

On the post-harvest loss project, we talked to more and more farmers about their food spoilage problems and there came a point where we had trouble understanding just how much of their crop goes to waste. We'd talked through it a few times but wondered if there was another way to learn. All the farmers we had asked about how much of their crops went to waste told us "None, they all get used." So, we decided to get visual.

Enter the bean counters. The goal with this method was to understand what portion of the farmers' crops went to market, what percentage went to feed them and their families, and what percentage spoils. We only had a sack of pinto beans and a notebook on which to spread them around. We put a mound of 75 beans in a pile and asked the farmer to group them into smaller stacks to represent how much of the harvest is consumed by his or her family, how much is sold, and how much goes to waste.

Though we got a great visualization of what percentage of crops spoil, we also learned that there was one category that we didn't even know about: crops that go to the neighbors. Not only did this give us an additional data point, it also made us realize that there's an informal sharing system among farmers in many Senegalese villages. This prompted all kinds of additional questions about how communities band together and what post-harvest crop loss might mean at a community level as well as an individual one.

This exercise also showed us that it was true that none of the crops were thrown away. Even the produce that wasn't sold to market was either consumed by the family, given to neighbors, fed to the animals, or used as compost. All crops that were grown had value in some way or another—however only some generated money for the farmer.

One of the huge benefits of this exercise is that you don't need a translator for the farmer to convey what he or she means. By going visual, by going analog, and by creating a simple but powerful tool you can communicate directly with someone whose language you don't speak. And, as mentioned, you're entirely likely to stumble upon an idea or dynamic that you had no idea was even in play. Best of all, you can adapt this method to any situation in which you want to see a visual representation of a percentage.

As we continue to work with smallholder farmers, we evolve our methodology and share new techniques with a larger community. We are especially focused on improving the methods related to prototyping, business design, and implementation.

Looking beyond the field

As we've worked with agricultural organizations, we've noticed that they have a tendency to focus only on the farming activities, crops, and income generated through agriculture of the families they work with. An important element of human-centered design is to understand the whole person—to see how livelihoods are connected with education, health, nutrition, access to basic services, and then to design for the person, family, or community as a whole, rather than segmenting his or her life.

In our work at IDEO.org, we've done some projects where we design a tool for the farmer or design one element specifically related to farming and increasing on-farm productivity. What we find much more interesting and impactful, is designing solutions that address a broader system. How might we support the farmer beyond his or her time in the field? How might we develop income-generating opportunities for non-farmers in rural communities? How might we consider the entire system and make sure we're designing for unintended consequences?

Prior to joining IDEO in 2007, I worked with a company in Kenya that was making artemisia for inclusion in ACTs (artemisinin-based combination therapies) to treat malaria. This company worked with approximately 7,000 farmers in Kenya, Tanzania, and Uganda to grow artemisia for processing and ultimately use in the drugs. The company was solely focused on the quantity and quality of the artemisia grown by the farmers. They didn't pay much attention to what they weren't growing on their land anymore or how growing a non-edible cash crop might affect the family's access to food or nutrition. They didn't necessarily think about how their payments to the farmers for the artemisia might not align with the payment of school fees or how to effectively help the farmers finance their inputs. Had the company employed a human-centered design approach, they might have been able to better improve the lives of the farmers while maximizing crop outputs.

In the fall of 2013, IDEO.org worked with the American Refugee Committee (ARC) to design a social enterprise to provide basic health services, clean drinking water, nutritional support, and agricultural financing and guidance in an effort to reduce under-five mortality in the Democratic Republic of Congo (DRC). ARC had determined that an integrated approach, rather than a bifurcated, sector-based approach, would be most effective in supporting the needs of women and their young children, and ultimately reduce under-five mortality from the 20 percent rate where it then stood. So we set our sights on the eastern DRC, in villages outside of Bukavu where the majority of people were farmers and most of their money came through selling crops.

After doing only a few days of interviews and getting to know a spectacular group of women, it was clear to us that we had so much to learn. We decided to work with a small group of women in a deeper way over the course of the four weeks in the field, rather than interviewing a breadth of people, like we might ordinarily do. We organized multiple co-design sessions with a group of seven women, choosing the participants from the women we had interviewed (Figure 9.3).

What was inspiring to us was that the women engaged in abstract role play activities about the health, water, nutrition, and agriculture enterprise so seamlessly and then provided us with feedback about the experience with absolute clarity. We knew they were smart and engaged based on our interviews with them, but we had been concerned that they would be intimidated by coming to the ARC office. Many of them had never ridden in a car to Bukavu and had never used a flush toilet. The samosas we served them for lunch were a real novelty. But despite this unfamiliar environment, the women were vocal, engaged, and open when it came to giving feedback.

The activities we ran were not much different than those we would run with CEOs in the States—they required imagination, creativity, critical and evaluative thinking, and generative concept building. At the end of the day, we saw one woman's notebook where she had sketched the ideas we and her neighbors described—it looked pretty similar to what I would see in the notebooks of my designer colleagues.

These women showed us the importance of power dynamics in their communities and reinforced the notion that control should not be centralized, or else someone in the community would become self-centered or greedy. When reflecting on how to determine ownership for the seed store for instance, one woman

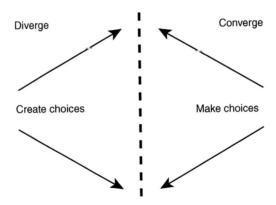

FIGURE 9.3 Human-centered design process in one in which we go through periods of both divergent thinking to explore possibilities and convergent thinking to make decisions and move things forward

told us, "One person should not own this shop. If he does, he will become boastful and will begin to charge us all too much for seeds." This insight led us to recommend structures of community ownership of the enterprises.

The women taught us the meaning of certain symbols, like the circle, which represents connection and harmony. They demonstrated how money is lent, at every turn, so that people could afford to pay for health care, seeds, or other basic services. When role playing, one woman was seeking seeds during planting season and didn't have the money on hand to buy them. She asked the seed seller to sell her the seeds on credit. The seller responded, "I can't give my seeds away to all my customers without getting money for them. I need to get money so I can buy more." To which, the buyer responded, "But I need to plant my field now that it's rained and I don't have any money today." The two finally negotiated a solution where the customer would pay half up-front for the seeds and the other half within two weeks. This role play helped us understand the importance of being able to provide services or sell goods on credit and led us to design systems to make this easier for the employees of these businesses.

It is due in great part to these co-design sessions that we wrapped up our time in the DRC with a much clearer vision of the system we are designing and how a whole host of community dynamics and a variety of services sit alongside an agricultural offer. Because we were able to share very early paper and role-playing prototypes with the women and get their feedback, we returned to San Francisco with a strong direction in terms of how to provide health, water, nutrition, and agriculture services to communities in the DRC.

Another example of looking at farm-adjacent business opportunities comes in our work with Arohona in India thanks to Grand Challenges funding from the Bill & Melinda Gates Foundation. Arohana had been working with dairy farmers in Southern India and wanted to start a business where farmers could finance the purchase of power tools and then rent them to their neighbors. This would both enable smallholder farmers to have an additional source of income and to increase productivity of farmers within the community.

The focus of the first research trip to India was to figure out what agricultural tools farmers needed to increase their productivity and then determine what business savvy the entrepreneurs would need to purchase and then rent out the tools. From there, we designed a business-in-a-box to allow the entrepreneurs to survey their neighbors to understand what power tools they might benefit from and how to structure their business to ensure it would be profitable. We developed the branding and communications, pricing tools and business models, and all other elements to start and run a successful small enterprise.

One observation that my colleagues had was that the livestock camps created by Arohana for its customers drew crowds of people unassociated with Arohana. People preferred the Arohana camps to other livestock camps because local community members hosted them, they brought in expert support, and allowed livestock farmers to share tricks of the trade with each other. This insight led us to develop a brand that builds on community participation rather than a service that only competes on price. Therefore, we designed a tool camp hosted by the community where people could fix their tools, learn how to use new ones, and share tips with one another as they expanded their businesses. This tool camp also serves as a way to recruit farmers to launch tool-lending businesses and helps them sign up farmers in need of power tools.

Because the business had been designed with the local community of farmers, it was easy for Arohana to launch the first pilot. They are now working in two communities and have come upon a huge learning: farmers prefer to hire someone to use the tool on their land rather than renting the tool and using it themselves.

Universally, we believe in the importance of understanding the farmer as a whole person and designing for him or her beyond the field. We also understand that oftentimes the product element of a business offering is the easiest element of the solution. But we continue to work to design the system around it, be it the business model, distribution model, branding, service provision, or repair options.

We have also learned that grasping farmers' motivations and aspirations is equally important as building their technical skills or providing them with new tools. We're working to share a few of the things we've learned about smallholder farmers that focus on how we can encourage strong farmers to grow their businesses and encourage others to create other rural businesses that support these farmers. We've come to this notion after seeing that market opportunities for crops continue to be limited and that increasing production universally will not necessarily increase income levels for smallholder farmers. Rather, we must consider the wrap-around businesses and other income-generating opportunities that people in rural communities can embrace to raise income levels for rural families across the board.

Seeds of success

For decades, many non-profits and community-based organizations have seen the value in talking with farmers and community members. Development scholar

Robert Chambers popularized a participatory approach to development work that has been a big inspiration for us. With our work, it's not only about engaging with farmers and asking them what they want and need, but it's also about gathering data about their behaviors and activities.

Doing both qualitative and quantitative research about farmers' behaviors helps us come to a point of view about smallholder farmers and allows us to make recommendations about how we can best support them.

Designing farmer-centric solutions is critical in terms of getting the uptake and impact an organization desires. However, it's not enough to just do this when one is initially designing a program. It's crucial to build in farmer feedback too. Digital Green is an organization in India that has done this well. Digital Green is committed to collecting data about which farmers watch the instructional videos they produce and which then adopt these practices on their farms. They have massive amounts of data about farmers and their practices, but, until recently, only Digital Green's leadership team and donors accessed it. IDEO.org worked with Digital Green to better understand how field-level staff could more easily collect the data and how that data could benefit the extension workers and the farmers. How could farmers learn what practices others in their community had adopted and what the results had been?

Making data both easier to collect and its outputs more accessible and useful is critical to seeing it have impact at all levels of an organization. Digital Green is now implementing the data-collection and reporting tools that IDEO.org designed so that they are more human-centric, easier to use, and more useful to stakeholders both within and outside of the organization.

At its core, we believe what is most important is to continue to spend time in the field, talking with farmers, asking them probing questions about what's working, what's not, and how things can be improved. Being farmer-centric requires getting constant feedback and continually iterating on one's approach.

Outside of data, there are other ways to gain feedback from farmers about the program, business, service, or product an organization has introduced. At the earliest stage, we run prototypes. These are rough, short-lived tests where we put an unformed solution into the hands of farmers and watch them interact with it and question them about their perceptions of it.

When working with Juhudi Kilimo in Kenya, we tested a concept of showing videos to farmers about new practices. What we found was that the farmers had questions once they were in process, and if the loan officer wasn't around when they had a question, it would go unanswered. We tackled this by creating a toll-free call-in number where farmers could call in and leave a message with their question. Once a week, an extension officer would return the phone calls and give the farmers the answers to the questions they needed.

We were able to prototype this idea in a weekend—we bought a SIM card, handed out cards with the number to farmers, gathered the messages for a few days, and then hired an extension officer to return the calls. We found that this approach was highly effective and created a rough business model to show Juhudi Kilimo the low cost to provide such a service.

Later in the process, we move to pilot tests where an organization runs the solution for a limited period of time—often one to three months—with a small number of farmers—generally fewer than a hundred. This allows us to see the solution in action, while being able to continue to adjust it based on what we observe and learn (Figure 9.4).

Along the way, we continue to seek feedback from experts as well. We show them the design solutions and get their feedback based on what they've seen work or not in other contexts. For example, when we shared the Asili social enterprise concept in the DRC with the Mercy Corps Innovation Team who have deep field experience, they questioned the membership model, saying that in their experience people won't pay a monthly fee for services. That type of critical feedback helps us question our assumptions and encourages us to continue to prototype.

Just as we learn from our partners, so too do we seek to inspire a more human-centered approach in them. And the uptake of human-centered design among our partners has been inspiring. When our project team arrived at Digital Green's office in Delhi, they saw the walls covered in Post-it notes and the team proudly shared stories of taking our online Course for Human-Centered Design. This is just one story of how partners have altered their methods and come to exciting breakthroughs thanks to a fuller embrace of our human-centered approach.

Moving forward, we have big goals. We want to better see the systems that affect the lives of smallholders. We will better measure and evaluate the impact of our work, and we'll strive to build more human-centered designers. But perhaps most importantly, we'll continue to talk to farmers, to see the world through their eyes, and to understand them not only as farmers, but as whole people.

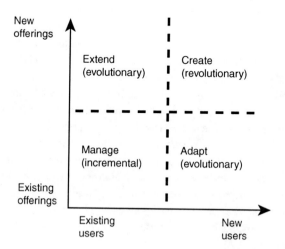

FIGURE 9.4 Human-centered design can bring out incremental, evolutionary, and revolutionary solutions depending on what the context calls for

10

TRUST, COLLABORATION, AND COLLECTIVE LEARNING

The experience in Namibia and Ethiopia

Synergos

SUMMARY

Synergos has worked for almost 30 years supporting initiatives that build collaboration between business, government, civil society, and marginalized communities. This case study examines its experiences in Ethiopia and Namibia, which shed light on how to shift mind-sets and behaviors in large bureaucratic organizations. Through a variety of approaches and feedback mechanisms, Synergos is helping build cultures of trust and learning. Its experience demonstrates that specific feedback tools vary depending on context, so no single approach fits all situations. However, regular engagement at multiple levels within a system appears to be required for cultural change to take hold.

At the core of changing mind-sets is the degree to which the values that support collective learning are cultivated by collaborating institutions and individuals within them. Various techniques to achieve this are explored in the case study. While collective learning can both enhance trust and collaboration and benefit from them, true effective learning in development projects needs to include formal "hard" data collection, collective qualitative learning, and informal personal learning. Personal learning and reflection are essential in building ownership of development initiatives, because they need to be consonant and coherent with collective learning. A culture of learning is therefore fostered when it is nurtured at all levels of an initiative or system, including not only senior leadership and mid-level professionals, but front-line staff and other stakeholders as well.

Introduction

Synergos helps solve the complex problems of poverty and inequality by promoting and supporting collaborations among business, government, civil society, and marginalized communities. Our role is to generate, test, problem-solve, and implement solutions that lead to sustainable change. Collective learning is an important element of our process for two reasons—it not only provides vital information to program design and implementation but also helps build ongoing trust among stakeholders.

Over the course of almost 30 years, Synergos has supported innovative initiatives in countries and regions including Brazil, Canada, Ecuador, Ethiopia, India, Mexico and the US–Mexico border, the Middle East and North Africa, Mozambique, Namibia, South Africa, and Zimbabwe. This global experience and our networks of international civil society leaders have led to knowledge of how to create participatory processes and engage multiple stakeholders in problem-solving seemingly intractable issues around poverty. Synergos is well aware of the challenges inherent in our process and we believe that the kind of change we seek to co-create with others only happens when efforts are made to:

- *provide learning* about "bridging leadership"—the capacity to help people come together across divides and work as partners;
- *build collaborations* that involve and respect the contributions of all stakeholders;
- *focus attention* on systems thinking—identifying root causes, system blockages, the interrelated factors that affect outcomes, and the resources needed for continuous improvement; and
- *use personal reflection* to connect people to their core values—enabling them to be open-minded, open-hearted, trusting, and most open to learning.

We find that this last element of helping people connect to their core values is often a vital early step in taking personal ownership of one's role in an issue. This is often followed by the creation of a collective ownership that engages with others and builds shared vision. Trust is essential and amplified, enabling a rapid exchange of ideas, prototyping strategies, and then work on scaling and sustainability.

Our approach to building partnerships includes the following tools: appreciative inquiry; reflection exercises; creating alignment; collaborative problem-solving; engaging a shared vision; learning to listen and accept feedback; stakeholder analysis and convening; developing roadmaps; and systems thinking (Figure 10.1).

We have learned that many of the problems we seek to address are complex and multi-faceted. In response, Synergos' processes are iterative, with the creation of an ongoing culture of collective learning essential to designing inclusive and systemic approaches. These processes are adapted to suit the culture and environment in which we work.

The two case studies we have drawn from—the African Public Health Leadership Initiative in Namibia and support for the Agricultural Transformation Agency and Ministry of Agriculture in Ethiopia—illustrate our approach to work

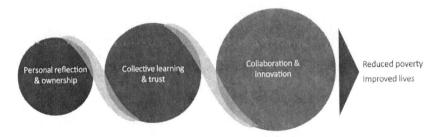

FIGURE 10.1 Synergos approach

with government agencies at national and regional levels. Both initiatives were funded by the Bill & Melinda Gates Foundation, and the learning from Namibia was used in the design for Ethiopia.

Brief background on work in Namibia and Ethiopia

Namibia

In 2008, Synergos launched the African Public Health Leadership Initiative (APHLI), a four-year project to strengthen the leadership and systems of the country's Ministry of Health and Social Services (MoHSS). APHLI primarily focused on alignment and renewal within the public health system and demonstrated that engaging different stakeholder groups and focusing on capacity can unlock potential and untangle complex systems. The initiative arose in part due to interest at the Bill & Melinda Gates Foundation in developing and testing replicable and innovative models to improve the leadership and performance of public health systems in developing countries, particularly in Africa. In response to this interest and interest among members of our staff and global networks, Synergos set about looking for a country to pilot this vision.

In Namibia, then–Prime Minister Nahas Angula responded enthusiastically to the idea, which was introduced to him by local civil society leader Len le Roux, a Synergos Senior Fellow alumnus. It was funded by the Bill & Melinda Gates Foundation. Synergos recruited highly respected local staff for the effort, including Len le Roux and Kasee Ithana (who returned to Namibia from South Africa to join this effort).

Early work included a detailed performance assessment of the Ministry, broad consultations across the health system to identify key needs, and pilot interventions at multiple levels of the system. These efforts purposefully aligned with, and supported objectives from, the MoHSS Strategic Plan 2009–13, including goals to improve stakeholder relationships, reduce malnutrition, and decrease morbidity and mortality rates.

This close alignment with existing government priorities allowed the project to maximize its impact on the government's intended outcomes, with a particular focus on maternal and child health. It was becoming clear that systemic blockages and not resources were the limiting factor in progress. In mid-2011, the MoHSS conducted a second performance assessment that revealed that our intervention had made strides in improving alignment around goals and strategy and shifting mind-sets and attitudes, but that more work still needed to be done around improving execution and the performance management of MoHSS strategies. After 2011, the effort continued with support from the US Agency for International Development and the Global Alliance for Improved Nutrition.

Major accomplishments in these efforts have included:

- increased collaboration and communication within the MoHSS through a Leadership Development Forum for the Ministry's top tier of officials as well as through workshops and events at other levels of the health system;
- a new infrastructure for communication and collaboration for child and maternal health at the regional level through the creation of Regional Delivery Units;
- improved access to health services, including through provision of antenatal care (ANC) clinics in shipping containers in both state- and NGO-managed facilities, and also through decentralization of ANC services from two hospitals to a larger number of clinics;
- increases in public education about, and demand for, maternal health services through radio drama shows;
- improvements in quality of care through in-service nurse training;
- reduced waiting times for ambulances in the city of Windhoek;
- upgraded maternal health information systems, which aligned several health information systems and cleared data entry backlogs; and
- expansion of the collaborative approach to the field of nutrition in 2010 through the Prime Minister creating the Namibian Alliance for Improved Nutrition, an independent trust with Synergos as its secretariat.

Ethiopia

In 2010 the government of Ethiopia created the Ethiopian Agricultural Transformation Agency (ATA) as part of its overall efforts to accelerate Ethiopia's agricultural development, grow the Ethiopian economy, and improve the livelihoods of smallholder farmers. This new government agency was part of the recommendations of a seminal diagnostic report commissioned by the Bill & Melinda Gates Foundation. The ATA was created to address two problems identified as key obstacles to achieving the national growth and transformation targets: low implementation and technical capacity within the Ministry of Agriculture (MoA), and poor coordination and alignment among the range of stakeholders and partners involved in agricultural transformation efforts.

The function of the ATA is to help build sufficient capacity within the MoA and not replicate or supplant it. The ATA promoted real and positive change by assessing the current state of Ethiopia's agricultural sector, working with key stakeholders in the system to identify the barriers to progress and prosperity for the country, and formulating strategies to address systemic bottlenecks. The ATA has done this by designing and supporting innovative, case-specific solutions aimed at increasing crop productivity, maximizing economic efficiencies, and streamlining market routes.

Synergos has been partnering with the ATA since its inception to provide robust and multi-faceted capacity building and organizational development support to both the ATA and MoA, in support of Ethiopia's efforts to increase agricultural productivity and improve the lives of smallholder farmers.

Through workshop engagements and strengthened institutional arrangements, the efforts of Synergos established certain fundamental conditions for the effective implementation of integrated actions in the agricultural system, the results of which will lead to unified ATA and MoA leadership teams with improved collaborative capacity. These include:

- building relationships and trust between institutions and with diverse stakeholders;
- improving alignment across programs within and between the ATA and MoA;
- equipping the ATA and MoA with strengthened competencies in leadership, management, facilitation, collaboration, communication, and stakeholder management; and
- enhancing overall implementation capacity.

The work is now in its third year. A foundation has been set for the ATA and MoA to collaboratively problem-solve as leaders of Ethiopia's agricultural sector and leverage the best from each organization. Synergos has designed engagements with the MoA and ATA as a capacity-building initiative for pursuing goals through improved alignment and collaborative problem-solving. The issue areas impacted thus far include the cooperative system, research and extension, soils, household irrigation, and the creation of a senior leadership team for executive-level coordination and accountability.

Start-up

The way a development initiative begins can often powerfully shape the way an initiative emerges over time and the attitude of participants toward collaboration and collective learning. It is far better to give time and thought on the front end than to try to fix things later. We have often felt significant pressure to "just get on with it" and to move quickly to action. Over time, we have come to appreciate that the eventual action will be more effective if we are sure that fundamental issues have been addressed first—including convening appropriate stakeholders, developing shared learning processes, and helping stakeholders arrive at a shared understanding of the problem to be addressed.

Each of our partnerships originated as a result of political will, in contexts where there is public pressure, citizen demand, and energy for change. In many instances such demands end up on the desk of senior government or civic leaders, who become champions for change and who then invite us in to catalyze action.

Without an invitation, or lacking the stamp of support from legitimate leaders within a society, we simply could not take the time to build the trust, relationships, and shared understanding needed to bring about significant change.

In Namibia, for example, we were invited in by the Prime Minister, who was alarmed by the skyrocketing maternal mortality rate in his country. In Ethiopia, the initiative was likewise invited in by the Prime Minister, who sought to bring about economic growth by transforming the agriculture sector.

Complementary forms of learning

Formal learning processes

Another vital element in our work is bringing together complementary forms of learning. One form, typical in large development projects, is rigorous data collection and analysis (Figure 10.2).

In the Namibia case, our project team included individuals from McKinsey & Co. (several of whom were medical doctors), who conducted a detailed assessment of the health system and its leadership, and also helped produce related reports on maternal health, child mortality, and child nutrition. The resulting reports were issued in 2008 and helped ground the project while also providing openings for the less traditional approaches to trust-building and leadership from Synergos and the Presencing Institute (PI). PI is a global action research community that works to facilitate innovation and change, which we engaged to support our work.

These reports included not only information about health but also qualitative input from participants in the health system itself. The project team made an extraordinary effort to interview users of the health system, regularly speaking with nurses, doctors, and women in ANC clinics, maternity wards, and villages to listen to their concerns and ideas and to reflect their input back into the partnerships' plans. We also strove to communicate these findings back to stakeholders themselves.

In Ethiopia, the Bill & Melinda Gates Foundation commissioned studies on output markets, irrigation, soil health, rural finance, and the seed system. This research informed an integrated study of the agriculture system, outlining problems and providing possible solutions. The report suggested the establishment of an independent unit to support the MoA to accelerate agricultural growth and augment the Ministry's work.

Synergos then conducted 50 interviews with key stakeholders on the federal and regional levels and visited two regions. These stakeholders had engaged in the diagnostic study. Their observations and feedback provided us with the basis to design how we engaged in Ethiopia and to co-create solutions with key stakeholders. Their observations included an overwhelming recognition of need for change and transformation in the agricultural sector. The diagnostic study and integrated report were seen to offer a way forward. At the same time, it was shown that the Bill & Melinda Gates Foundation had a remarkable opportunity to catalyze change in Ethiopia's agriculture sector. There was universal praise for the foundation's consultative approach.

FIGURE 10.2 Collective learning at the service-delivery level was essential in improving the ambulance service in Windhoek

These formal learning processes served several goals. They demonstrated intellectual rigor appropriate in work at the scale proposed in each country, which was important for buy-in. They provided a shared basis for further discussion among stakeholders. And, insofar as interviews, broad consultations, and communication back to stakeholders were used in both initiatives, they served to begin to bring disparate voices into the process and to demonstrate that collecting such voices was essential to success.

Personal and collective learning

But formal studies are rarely enough. In both Namibia and Ethiopia, Synergos also employed processes to collect learning in more personal ways, helping develop personal ownership, self-reflection, and co-creation of solutions.

In Namibia, the key theory that guided the effort was Theory U (or "the U Process"), a social technology to generate insight, manage change, and generate solutions to difficult problems developed by Otto Scharmer of the PI and MIT as well as Peter Senge, Joseph Jaworski, and Betty Sue Flowers. Based on a simultaneous effort to build leadership capacity and stimulate system change, Theory U helps participants in a multi-stakeholder process shift the nature of institutional relationships to enhance collaboration. Activities guided by Theory U focus on cultivating shared experiences and understandings, renewing personal commitment and energy, developing leadership skills, and identifying, testing, and refining innovative solutions to persistent challenges (Figure 10.3).

In Namibia, this process included five phases that guided the journey for change:

- "sensing" that engaged Namibian leaders and partners in assessing the Namibian health system;
- developing curriculum for staff from Synergos, PI, and McKinsey to use in informing change processes;
- helping build leadership skills and fostering innovation;
- planning and implementing pilot innovation projects; and
- working towards replication and sustainability.

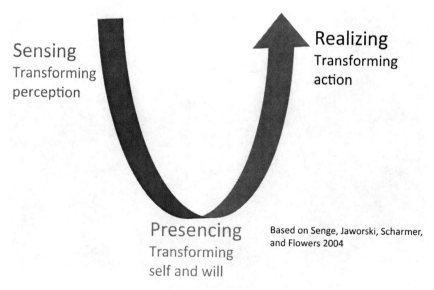

Sensing
Transforming
perception

Realizing
Transforming
action

Presencing
Transforming
self and will

Based on Senge, Jaworski, Scharmer,
and Flowers 2004

FIGURE 10.3 Theory U

In practice, the sensing activities included brief immersion in the health system, including efforts to learn about the system from the perspectives of others. Examples included culture surveys and "in your shoes" activities to re-connect MoHSS officials with the system from the eyes of a user by their riding in an ambulance or waiting in a clinic. These experiences proved vital in developing personal ownership and openness to ongoing collective learning.

In Ethiopia, Theory U also helped guide our work, and we also engaged the PI as a resource. One of the key early personal and collective learning activities was the ATA learning journey held in the Rift Valley area, where subsistence agriculture is widely practiced and agriculture is the main source of income. The purpose of the journey was to expose 49 ATA staff, many of whom were foreign nationals or from the Ethiopian diaspora, to the lives of smallholder farmers in order to increase understanding of the poverty issues these farmers face (Figure 10.4). ATA staff were assigned to stay with the families for 48 hours. These families were introduced to Synergos through a community-based organization. Synergos spent several days meeting with the families, explaining the project objectives, and ensuring that we were extended an invitation to stay.

Synergos used this phase of assembly as an opportunity to engage farmers in the initiative by telling them directly about the diagnostic study and receiving their input and feedback. The dialogues were fruitful as the farmers were both inviting and healthily skeptical about the imposition of one more big idea.

We worked with the ATA staff, explaining the value of learning through immersion, encouraging them to sense, observe, and be present throughout their host family stays.

FIGURE 10.4 The first Ethiopian ATA learning journey exposed 49 staff members to the lives of smallholder farmers

At the end of the stay, the staff shared their observations in a reflection session in the following three areas:

- They experienced the difference in defining poverty through an organic process based on their first-hand experience versus merely accepting the academic definition of poverty.
- They shared the "moments of the truth" they had in their experience with the farmers.
- They shared experiences that inspired and reconnected them to their commitment to the mission of the ATA and to the smallholder farmers.

The ATA staff acknowledged that the learning journey gave them the opportunity to have a direct experience with smallholder farmers and their families as most had never seen a farmer or been inside a farmer's house before. They attested that the learning journey experience helped them to understand better why the ATA was established and why its work is so important. They recognized that farmers are knowledgeable about their work and their needs. Each ATA staff member greatly appreciated the hospitality and kindness they received and were touched by the generosity of spirit of the farmers.

A significant result of this learning journey is that the ATA has since incorporated the concept of a learning journey into its organizational culture, calling them "home stays." These home stays are conducted in the areas where they work with the aim of inspiring and eliciting the experiential knowledge that comes from this process. This learning activity is now embedded in the ATA's culture and processes.

Strengthening collaboration

Initial collective learning experiences set the stage for deeper collaboration, but such collaboration could not happen on its own. Synergos uses specific social technologies to deepen trust and sustain a culture of learning and feedback. In many cases, this work helps project participants be more open-hearted with their self-knowledge—leading them to become better leaders, better at supporting collaboration, and more open to learning.

In Namibia, an example of this came early in the project. The then-Permanent Secretary (PS) of the MoHSS, Kahijoro Kahuure, began to meet and engage with members of the project team, beginning a mentoring relationship. During this period, the PS was very keen on the idea of leadership and transformation training for his senior team, which comprised 24 of the top staff of the MoHSS. This did not seem particularly different or innovative at the time, but the project team responded to the PS's motivation. An initiative called the Leadership Development Forum (LDF) was conceived, focusing on a leadership and management initiative around the MoHSS leadership team (Figure 10.5). Not a part of the original project design, the LDF started as an exercise to build and align the top leadership

FIGURE 10.5 Learning activities at the Leadership Development Forum

team. The LDF team is composed of 24 staff members from the top tiers of the MoHSS: the PS, the Deputy PS, three undersecretaries, six national directors, and 13 regional directors.

The first LDF meeting was an important event in the story of the APHLI. The design of the gathering was carefully crafted to bring the group together for the first time and define the purpose of the LDF. It was also important to engage the senior cohort responsible for the Namibian public health system in the results of the health assessment and the MoHSS review. During the meeting the LDF team was given the opportunity to experience the landscape of their own health system through a series of explanatory posters and materials put together by Synergos. The results of the assessment and review were shared using strong visual material. This, coupled with deep and innovative team building, had a profound effect on all those involved.

The LDF went on to be a quarterly, collaborative, retreat-style event that was held regularly during the project period.

At the highest level, the result changed leadership and communications style within the MoHSS, enabling both better communication between different parts of the Ministry, and also within each part. Several members also noted that through the LDF the fear of hierarchy was broken down and trust between top team members was established. LDF members further noted that the work with Synergos had:

- brought people together—created real connectivity;
- led to an attitude change and culture shift—a new way of working;
- allowed for self-evaluation, exploration, criticism, and the acceptance of advice;
- encouraged members to be open to external advice and advice from colleagues; and
- encouraged members to question the health system and their own role within it.

As then-Deputy PS Dr. Norbert Forster stated:

> We've already shown a remarkable difference in the working atmosphere, improving the environment, the frequency of communication, the openness of communication, and the preparedness of our management staff. We are thinking about solutions and we are designing solutions.

It is worth noting that not only was the LDF able to help the health system be more responsive, its creation was in response to an emerging demand from project participants to Synergos, rather than a pre-planned activity.

Ethiopia

The creation of the ATA as a government agency to support the MoA in catalyzing action and transforming the sector was an unusual step for Ethiopia. The standard practice is typically to form a temporary team or task force in order to accomplish certain objectives. In the build-up to the establishment of the ATA, there were many consultations with officials and staff from the Ministry who offered their input and opinions related to its unique role and contribution.

However, when it came to implementation of the areas of work identified by the ATA and MoA, there was confusion and misunderstanding around roles, responsibilities, and mandates of the various departments within the MoA. Eventually, these misunderstandings created tension and conflict between different departments of the Ministry and with the ATA. It became apparent to MoA and ATA leadership that they needed to address these issues, build trust, and create alignment in order to achieve the greater common purpose of transforming the Ethiopian agriculture sector. Synergos was tasked with supporting both institutions and their staff to go through the training on leadership skills and to help create human and institutional synergy between the ATA and the various departments within the MoA. To this end, efforts were made by all stakeholders to achieve personal and institutional change and, ultimately, to contribute to the objectives of improving the lives and livelihoods of the small-scale farmer.

Creating a foundation for collaborative learning to bridge the divides of misunderstanding and mistrust required a series of strategic workshops that opened space for shared learning, and identification of problems, and subsequent co-creation of solutions (Figure 10.6). This started at the highest levels with the senior leadership

FIGURE 10.6 Aspirations from a Ministry of Agriculture workshop

in the ATA and MoA, moving to directors in the MoA, and then focusing on staff working on specific issue areas, including soils, research and extension, and household irrigation, as well as from the Federal Cooperative Agency.

In all these workshops it was essential to bring in the voices of the participants, and this occurred through interviews with the Minister and State Ministers and with other stakeholders in the system. The workshops built off the interviews and were designed in a way that recognized this was a new experience for many of the participants and that the participants were going to learn to problem-solve in a different way: using their heads, hearts, and hands. The genesis of the ATA was examined and the objectives were laid out by the State Minister who attended and participated. Having the engagement of high-level leadership (including the Minister and State Minister) demonstrated the importance of the program and ensured participation. It also provided us with leeway to conduct workshops at multiple levels in the system.

The design of a workshop was usually for three consecutive days, with participants guided in sharing their personal journeys that connect them to the MoA's mission (Figure 10.7). They were provided with tools to reflect on what was block-ing them from being innovative and to identify leverage points to initiate change. When the participants were guided to reflect on the past, envision the future, and give their insight about the MoA and the Ethiopian agricultural sector as a whole, some of the following themes arose:

- Subsistence farming is ending and commercial farming is emerging.
- Traditional agricultural technologies are ending and mechanized agriculture is emerging.
- Full dependence on rain-fed agriculture is ending and irrigation-based farming is emerging.
- Top-down thinking and planning are ending while a bottom-up and partici-patory approach is emerging.
- Exclusion of the private sector is ending and private sector participation is emerging.
- Marginalization of women and youth is ending while empowerment of women and youth is emerging.
- Reluctance to adopt new technologies is ending and ICT-based technologies and innovation are emerging.
- Undermining natural resource management (NRM) is ending and NRM-focused projects are emerging.
- Needs-based production is ending and demand-driven production is emerging.

FIGURE 10.7 Toy blocks and craft materials used in an exercise to create shared understanding of the agricultural system

After this examination of the system, participants were encouraged to examine what parts of their old belief system/way of being needed to subside and what new way of being needed to emerge. Exercises related to listening and conversing, advocacy and inquiry, and "dialogue walks" with colleagues helped participants to see themselves from various angles, using toy blocks and craft materials to build a representation of the current situation and develop future possibilities. Many of the participants acknowledged that they had never had the time and opportunity to look deeper into themselves and question why they were doing the work they do and if they are happy about their work. Some of the personal issues raised and discussed included apathy; fear of losing one's job; skepticism about change and new ideas; distancing oneself from taking initiative; and leadership's inability to hold space for others to grow.

Regarding collaboration and coordination between the ATA and MoA, the directors jointly agreed that:

- there is a lack of communication between the ATA and different departments in the MoA;
- the value added by the ATA was not clear to many MoA directors and staff;
- there is no clarity of roles and demarcation between the two institutions;
- MoA directors think that the ATA has moved to implementation of projects in different parts of the country instead of focusing on new research, looking for new technologies, and building the capacity of the MoA;
- ATA directors believe that MoA directors and staff are not meeting deadlines for joint deliverables;
- there are significant differences in organizational culture;
- ATA directors think that the MoA staff have less understanding about the pressing tasks and new responsibilities that are coming to the ATA from the Transformation Council.

Finally, after candid and difficult conversations about the above issues—including fears, disbelief in new possibilities, and judging one another without making an effort to close the gap—the directors agreed to work closely to suspend these misunderstandings. Accordingly, they created a leadership team from the two institutions to work with Synergos to promote and extend the same kind of joint workshop and learning to all departments in the Ministry and across all major departments in the ATA, which included Extension, Input–Output, Soil, Irrigation, Research, and the Federal Cooperative Agency. Synergos has also been invited to conduct similar workshops in the four largest regions with the respective bureaus of agriculture.

Collective learning at all levels

Processes used to build a culture of learning are essential not only at the initiative-wide level, but for particular sub-projects within them. We thus used similar approaches in particular projects within the Namibia and Ethiopia initiatives.

In Namibia, discussions within the LDF and with others in the health system led the LDF members (including the PS) and Synergos to identify maternal health as an area of the health system in need of attention. Maternal health services and, specifically, the delivery of services, needed strengthening. Maternal health was high on the government's agenda as it is one of the Millennium Development Goals. Data showed that Namibia was moving away from its goal of reducing maternal mortality by 75 percent by 2015.

Five workshops were held with a group consisting of 17 members (15 women, two men), 11 from government and six from non-governmental organizations. The group from government institutions included seven registered nurses, two lecturers, an education officer, and one deputy director.

This Maternal Health Initiative (MHI) aimed to cover four critical issues within the public health system's maternal health practice:

* demand;
* supply;
* quality; and
* enablers of effective service delivery.

Initially, the maternal health group divided themselves into three work streams: community mobilization, operations, and skills and capabilities. These groups would design and implement prototypes addressing the four key issues. Each group comprised participants with appropriate skills, positions, and experience to contribute to the particular work stream.

Each work stream was supported by APHLI consortium members who mentored and trained the group and its individual members. All MHI participants were trained in both Theory U and bridging leadership, by PI and Synergos staff respectively.

The MHI was located within the Khomas Region, a geographic area including Windhoek, the capital city. The intent was for the Khomas Region to serve as a prototype where innovative ideas would be implemented, tested, and—if successful—piloted and refined in more regions. The process followed at this point of the APHLI has been the basis for the roll-out of the project to seven additional regions with an aim to reach ten regions by late 2014.

The Khomas MHI developed 11 initiatives around the four areas of demand, access, quality, and enablers of maternal health care. Examples of these initiatives included:

* radio drama series on maternal health in "soap opera" format to reinforce the maternal health messages of radio shows (demand);
* shipping container ANC clinics—providing ANC clinic space and services by procuring and equipping a renovated shipping container at one state clinic and one NGO-managed health center (access);

- ANC decentralization from two hospitals to 13 clinics, with services offered at additional public health-care facilities in the Khomas Region (access);
- in-service nurse training, which provided accredited maternal health training sessions for continuing professional development of nurses and doctors (quality); and
- upgrading maternal health information systems, which aligned several health information systems and cleared data entry backlogs (enabler).

These initiatives were developed in response to needs identified by front-line and mid-level actors in the health system. Through the leadership development and collaborative processes, actors in the health system became better able to elicit information about the underlying issues and build working partnerships. As one mid-level staffperson in the MHI put it:

> The communication skills have taught me not to be above my subordinates, [but] rather to sit down with them. Even when I am very stressed now, I have learnt to control myself because of those communication skills ... So, we have got more of a teamwork atmosphere going, because we bring everything to the table and discuss it together. So, there is that freedom of participation, and we can speak with each other peacefully.

A front-line health worker pointed to an increased ability to simply learn from expecting mothers themselves:

> Before we were very short-tempered. Even me, I really had to hold my tongue ... and you always ask the clients to please limit their stories because if someone comes with a long story you just don't have time. Now we are able to say, "Mama, talk" ... We also have time to give them much more information about why they have to go to the doctor and all these things.

Helping health workers and MoHSS staff increase their personal capacity to welcome and elicit feedback from others in the health system, including clients, is a key part of APHLI success.

It is also worth noting the vital role of improved information in making the health system more responsive to feedback. Initiatives on demand and access increased the numbers of expecting mothers seeking antenatal services, requiring the health system to respond to their needs earlier and more effectively. Improvements in information systems are also a vital component in enabling front-line health workers and their managers to develop more effective approaches to their day-to-day work.

This phase of the project produced significant results. The clinical results of the innovations were all positive and other key results included:

- radio programming reaching an estimated 500,000 listeners;
- ANC services decentralized from the two main hospitals in Windhoek to 13 clinics in the Khomas Region, with an increased in demand for services, including in the vital first trimester of pregnancy; and
- change measures at one of the main hospital's ANC clinic that resulted in reduced waiting times and better conditions for patients.

It is also worth noting that some of these innovations brought about new pressures on the health system. For example, while decentralization of ANC to clinics significantly reduced the workload of the two major hospitals, staff at clinics reported that providing new services had significantly increased the workload on staff. This is an example of the sort of generative complexity that responsive development efforts must be prepared to address. Ongoing learning is essential to such responses.

In Ethiopia, the initiative is just now moving down to regional and local levels, so the process of collective learning, trust-building, and collaboration is just beginning at those levels. An early example at the regional level is an effort to improve collaboration between the MoA and the Bureau of Agriculture of Oromia Region. Building upon a 2014 workshop using Theory U, a joint vision for alignment and collaboration is being created. This workshop included extensive "in your shoes" exercises—playing the role not only of staff of other government entities but also of farmers—to enable participants to individually and collectively gain a better understanding of the challenges they face. What is noteworthy is the degree to which ongoing information sharing is considered vital to collaboration. As one participant put it, "Challenges exists because we have information gaps. As we innovate there are secondary generation problems that emanate."

Conclusion

What Synergos has learned from Namibia and Ethiopia is that it always takes more time to build the necessary trust for collaboration and collective learning which will lead to shared solutions in complex health or agricultural systems. The processes and tools we use recognize that for many of the problem holders it is often the first time they are being asked to observe the system they are seeking to change, step into the shoes of others, and reflect individually and collectively on what they have learned—and then experiment with solutions they own. We help build trust, collaboration, and collective learning that complement each other.

Synergos takes a long view in transforming complex systems and in providing the necessary support in unpacking the root causes to the problems in the system and creating iterative feedback loops at all levels of engagement, recognizing bridging leaders who hold the intention that collaborative problem-solving will impact the marginalized communities we seek to support—mothers and their families and smallholder farmers (see Box 10.1).

BOX 10.1 SYNERGOS AT A GLANCE

- *Overall organization description*: Synergos is a global non-profit organiza-
  tion that helps solve the complex problems of poverty and inequality by
  promoting and supporting collaborations among business, government,
  civil society, and marginalized communities.
- *Time frame/founding date*: 1986 (initiatives covered in chapter run from
  2008–present (2014)).
- *Latest annual budget*: $14.7 million.
- *Countries of operation*: Brazil, Canada, China, Egypt, Ethiopia, Jordan,
  Lebanon, Mexico, Morocco, Mozambique, Namibia, Nigeria, Palestinian
  Territories, South Africa, and the United States (plus work with network
  members from an additional 32 countries).
- *Current number of staff*: 49.

Bibliography

Davis, A. (2011). "The African Public Health and Leadership Initiative: A Story from
    Namibia." Discussion Paper. New York: Synergos.
Ethiopian Agricultural Transformation Agency. (2013). *2012 Annual Report: Transforming
    Agriculture in Ethiopia*. Addis Ababa: EATA.
ICF Macro. (2011). "African Public Health Leadership and Systems Innovation Initiative:
    Final Evaluation Report." Calverton, MD: ICF Macro.
Scharmer, C. O. & Senge, P. M. (2009). *Theory U: Leading from the Future as it Emerges: The
    Social Technology of Presencing*. San Francisco, CA: Berrett-Koehler.
Senge, P. M., Jaworski, J., Scharmer, C. O., & Flowers, B. S. (2004) *Presence: Human
    Purpose and the Field of the Future*. Cambridge, MA: Society for Organizational Learning.
World Health Organization. (2000). *The World Health Report 2000: Health Systems: Improving
    Performance*. Geneva: WHO.

CHAPTER SUMMARY

Type and frequency of key feedback tools

Our focus is on building a culture of trust and learning; specific feedback tools
will vary depending on context. Examples of tools we use to develop and sustain this culture include:

- regular (approximately quarterly) senior leadership meetings to focus on
  transformation;
- cross-sector, cross-institution, cross-level workshops;
- personal mastery/self-awareness tools including journaling, dialogue
  exercise, time in nature, meditative practice;

- learning journeys and "in their shoes" exercises;
- building an organizational culture that fosters collective learning: the backbone organization itself must have values that support collective learning;
- personal reflection exercises to develop sense of ownership; and
- Theory U and other social methodologies that frame and support building alignment and collective action.

Five key lessons learned (centered on the collective learning themes identified at the workshop)

- Collective learning can both enhance trust and collaboration and benefit from them.
- Effective learning in development projects should include both formal "hard" data collection, collective qualitative learning, and informal personal learning.
- Personal learning and reflection are essential in building ownership of development initiatives.
- Personal learning and reflection are a complement to collective learning.
- A culture of learning should be created at all levels of an initiative or system, including not only senior leadership and mid-level professionals, but front-line staff and other stakeholders.

11

PROMOTING INCLUSIVE DEVELOPMENT THROUGH A PROCESS OF LEARNING AND MUTUAL ACCOUNTABILITY

Preliminary insights gained from the experience of FOSCA[1]

Fadel Ndiame, Emma Kambewa, Mary Njoroge, Pauline Kamau and Samuel Sey[2]

SUMMARY

Farmer Organization Support Center for Africa (FOSCA) is a program within the Alliance for a Green Revolution in Africa (AGRA) that works to build the capacity of farmer organizations to more effectively serve their members. This case study examines concepts of accountability and the inherent tensions in the competition for resources that typically characterize many development initiatives and organizations. This chapter illustrates the challenges of setting up both vertical and horizontal accountability systems in the context of AGRA-supported projects. From its experience with value chains in Kenya and in Mozambique, FOSCA is learning about the transformation of smallholder agriculture by facilitating the alignment of the goals and strategies of different stakeholders. Some specific challenges associated with promoting horizontal accountability systems among development partners include linking the actions and interventions of different institutions across different time horizons, and the need to build on prior investments made in a specific locale to learn from their success and failures.

Overcoming the initial fear and resistance of the different actors to cooperate was an important part of its learning, as was the need to facilitate the development of a new conceptual framework to replace outmoded mental models. By transparently defining acceptable roles and responsibilities for each constituent, FOSCA is learning about successfully facilitating the building of mutual accountability systems that enable different protagonists to access resources and account for the results and achievements for which they took responsibility. Iterative processes that entail joint planning, reviews, and learning activities are helping collaborating institutions to move away from the traditional competition for resources, in favor of cooperative strategies that are equally results-oriented, and striving to see these embedded at the level of organizational culture.

The sense of empowerment among farmers—what FOSCA calls "voice"—remains critical. As smallholder farmers increasingly gain the sense that they are able to take hold of their destiny, act in their own interests, and properly manage their own affairs, then greater levels of cooperation are achieved, and results delivered.

Introduction

This chapter discusses key challenges and opportunities associated with building an inclusive value chain and facilitating the processes of learning and mutual accountability among different protagonists. It builds on the experience acquired by the Alliance for a Green Revolution in Africa (AGRA) during the implementation of programs aimed at producing a blueprint for the systemic and sustainable transformation of smallholder agriculture in sub-Saharan Africa (SSA). It also analyzes the conditions under which effective learning and accountability systems would contribute to the successful delivery of agricultural development programs in the region.

The chapter starts with a brief analysis of key dimensions of the accountability challenges inherent in most planned development interventions aimed at transforming the smallholder agricultural systems in SSA. That analysis is followed by a review of three case studies focused on how accountability challenges materialize in the context of the work of AGRA, and the types of approaches used to promote a more inclusive development scenario. The final part of the chapter presents lessons learned and recommendations that highlight programmatic and institutional requirements for building and promoting robust learning and mutual accountability systems—prerequisites for inclusive development, whether in SSA or elsewhere.

Background

The accountability challenge

Rural development interventions are channeled through an array of intermediaries that are typically selected on the basis of their capability to reliably deliver services and accurately account for the use of resources. Accountability can be defined in many ways, depending on context. In this chapter, accountability is defined as the *obligation of an individual or organization to account for its activities, accept responsibility for them, and to disclose the results in a transparent manner.*[3] It also includes responsibility for financial and other types of entrusted resources.

The focus of this chapter is on accepting responsibility for the activities meant to bring about development, especially for the poor. For instance, most donor agencies rely on locally based institutions to carry out interventions on their behalf. Such locally based institutions can include international non-governmental organizations (NGOs) that have local offices or representatives, public institutions, locally registered private business entities, and so on. In practice, these categories of actors can differ significantly in terms of geographic locations, institutional capacities, and the level of power, authority, and control over resources implied by these differences. By bringing numerous project implementers into the equation, competition for donor resources often overshadows collaboration, potential synergies, and the alignment of expertise within the development space, as well as opportunities to leverage additional resources.

In such situations, which are not unusual in the development arena, accountability questions often arise, especially as they relate to accountability to *whom*, *why*, and *how*, and they are often answered in ways that reflect the competition for resources and a sense of dependency on the part of beneficiaries.

Why do local institutions compete for resources?

Most development partners and donors are not based in developing countries, and therefore need local institutions capable of providing timely project results and transparent accounting for resources. Unfortunately, this need for accountability does not always extend to accountability for project impact. Well-written reports enhance the credibility of local organizations and encourage donors to entrust additional resources to them. This narrow view of accountability is built around outputs and resource management, and often undermines the accountability of the project-implementing institution to intended project beneficiaries, such as rural communities—all too often to the extent of denying intended beneficiaries a voice in identifying and prioritizing their needs.

Clearly, local organizations should be accountable to donors on a number of issues, including whether financial resources provided were used according to contractual obligations. They should also be accountable to the beneficiaries, especially rural communities, as to the positive as well as negative impacts of the interventions made with the resources provided. Unfortunately, this latter dimension is rarely enforced because of the power imbalance between local organizations and rural communities who tend to lack a common voice and the resources needed to hold local organizations to account. Today, development interventions tend to be top-down, with beneficiaries on the receiving end usually having no *droit du regard* or questioning authority.

Considering that no single organization can solve all development problems facing the poor, collaboration and an integration of one another's expertise and resources are needed. Collaboration and integration call for horizontal accountability among local organizations, for the use of resources as well as the contribution and attribution of development achievements. Horizontal accountability remains elusive, due at least in part to the fact that local organizations compete for donor resources. This contributes to the fact that accountability between donors and the rural communities they want to help is the least developed of all.

For development and grant-making organizations such as AGRA, the overall performance metrics for evaluating local organizations tend to emphasize their ability to demonstrate financial prudence and quick results. This logic creates an advantage for more formal and established institutions and NGOs. However, whether these organizations are always best suited to deliver needed services and produce usable results for marginalized beneficiaries tends to be a secondary selection criterion.

This situation is typical of a pattern of relationships and accountability systems that does not facilitate a culture of collaboration. The incentive for each layer of players is therefore to emphasize and celebrate its unique role in the support chain, and therefore be allocated more resources as a critical agent of change. An appropriate label for such a pattern of relationships is illustrated in Figure 11.1—"my organization, my results, my entitlement to resources."

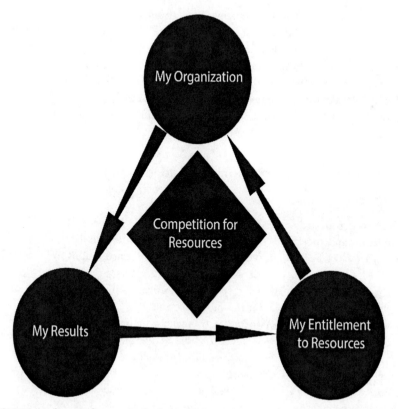

FIGURE 11.1 A typical pattern of relationships among local development organizations

In other words, conventional forms of development interventions create account-ability challenges because of their propensity to create power imbalances, competition among local development partners, and a mind-set of dependency and marginality among beneficiaries.

Sense of dependency

The charitable purpose of most development interventions is to bring about short- and long-term benefits, especially to the poor. In return, the beneficiaries are expected to become self-sufficient in the long run. In reality, however, ben-eficiaries often become more dependent. On the one hand, some organizations are so focused on their own survival that the driving strategy is to maintain the status quo, and continue to use the plight of the poor to ensure a never-ending stream of funding from donors. On the other hand, some beneficiaries become so used to continuing financial support that they lose the motivation to become self-sufficient. Instead they highlight their problems and challenges as a strategy to qualify for even more development assistance. While this assessment may seem rather harsh, it is true that most projects have no realistic exit plan and therefore propagate dependency.

In other words, while the principle of accountability is noble and good, its implementation can be tricky in situations where there is a large power imbal-ance between those providing support and those receiving it. True accountability should therefore be bi-dimensional, with project implementing agencies being accountable both to their donors and to the communities they claim to serve. The difficulty of systematically embracing this bi-dimensional approach, illustrated in Figure 11.2, is acknowledged, but there are successful case studies from the experi-ences of organizations such as AGRA (see below).

AGRA'S approach to accountability and learning

Background

AGRA was founded in 2006 through a partnership between the Rockefeller Foundation and the Bill & Melinda Gates Foundation to fulfill the vision of an Africa that can feed itself, as well as make significant contributions to feeding the world. AGRA's vision of success is premised on a broad-based alliance of key stakeholders, including national governments, African farmers, private sector enti-ties, NGOs, civil society, and many others.

AGRA operationalizes its mandate by making grants and providing technical assistance to a range of organizations that are active in different segments of the agricultural value chain: training; research; production; post-harvest processing; commercialization; and consumption. Thus AGRA's vision of a uniquely African Green Revolution is based on investments at strategic points along the value chain that will sustainably unlock resources and create wealth for those working along the value chain, including smallholder farmers (SHFs).

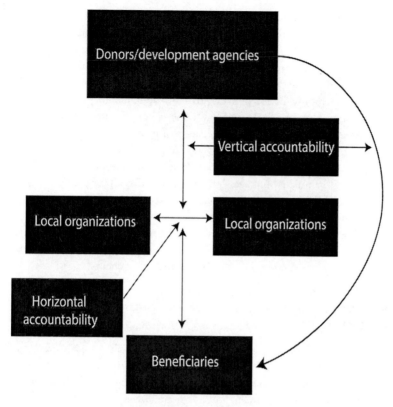

FIGURE 11.2 Bi-dimensional (vertical and horizontal) accountability

AGRA has identified indicators for measuring the success of its collaborative efforts with partners in the short- to medium-term. These include: the reduction of food insecurity by 50 percent in at least twenty African countries; a doubling of the incomes of twenty million SHFs; and the development of policy and institutional frameworks favorable to sustained improvements in agricultural productivity in at least fifteen African countries by 2020.[4]

In 2012, AGRA reviewed its strategy and emphasized the need to build partnerships with national governments, donor organizations, and large-scale private sector entities in order to scale out innovative solutions to African agriculture challenges. AGRA's core activities were expanded to include convening and knowledge management as key anchors of a scaling-out strategy.

As part of its agenda to improve the incomes and the livelihood opportunities of African smallholders—especially of women and youth—in 2010 AGRA set up the Farmer Organization Support Center in Africa (FOSCA). The strategic objective of FOSCA is to enhance access to quality, demand-driven, and income-enhancing services by SHFs through strong farmer organizations (FOs). Effective and well-structured FOs provide the support system through which SHFs access vital services that are critical for increasing incomes and improving livelihoods.

FOSCA's theory of change envisages strong FOs as enablers for farmer aggregation and collective access to input and output markets, finance, information, and new technologies and skills.

To date, FOSCA has worked on empowering SHFs so that they can seize opportunities associated with the development of more lucrative value chains. It has also strategically invested in approaches designed to enhance collaborative relationships between SHFs and key value chain players, including small and medium-sized enterprises (SMEs), aggregators of produce, input dealers, and agricultural mechanization and post-harvest service providers.

Furthermore, and through joint investment undertakings with other AGRA programs, it has stimulated linkages between extension support services and FOs, and the latter have been enabled to facilitate community extension delivery systems through their aggregated platforms and networks. Finally, tailored capacity strengthening of FOs informed by profiling exercises has resulted in increased engagement of FOs with financial institutions, giving them greater access to financial support for selected commodity activities and value chains.

Some strategic challenges and opportunities associated with the work of FOSCA

The major challenge associated with the objective of facilitating a more open and inclusive development scenario is how to improve the currently dominant model of planned development projects, with its attendant logic of accountability and engendered mind-set of dependency highlighted above.

Figure 11.3 outlines the key principles that underpin the search for an alternative narrative of inclusive development interventions.

In principle, and building on the experience of AGRA and others, promoting effective collaboration entails a different culture of cooperation, based on the logic of "obligation of results." AGRA's approach to the problems of competition for resource and creating dependency revolves around two major thrusts: first, program integration for the delivery of demand-driven and income-enhancing solutions to SHFs and other value chain operators; and, second, amplifying the voice of farmers and their capacity to meaningfully participate in the co-creation of wealth.

This approach is illustrated below by two case studies: (i) the development of a banana value chain in Kenya; and (ii) the integrated development of the Beira Corridor of Mozambique.

Case studies

Building an inclusive banana value chain in Kenya

Background: the Banana Growers Association of Kenya (BGAK)

The formation of the Banana Growers Association of Kenya (BGAK) was one of the deliverables from TechnoServe International, which received funding from

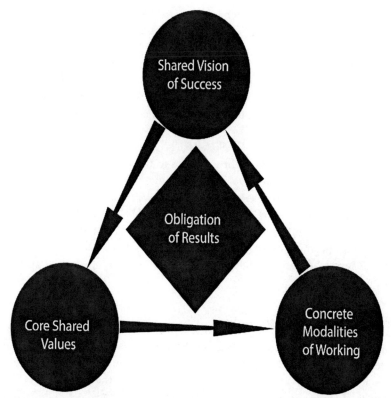

FIGURE 11.3 Underlying principles of an inclusive development model

AGRA in 2008. BGAK is the national banana farmers' association that was registered in 2009 under the Societies Acts Laws of Kenya CAP108. It has countrywide scope, focusing on all banana-growing areas in Kenya. It has contact offices in eight regions, democratically elected committees, and a management board of nine members. The Kenya National Federation of Agricultural Producers (KENFAP) officially launched BGAK in December 2010 as one of its commodity associations, the purpose of which was to bring together the main players of the banana industry. KENFAP provided overall technical support in developing a BGAK strategic plan and also committed to supporting the plan's implementation.

However, due to unavailability of funds, KENFAP was not able to provide the support required to ensure that BGAK became an authoritative autonomous body capable of achieving its mandate. For this reason, in 2012 KENFAP approached AGRA for a grant of US$299,920 for two years to strengthen BGAK. This was approved in June of the same year and the project will close this year. The project is being implemented in four counties in Kenya—Embu, Kirinyaga, Meru, and Muranga. FOSCA/KENFAP will use the results of this phase to help extend BGAK to other counties in subsequent projects; an appropriate resource mobilization strategy is being readied to attract additional investors in the future.

Prior to AGRA's support to TechnoServe in 2008, there were previous investments that laid the foundation for establishing BGAK:

- In 2003, Africa Harvest (with support from the Rockefeller Foundation) was able to build a comprehensive, functional value chain in support of banana production in Kandara, Maragua, and Meru. By 2006, 2,500 farmers were trained and organized into fifty Producer Business Groups that aggregated the bananas for sale and transport.
- In 2006, with support from Rockefeller, TechnoServe was funded to deepen the initial phase by working through FOs to build awareness, provide agronomic training, and improve access to inputs. Of importance during this phase of funding was that market failures were addressed directly through the formation of Market Service Centers to link farmers directly to urban wholesalers and institutional buyers. This removed up to three layers of opportunistic middlemen between the farmers and wholesalers, increasing the incomes of many farmers and enabling them to properly invest in their land and in their crops.

Accountability issues of the project

This is a typical donor-funded project, which has five levels of accountability and at each level there is dual accountability (see Figure 11.4). As indicated in the figure, accountability flows in two directions: from the right to the left, and vice versa. Accountability from the right to the left is largely accommodated; flows from the left to the right are not necessarily efficient and the parties on the left do not have a real motivation to be accountable to those on the right. After all, they are the "donors". Even when an entity on the left is not providing finances, they may be providing technical assistance or serving as a link to resources in one way or another, which puts them in an influential position and may hinder their sense of accountability.

For the group on the right, their subsequent support, whether it is financial or through technical assistance, is largely dependent on being accountable to the group on the left, which to a large extent means complying with what was agreed upon through a contract, a grant, or such other support that donors would typically provide. The secret to unlocking the real value of the entities on the right lies in empowering them to hold those on the left truly accountable, which can happen if they own the process and buy into it to the extent that they would still run with the project even if the group on the left did not provide financial support. The various levels of accountability are described below.

AGRA to BMGF

The approval for use of any funds is supported by a proposal, accompanied by an activity-based budget and a Key Performance Indicator Table that helps the AGRA Project Manager set targets with the beneficiary, in this case KENFAP.

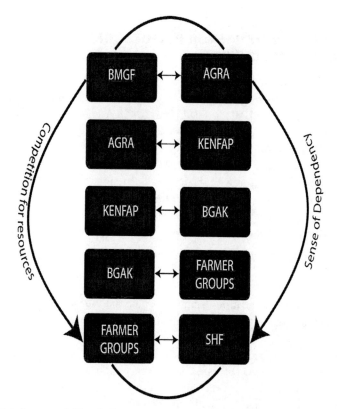

FIGURE 11.4 Accountability challenges in development intervention

Reports to BMGF are based on deliverables reported by KENFAP and verified by the Project Manager. Variances are tracked and adjusted during the project implementation period. To further enhance this project, the AGRA Monitoring and Evaluation (M&E) Team verifies the data received through the use of an Indicator Performance Tracking Table (IPTT) (see Box 11.1), a tool that assesses quarterly targets versus achievements.

BMGF's accountability in this context would be measured by subsequent investment in FOSCA to continue this kind of institutional development, while allowing for variances during project implementation.

KENFAP to AGRA

IPTTs from KENFAP are submitted to AGRA on a quarterly basis, and financial and narrative reports on a bi-annual basis. Disbursement of subsequent funds depends on the reports being consistent with activities on the ground and incorporation of any adjustments made. In addition, the Internal Audit Unit of AGRA conducts random audits of projects that have been in operation for about two

---

BOX 11.1 THE INDICATOR PERFORMANCE TRACKING TABLE (IPTT)

The IPTT tool was developed by the AGRA M&E Unit to assist AGRA management, programs, and grantees track their achievements against stipulated indicators. The IPTT is filled by the AGRA grantees and enables the programs to aggregate achievements across all their projects, which in turn informs the AGRA Strategic Dashboard updates.

The process of developing the IPTT starts with the project roll-out. Grantees are familiarized with the tool, which is also mentioned in the grant agreement. The project indicators in the Key Performance Indicator (KPI) Table are captured on the IPTT and annual and project targets. This then enables the project to capture data every quarter as per the project indicators.

---

years, and the recommendations from such audits are used to strengthen the institution while helping AGRA in deciding on subsequent investments.

The best illustration of AGRA's accountability to KENFAP is the banana conference that was held on October 23, 2013. At the conference, farmers were allowed to articulate their challenges and successes through a panel discussion. As a result, AGRA was able to hear firsthand from farmers the extent to which this project has facilitated their banana farming business.

KENFAP to BGAK

At the beginning of the project, there was a lot of awareness-building about the project—AGRA's expectations, KENFAP's expectations, and how BGAK's role is crucial to ensuring the success of the project. This has enabled BGAK to be open to AGRA when these expectations are not met. For example, in 2012, BGAK rejected the planning of a Board of Directors meeting for BGAK because KENFAP had not consulted BGAK on the dates of the meeting. Such actions may seem inconsequential, but the fact that BGAK can say no to its "mother" organization is because they have matured to the level where they feel such important decisions as a Board meeting should be self-driven and not imposed. This simple action speaks volumes about empowering farmers.

BGAK to individual farmers

Each sub-group under BGAK has its set of rules with which all members must comply. For example, in Kirinyaga one of the sub-groups expelled a member who had missed four meetings in a row. In addition, when bananas are collected, traders pay up front into the group's account, and for the aggregated bananas to be collected, bank slips must be provided to the group's Chair. The group's Treasurer then prepares a summary of the amounts payable to each individual, depending on the weight of bananas that each farmer supplies. This is perhaps the best illustration of dual accountability: the leadership has to ensure that the bananas are weighed on arrival, individual weights are recorded, and then payment is made based on the weights supplied; the farmers have the responsibility to ensure that the recorded weight is accurate to avoid conflicts during the disbursement of funds.

These various levels of accountability are only successful to the extent that individual farmers are empowered enough to understand their role at each step of the farming business. For example, farmers have to ensure that bananas are delivered at an agreed time to the collection center. BGAK must ensure that the trader will collect the bananas at the agreed time since there are no cold storage facilities and therefore delays in collection will lead to huge post-harvest losses. KENFAP's role is all-encompassing—to ensure that farmers are producing the right quality through training in agronomy and the use of demonstration plots, and that farmers have the requisite skills to negotiate effectively with traders to ensure they achieve maximum gains from their farming business.

Another way that FOSCA is trying to build this mutual accountability is through the Capacity Performance Index (CPI), a tool that FOSCA uses to assess the baseline capabilities of an FO and then empower the organization itself to apply the tool over time. This enables the FO track its progress and understand where it is falling short. It also enables the FO to understand what it will take to move toward sustainability, which rests on enhancing operational efficiencies as identified using the CPI assessment.

Quick wins

The objective of the BGAK project was to strengthen the association so it can provide more efficient services to its members. We have begun to see positive results emerging from this work because the governance structure of the banana value chain is quite transparent. Farmers are becoming more confident about joining the association as they realize the emerging opportunities at different steps of the value chain. This growing confidence is a result of an array of interventions, but the main one is coaching and mentoring, especially of the farmer leaders.

A year ago, farmers were focusing on their weaknesses and how they hinder growth, but now, thanks to the realization of value chain efficiencies, they are negotiating a loan with a bank to fund an irrigation project. This is a typical example of how objective feedback from different stakeholders can help shape the thinking of FOs.

Furthermore, thanks to agronomic training through the use of demonstration plots, coupled with the establishment of banana nurseries in each county to allow farmers easier access to clean planting materials, productivity has increased significantly. Farmers are selling significantly larger volumes and therefore have put in place a cashless system through which traders pay them by producing bank deposit slips. The group's Treasurer then sends a schedule of beneficiaries to the banks for disbursement to individual accounts.

This level of accountability by the association is a testimony to how focusing on the softer side of issues (transparency, accountability, trust) and having the right leadership at the helm can propel such organizations to success. Member farmers have received training on entrepreneurship that enables them to determine their input–output costs and benefits, and therefore determine profits. Perhaps the best indicator of the value added by our interventions has been the willingness of member farmers to pay for services rendered.

Following several years of investing in generating new planting materials based on cutting-edge tissue culture technology, AGRA followed up with investments in marketing facilities and infrastructure. The idea has been to provide targeted farmers with lucrative markets that would trigger greater adoption of the new technology. These investments were subsequently followed by a specific initiative aimed at building an organizational platform that would enable farmers' participation in a lucrative value chain.

This case illustrates how AGRA was able to build on prior investments in research and market development to expand the program into the development of an organizational platform capable of amplifying the *voice*, generating *visibility*, and adding *value* for banana producers in selected districts in Kenya.

Promoting an integrated value chain-based program in the Beira Corridor in Mozambique

In 2012, AGRA funded a project entitled "Enhancing the Value Chain Approach to Agricultural Production for Improved Smallholder Farmer Livelihoods in the Central Region of Mozambique." This project illustrates how donors can enforce both vertical and horizontal accountability, while at the same time reducing competition. In practice though, setting up this type of program entails many changes that relate mainly to the need to facilitate collaboration among project partners and to avoid unnecessary competition.

The next section illustrates the processes used by AGRA in order to promote integration and mutual accountability on the ground.

Subsequent discussion centered on the identification of key value chains in the localities in the Beira Corridor, especially where the organizations faced similar challenges, opportunities, and risks, and had similar approaches to improvement. The focus of the discussion was then on the need for collaboration between different protagonists, including SHFs, in order to bring about significant transformation of the incomes, food security, and livelihoods of the target population. The discussion on partnership entailed an initial brainstorming on the identification of benefits, fears, and hurdles, and core values and principles of effective partnerships. Whereas the five organizations realized that they had unique competencies, they also noted that to solve the identified value chain challenges, there was a need to include other partners that would bring skills no one among the five had, for example seed production capacity. Two more partners were brought into the workshop to fill the gaps identified.

Structures of the meetings: Each of the bidding organizations was represented by two members. AGRA took a facilitative role, while the representatives of the organizations developed the program structures, and defined and assigned roles and responsibilities according to their capabilities relative to the project framework (i.e., addressing farmers' issues, ranging from inputs, production, post-harvest handling, and marketing, plus capacity building as a crosscutting issue). They organized themselves into three groups focused on production, marketing, and capacity building, and chose one organization to serve as the group leader.

The meetings accomplished a number of key objectives. The members of the newly established Consortium agreed on the project implementation structure, as shown in Figure 11.5. They assigned responsibilities based on their organizational strengths, thus complementing one another rather than trying to compete against each other. Accountability, mutual support, and cooperation fortified the Consortium and the final product was a "mega" project targeting 40,000 SHFs. Through this collaboration, the resources (time, money, human resources) required to develop five separate projects from the initial concept papers were redirected (and greatly reduced) to meet the main value chain needs of farmer beneficiaries with one initiative. This was a good lesson for AGRA, and the process has since been replicated in Tanzania.

Aligning local organizations' expertise

One way to promote collaboration and minimize competition is to facilitate a process where local organizations get to know each other and align their expertise. Only when they know that their services, expertise, and competencies are complementary, would they realize that competition is in the first place not essential. Box 11.2 summarizes the process followed.

Such an iterative learning process enabled the five organizations to gradually construct *a shared narrative* on effective ways to intervene in the target areas in order to unlock value for SHFs. This common *voice*, which incorporated the *vision* and *values* shared by the different protagonists, including AGRA, became the basis for the formulation of a collaborative program in the Beira Corridor.

Sharing responsibilities to deliver complementary services

The major levers of integration and change included: geographic focus; training of farmers; strengthening of farmer organizations; improving productivity; strengthening participation in agricultural value chains; and strengthening the institutional capacity for program delivery. These crosscutting issues are crucial for achieving the thematic objectives, and subsequently the overall project goal. Further discussion on the project strategy resulted in the operational framework represented in Figure 11.5.

BOX 11.2 FACILITATION PROCESS USED FOR THE FORMULATION OF AN INTEGRATED PROJECT IN MOZAMBIQUE

Initially, five organizations submitted individual concept notes to different programs in AGRA. Instead of responding to the individual notes, AGRA decided to invite the prospective partners to a project formulation workshop that would lead to the formulation of an integrated program in which each partner will play a role based on recognized competences and potential contributions by the other parties involved. Two sets of workshops were subsequently organized, during which the prospective partners shared detailed information on their organizational goals, objectives, geographic focus, services provided, beneficiaries, and lessons learned during their work in their target areas. This process enabled the different partners to discover shared values and priorities, and to identify one another's strengths and logical opportunities for collaboration.

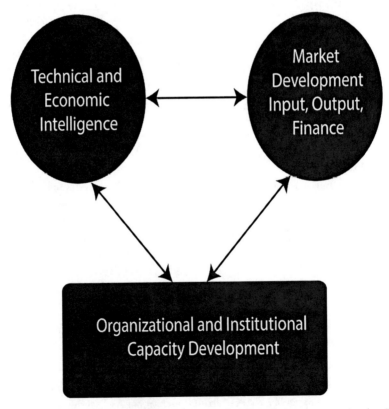

FIGURE 11.5 Key components of the integrated value chain program in the Beira Corridor, Mozambique

The result of this analysis was the identification of an overall strategic approach to an integrated program in Mozambique based on the following value proposition: *"A concerted integrated value chain approach driven by a network of competent professional organizations that are committed to achieving results and holding each other accountable."*

The proposed program included a wide range of interlinked activities related to the improvement of the agricultural value chain. In addition to the need to create awareness and facilitate the adoption of improved technologies, the program also highlighted the objectives of: (i) building the capacity of farmers in leadership and governance, business skills, entrepreneurship, and management; (ii) supporting rehabilitation and equipping of warehouses, strengthening umbrella organizations of FOs; (iii) linking FOs to financial service providers; (iv) ensuring integration of production; (v) developing marketing and capacity-building components within the value chain; (vi) promoting documentation of lessons learned; and (vii) sharing knowledge between implementing organizations and supporting broader policy design- and policy implementation-related activities.

This shared mental model of the interventions needed provided the broad framework around which the roles and responsibilities of each participating organization could be situated.

The members of the new Consortium decided to implement the proposed program based on the principle of shared responsibilities in specific geographies and for specific thematic areas. Selected organizations were identified to operate as thematic leaders, while each participating organization was assigned the role of implementing the full program in the geographic areas in which they operate. In addition, the thematic leaders (markets, production, finance, capacity building) will backstop project implementers operating in different localities, to make sure that all the thematic aspects of the project are dealt with consistently across the different project localities.

Figure 11.6 illustrates how the principles of co-learning and mutual accountability were embedded in the design and operational architecture of the program.

By combining full responsibility for the implementation of the integrated program in the different geographies with a leadership role in a specific thematic area, the members of the Consortium were committing themselves to cooperating with and supporting each other for the successful delivery of the project. This specific program design compelled the participating organizations to engage in a set of bilateral relations that needed to be harmonized by a coordinating entity, which in turn would be fully accountable for achieving the overall goal of the project.

Identifying the goal holder

One question that arises in accountability is "to whom?" The integrated project first promoted horizontal accountability among the seven partners by enabling them to understand that challenges in selected value chains would not be solved by one partner, or by interventions in one part of a given chain. It was clearly understood that challenges ranged from production, extension, farmer organization

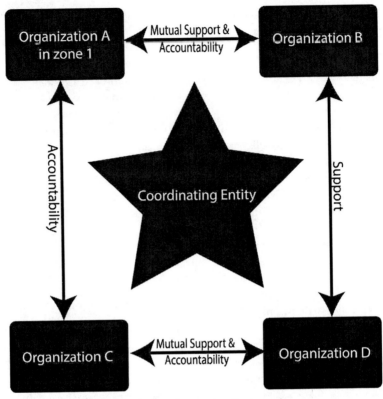

FIGURE 11.6 Beira Corridor's program integration framework

capabilities, and effective linkages to markets. This meant that failure to address an issue at one stage of the chain would have a multiplier effect along the whole value chain.

Consequently the success of interventions implemented by one partner or partners at one place in the value chain would contribute to the success of the other partners. Focusing on this interdependence and having it fully understood by the partners made clear the need to have one organization that would take responsibility for ensuring that all partners do their part and together all partners would deliver.

Considering that partners were now aware of each other's competencies, they were left to deliberate without AGRA's influence to choose a coordinating organization—the "goal holder"—and pledged to cooperate fully with that partner. The role of the coordinating organization was defined as:

> The main convener, responsible for facilitating exchanges of information, lessons learned, and preparing reports to be discussed with the AGRA Team, represented by the AGRA Country Officer. The project coordinator will also

convene the different project implementers on a quarterly basis in order to share their progress reports and to update each other on important developments related to the technical and economic conditions of the project (i.e., the sharing of technical and economic intelligence).

In practice, and beyond the formal agreement to collaborate for the successful implementation of the project, program stakeholders identified some specific tools and mechanisms aimed at enforcing the partnership. The next section provides additional information on the specific ways in which accountability and learning were enforced in this project.

Enforcing accountability and responsibilities

Even before the project was officially launched and funds were disbursed to the project goal holder, partners in the initiative agreed to sign memorandums of understanding with Concern Universal outlining their commitment to work together for a common goal. The memorandums outlined the conditions under which funds and other resources would be disbursed to individual partners. To ensure transparency in all processes and accountability to each other, especially for producing results, partners agreed that Concern Universal should undertake preliminary assessments of their management systems, including accounting systems, to identify weaknesses and strengths and above all to harmonize the systems. All partners agreed to avail their management systems for due diligence and committed to adopting a standard management system that Concern Universal deemed appropriate for synchronizing the reports to AGRA. This was critical to assess the partners' readiness to receive and manage funds for project activities.

The goal holder was also tasked to advertise all technical positions for the project in a transparent and competitive recruitment process. All partners were free to attend interviews and orientation of new staff. Once preliminary assessments were done, the goal holder held a project inception workshop within a month of the start of project activities, during which Concern Universal presented to all partners the results of the assessment it conducted, and the next steps in harmonizing project tools and management systems.

Quarterly meetings to develop the IPTT

One critical decision made was to have regular meetings. Whereas AGRA requires six-month reports from the project, partners considered this to be too long a period for timely information sharing; instead they opted for quarterly reports to keep each other updated on how activities were progressing. During this period, the goal holder prepares the agenda, which focuses mainly on partner progress reports relative to agreed action plans, and on sharing of any success stories or lessons learned. Each thematic leader presents their progress and work plan for the next period. The dates of these meetings are chosen to enable the goal holder to consolidate the results and report to AGRA in a timely manner. To ensure consistent engagement with AGRA, the Country Officer and other Program Officers have been encouraged to attend at least some of the quarterly meetings.

These meetings enable the members of the Consortium to jointly develop the IPTT, which is a key tool for learning and is regularly shared with AGRA to track the extent to which the project is meeting its quantitative and qualitative targets.

The strengths of the tool are that both AGRA and the grantees are able to assess their performance on a continuous basis (achievements against targets). Once the indicators are captured in the first report of the project, thereafter it only requires updating. It also enables AGRA to continually update its achievements against its strategic goals, thus making for more efficient strategic reporting.

One observation about these quarterly meetings has been the openness and candid discussions that take place during the sessions. It is impressive to note how partners hold each other accountable and also celebrate each other's roles where progress has been made. The Mozambique program is now in its second year of operation and the team is able to deliver on its collective and individual responsibilities on the basis of the collective learning and mutual accountability systems that have been put in place.

To date, partners have appreciated the role Concern Universal is playing in supporting each partner to implement its activities, including putting office management systems in place that have enhanced the ability of partners to remain accountable and submit reports on time. Partners who did not have proper accounting systems in place have been supported in strengthening that aspect of their management capacity, for which they are thankful.

Early results and lessons learned

The learning and collaborative processes initiated in the context of Beira Corridor have provided the following early results from the project.

Capacity building for increased productivity: A total of 109 demonstration farms focused on the use of integrated soil fertility management (ISFM) have been established to mobilize, train, and raise the awareness of SHFs and FOs on the benefits of improved seeds and fertilizers. The approach to sensitization and awareness creation relied largely on radio programs, aired on weekends, when farmers are expected to be home. The content of the programs cover: dissemination of information on ISFM; interviews with ISFM experts or farmers already applying such practices; and agricultural market information, including the advantages of collective marketing, post-harvest handling, and information from input and output markets and agrodealers.

During the course of the first seasons, over 12,000 farmers have been trained in ISFM and have applied the ISFM approach on 29,241 hectares; it is expected that by the end of this season they will produce approximately 214,700 Mt of various products, including maize, beans, soybean, and sesame.

Production of certified seeds: The two private seed companies, Dengo Commercial and Nzara Yapera, have produced and distributed 800,000kg of maize seeds, 12,800kg of sesame seed, and 43,750kg of beans.

Marketing: Over 7,000 farmers have been trained in post-harvest handling, and nine new storage facilities have been established while another seven were rehabilitated in 2014. Engagement meetings between FOs were facilitated and four bulk buyers have committed to buying 12,000 Mt of maize, 8,000 Mt of soybeans, and 200 Mt of beans during the coming harvest.

Strengthening FOs: Over 9,000 farmers have been organized into groups, and their leaders trained in group dynamics, business planning, and governance and management. The leaders who have been trained are in turn training member farmers, following a "training the trainer" approach.

As a result of this training, the farmer groups have developed a total of 184 business plans, with 182 of them submitted by the groups to Micro-Credit Bank. Of these, 110 were approved and 102 of them accessed credit amounting to about US$106,000. The credit enabled farmers to access good quality seeds and fertilizer, giving rise to the expectation that about 76,800 Mt of various crops will be produced, including maize, sesame, soybean, and beans. This could result in additional income of US$352,920 in the first year due to the higher productivity, the ability to aggregate produce for processing and sale, and stronger links with bulk buyers.

Challenges: During the first annual AGRA-partners review meeting, held in March 2014, the Consortium reflected on their gradual change in mind-set: initially they were reporting challenges because some of the partners were not used to strict reporting requirements and formats. They therefore viewed the lead partner as imposing extra work on them. This however was gradually and firmly addressed by all the partners, with the understanding that it is part of the accountability, cooperation, and support they all agreed to when they set up the project. They also understood that the lead partner is reporting on behalf of all of them to AGRA, and hence the need to meet the expected reporting standards and requirements, including timelines. So by the time the March annual meeting was held, the concern had been resolved and they were only bringing it to AGRA's attention as part of the initial "teething" process.

Another challenge was that the two seed companies were not keen to produce a certain variety of maize seeds that the farmers were interested in, yet the project could not bring other seed companies on board from outside the Consortium. This issue was discussed at length during the meeting with AGRA, and it was decided that new seed companies could be requested to produce seeds.

Despite these two challenges, the Consortium has worked very well and the early results emerging from the various components are very encouraging.

Institutionalization of the integrated approach within AGRA: Although the project development process was transparent, it was the first of its kind for AGRA. Therefore, AGRA management had to be briefed and convinced that it would work. Many questions were raised during the submission of the program for approval to AGRA's Management Committee, including concerns about the technical competence of specific organizations and their ability to handle some technically difficult activities. In addition, the role of the coordinating organization in ensuring harmonious operation of the integrated program was questioned.

The AGRA team that defended the proposal acknowledged the relevance of the questions raised. However, it emphasized the fact the collective experience of the participating organizations, and the co-learning and collaborative processes that have been put in place, will, in the end, determine the extent to which this program will succeed or fail.

For AGRA as an organization, this first experience of alignment and integration around commonly defined goals and responsibilities has set the stage for more program integration within AGRA itself.

Concluding remarks

The transformation of smallholder agriculture entails an initial challenge of connecting dots and facilitating the alignment of the goals and strategies of different stakeholders. The experience of AGRA's programs analyzed in this chapter enables us to draw some general conclusions on the issue of accountability and mutual learning in the context of inclusive development interventions. The specific challenges associated with promoting horizontal accountability systems among development partners include:

- linking the actions and interventions of different institutions across different time horizons. As was shown in the case of the banana value chain in Kenya, there is often a need to build on prior investments made in a specific locale and to learn from their success and failures;
- overcoming the initial fear and resistance of the different actors to cooperate, as was the case in the Beira integrated program in Mozambique;
- facilitating the development of a shared mental model;
- defining acceptable roles and responsibilities; and
- building mutual accountability systems that enable different protagonists to access resources and account for the results and achievements for which they took responsibility.

The whole accountability exercise needs to ensure that the expectations of all parties are addressed, and that the achievement of project goals will depend on all parties (implementers and recipients) doing their bit. In summary, AGRA was able facilitate a process of program design, implementation, and evaluation, which is essential for moving away from the traditional competition for resources, and for bringing about a results–oriented culture and mind-set. These outcomes were achieved through iterative processes that entailed joint planning, reviews, and learning activities.

Building on the experience of AGRA, one of the ways the accountability principle makes sense is if farmer groups grow in their governance capacity and are effectively empowered to the point of taking their future into their own hands.

This will include them embracing the responsibility to act on their priorities and insisting on impact-oriented results. If a farmer group lacks solid internal accountability mechanisms, it cannot be good at holding others accountable (including politicians). Overall, the sense of empowerment among farmers—what FOSCA calls "voice"—is critical: smallholders must increasingly gain the sense that they are able to take hold of their destiny, act in their own interests, and properly manage their own affairs.

An organization like AGRA can use its convening power to facilitate the development and amplification of the "voice" of local organizations. As we have seen in the cases examined here this outcome is intimately linked to its willingness to subject its program to a learning process to enable the construction of voice for project participants. This approach would, however, require a delicate balancing act between grant making, capacity building, convening, and knowledge-management activities in order to catalyze a self-driven mind-set among development actors involved in Africa's agricultural value chains.

Notes

1 Farmer Organization Support Center in Africa (FOSCA).
2 The authors acknowledge the guidance, support, and contributions of Dr Njeri Gakonyo, Prof. Ola Smith, and Dr Roy Steiner who reviewed the first draft of this chapter and provided some useful guidance and suggestions. This version of the chapter also incorporates the results of discussions with the participants at the writers' workshops held in Seattle on May 14–18, 2014. Tiff Harris completed the final review and editing of the document. We thank the reviewers for their contributions. However the primary authors of this paper take full responsibility for any shortcomings of the document.
3 Read more: www.businessdictionary.com/definition/accountability.html#ixzz3622Clgk0 (accessed September 27, 2015).
4 www.agra.org.

Bibliography

Africagrowth Institute. (2014a). "Baseline Survey Report on Smallholder Farmers in Selected Countries in Sub-Saharan Africa." Organizational report published on www.agra.org.

Africagrowth Institute. (2014b). "Profiling of Farmer Organizations and Service Providers in Selected Countries in Sub-Saharan Africa." Organizational report published on www.agra.org.

AGRA. (2013). "Transforming African Agriculture through Partnerships." Organizational report published on www.agra.org.

Ndiame, F. (2008a). "Empowering Rural Communities through Wealth Creation: The Experience of the W.K. Kellogg Foundation in Southern Africa." *Africa Growth Agenda* 5 (4).

Ndiame, F. (2008b) "Building the Capacity of Rural Communities in Southern Africa: The W.K. Kellogg Foundation's Zoom Site Process." Organizational report published on www.agra.org.

12

LEARNING THROUGH FEEDBACK LOOPS

Lessons from Kenya Markets Trust

Mike Field, Anna-Paula Jonsson and Mehrdad Ehsani

SUMMARY

Kenya Markets Trust (KMT) manages the Market Assistance Programme (MAP), which is a multi-donor-fund initiative that aims to reduce poverty in Kenya by making markets work for the poor. This case study describes how their approach maps out the system dynamics of a market and uses feedback loops to alter behavior and incentives in order to create a more inclusive market value chain.

KMT is learning about how feedback loops are central to restructuring incentives and hence behaviours in a market system. While the demonstration effect of successful business models for agro-dealers created competitive firm-to-firm pressure, the response by other firms was most often not to adopt the practices to copy these economic successes. More often agro-dealers felt threatened by the success of another and they actively used their network to try to impair the gains being made by the customer-oriented agro-dealers. As a result it became impossible to imagine how competitive pressure alone could be the lever to scale up, let alone catalyse systems-wide behavioural change. For wider systemic change, multiple feedback mechanisms are needed, and they need to be aligned to reinforce the competitive pressures for positive change. Experimentation with marketing, ICT and media services has shown promise to create the appropriate ether around which the competitive firm-to-firm pressures would become more powerful and catalytic.

KMT's experience has yielded other important lessons, including one area of learning among the market actors themselves. Agro-dealers and service providers such as marketing, ICT and media firms learned the importance of being customer-oriented and by working together started to develop a system ability to learn and adapt. In the final analysis a market system that is able to find solutions to future problems without external support is more likely to grow and survive while reaping sustainable pro-poor benefit flows.

Introduction

Feedback mechanisms make up one of the cornerstones of any well-functioning market, so much so, that we often take it for granted. In developing markets many of the institutions that enable effective feedback are missing. Take for example consumer protection, regulatory oversight and investigative media. Without such institutions, instances of counterfeit, fraud or other distorting market behaviours, will seldom reach the wider market's eyes and ears, hence enabling its agents to carry on with predatory, sometimes illegal, behaviour as their normal way of operating. In markets where feedback is easily deterred, market actors tend to adhere to shorter-term rather than longer-term strategies. And the chances for pro-poor market development? Well, poor. In this chapter we will discuss the lessons learned on social feedback loops from the Kenya Market Assistance Programme (MAP). MAP is a multi-donor-funded development project that works to improve effectiveness in private sector markets to generate inclusive wealth creation in rural Kenya.

Feedback loops are part of all effective markets and a concept that can be traced back to classical economic thinking in the form of Adam Smith's 'invisible hand'. Essentially, they are the mechanisms, systems and channels through which self-regulating behaviour occurs in a marketplace. Perfect self-regulating behaviour, however, can only occur in perfect market conditions. *Ceteris paribus*, no markets are perfect, but some are more ineffective than others. The idea may thus be old, but it has not been an integral part of development strategies until recently. Thinking around how change in market actors' behaviour is catalysed and adopted on a large scale has begun to shift lately. Much of traditional thinking around economic development has focused on the individual's (person or firm) capacity to change its own environment, or market system, in this case. Recent thinking has begun to focus increasingly on how the institutions that make up a market system, i.e. the rules, norms and mechanisms that create and sustain certain behaviours (the invisible hand, if you wish), can change its market actors and hence the inclusiveness of these markets.

A focus on the individual rather than the system fosters development strategies that target market-wide issues with narrow solutions aimed at correcting a malfunction for the individual. The underlying causes, often traced to market-wide institutional inefficiency, are overlooked, and durable change cannot be obtained. For example, a farmer is cheated on the price of improved seed in a rural inputs shop. Let us assume that the shopkeeper's stunt was not a one-time event, but an endemic manifestation of lack of social feedback loops. While providing the farmer with legal support and advice may eventually return him the money, this intervention of itself is unlikely to change the underlying reasons why the shopkeeper chose to cheat the farmer. It is also unlikely to create sustained change that would reduce the risk of the farmer, or other farmers, being cheated again because the lack of feedback loops rewards this kind of behaviour. Our experience has been that market systems that self-regulate ineffective behaviours such as those mentioned above exhibit greater growth, investment, sales and similar performance indicators and hence are all more likely to reduce poverty. By defining sustainability in the context of a system's capacity to uproot 'bad' behaviour, there is also an inbuilt perspective that donor programs should not be permanent fixtures in a market system, and special care should be taken to limit dependency or to act in such a way that a system's internal capacity isn't limited or reduced.

Our story below aligns with two shifts observed in development thinking, one with regard to how the institutions driving economic growth must function to result in poverty reduction, the other in relation to how sustainability of change is defined. Our experience with MAP seems to indicate that development strategies that target a change on a systems level have a better chance to produce sustainable poverty reduction than development strategies that seek to directly influence individuals' behaviour. Below, we chart our learning in trying to use feedback loops in rural Kenyan markets and the observed shifts (or lack thereof) in the behaviour of both firms and individuals which have implications for the institutional and market failures that exist.

MAP at a glance

The Kenya Market Assistance Programme is implemented by the Kenya Markets Trust, a non-profit organization that seeks to transform the performance of key markets so that they can function better and improve the lives of those participating in them whether as producers, employees or consumers. MAP is implemented in cooperation with Adam Smith International and co-funded by UKAID, Gatsby Charitable Foundation and the government of the Netherlands.

The MAP strategy encourages 'farming as a business', and the shift from subsistence to market–oriented commercial production by small-scale farmers. To facilitate this shift and enhance productivity, the programme has focused on increasing farmers' access to, and application of, modern farming technologies and inputs. A particular focus has been on seeds and fertilizers, which are distributed mainly through agro-dealers. Being the focal point linking input supplies to farmers, agro-dealers lend themselves as natural partners to work with more inclusive agro-inputs markets. Partnering agro-dealers have seen a 50–100 per cent increase in sales since the programme began two years ago.

Improving the incomes of Kenyan farmers

Kenya's agricultural productivity levels have long been lower than those of other African peer countries (Figures 12.1–12.3). Relative to world averages, the average yield for Kenyan coffee is 28 per cent, for maize 46 per cent, cotton 31 per cent, sorghum 45 per cent and vegetables 60 per cent (FAOSTAT 2013).

Access to, and appropriate use of, agricultural inputs such as seeds, fertilizers, pesticides and animal health protection is often cited as one of the biggest challenges facing small-scale farmers in Kenya as it undermines increased productivity and quality of output. Although fertilizer use in Kenya was higher than in other East African countries, it was only one-sixth of that used in India and Brazil, and half of that of South Africa and Zambia. Fertilizers are vital for improving the growth of crops, but over the last decade their use has stagnated in Kenya.

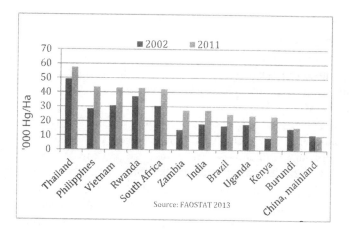

FIGURE 12.1 Kenya's maize yield benchmarked against other countries

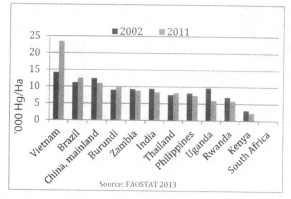

FIGURE 12.2 Kenya's coffee yield benchmarked against other countries

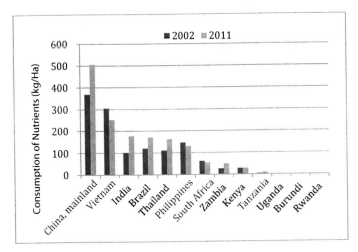

FIGURE 12.3 Kenya's fertilizer use on arable land benchmarked to selected countries

At the commencement of our programme we engaged in focus group discussions with smallholder farmers to better understand the underlying issues behind this dynamic. It emerged that smallholder farmers' access to information was one of the key constraints. Farmers who were not aware of how inputs could be used to enhance their productivity or to decipher between effective and less effective inputs (including counterfeit inputs) were risk-averse to testing inputs.

Conversations with agro-dealers brought to light that it is common practice across Kenya to regard good business as maximizing profit from each transaction taking place. As a result short-term gain has come at the expense of long-term growth. Customer support seldom seemed to have been valued, leaving farmers without information on correct usage for better crop and soil management, and sometimes with a feeling of intimidation and exploitation. Hence agro-dealers, taking little interest in farmers' preferences, needs and potential to become repeat customers, have been unable to make strategic and efficient choices when selecting and stocking products. Our assessment was that the agricultural inputs sector is characterized by retail businesses with limited strategies for growth, lack of trust between retailer and farmer, and farming communities without the knowledge they need to optimize the potential of their land and this has led to a market system that fails to effectively deliver pro-poor growth.

Key constraints in input supply retailing

We conducted a series of interviews, focus group discussions and surveys with market actors to understand the underlying constraints in inputs supply retailing. Each actor experienced his or her own challenges.

Based on the findings (see Figure 12.4) we developed a number of strategic interventions to address the constraints standing in the way of a more efficient input

Farmers
Only 50% of rural farmers participate in commercial farming

? Lack of knowledge, semi-literacy & capital

Small land

Physical distance to stores ~ restricted choice as a consumer

Agro-Dealer
SHOP

NO FARMER outreach

10,000 estimated agro-dealers in Kenya

Exclusive deals with certain exporters

Counterfeit & out-of-date products

$ Lack of capital to meet a spike in demand resulting in empty stock

Over 70% of the agro-dealers had not undergone any training in the safe use and handling of agro-chemicals

Distributor & Importers
Some 'sales' rep sold directly to farmers this cannibalized sales of local agro-dealers

Sell out of key products

2/3 distributors per town

Seed supply is dominated by one company

FIGURE 12.4 Challenges faced in retailing of agricultural inputs

supply market. In line with systems thinking, we sought to design interventions that would catalyse change, i.e. fostering change without becoming a permanent part of the system, with an obligation to exit the market without leaving a vacuum when the programme reaches its conclusion. In this regard, interventions were not only guided by what the programme could do, but also by what the programme should *not* do.

Understanding and applying feedback

Donella Meadows, a renowned systems thinker, describes her perspective on feedback:

> Feedback means, basically, giving people quick, accurate, emphatic information about the results of their own actions. A seller who sets a price too high gets no customers. A politician who thwarts the public gets no votes. Feedback can promote quick learning.

The reason the market system and democracy work badly, when they do, is that feedback is often distorted and delayed, sometimes inevitably, often deliberately. Politicians and merchants dominate the media with information that is – well, let's just say inaccurate. Prices don't carry full information about actual costs, especially environmental costs. The world is full of incomplete, late, deceptive feedback. According to Meadows (1992):

While an important component of feedback is information, we have since learned that there is another more complicating aspect to feedback within complex social systems. First of all feedback comes from multiple sources and they have differing strengths (depending on how the source is valued) which could either reinforce or counterbalance existing notions. We observed that information available to the actors in the inputs market system were not valued in a rational or logical way. What seemed to determine how actors consumed and processed information, and consequently how their behaviour was influenced, was determined by institutional (regulatory, cultural, economic, social, etc.) biases.

In Kenya's case, our perception was that social and political networks, commonly generated by ethnic and social hierarchy, were what dominated behavioural change. We also noted that while consumers have feedback loops through purchasing habits and their ability to complain, these feedback loops were very weak in practice. To counter existing biases, we postulated ways that we could align other feedback loops in support of consumer and business change, as a powerful lever to push back on dominant social and political feedback loops that entrenched predatory thinking. Our theory for modifying these biases included the use of radio. Radio stations could hypothetically broadcast information of any kind, without a guarantee that listeners would value it. However, if a radio station increased its credibility with listeners, farmers would be more sensitive to its influence, and we would have a more powerful tool to counter existing social and political biases. Take for example the sale of counterfeit products by an agro-dealer to farmers. If the access to information about the performance/behaviour of agro-dealers was valued by farmers, a radio station could present itself as a very powerful feedback mechanism on the sale of counterfeit products, generating social pressure with the potential to change agro-dealers' behaviour.

By dissecting the feedback loops that drive the collective behaviour of agro-dealers in Kenya (Figure 12.5), we began to define which feedback loops were,

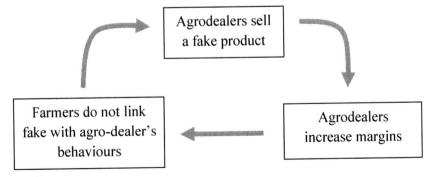

FIGURE 12.5 A common causal loop in the Kenyan agro-inputs distribution system

or could be, influential enough to influence behaviour in a pro-poor direction. Through this process we targeted resources around specific feedback loops with a view to catalyse specific behavioural changes understood to have the greatest impact on inclusive growth.

Learning to catalyse and scale up feedback loops

In this section we look at practical examples of the experience of the MAP team using three social feedback mechanisms developed in our interventions in the Kenyan inputs supply market. Each feedback mechanism targets a specific malfunction in the inputs market by creating the means to exert systemic pressure to reward 'good' (pro-poor) behaviour and sanction 'bad' (unfair) business behaviour (Box 12.1). To bring about durable change, MAP leveraged feedback loops at multiple levels and between multiple systems. As MAP is ongoing this chapter is written from the perspective of our hypotheses, observations and key lessons to date.

To understand whether interventions are having the desired effect on creating feedback loops, we integrated an M&E framework into the intervention process via results indicators that we believed indicated signs of change in the systems and resulting outcomes. Behavioural patterns that would indicate wider system change included the level of investment made by an agro-dealer in sales events to promote products and know-how to customers. This, for example, indicated that the agro-dealer saw the value in informing, educating and/or connecting with their customers.

BOX 12.1 MAP THEORY OF CHANGE

The main goal of MAP's work with agro-inputs market systems is to catalyse a shift from a dominant trader-based retail strategy which values short-term profits to a customer-oriented strategy. Customer-oriented retail networks align incentives of input firms, farmers, processors, service providers, etc. since the business model is geared towards volume of sales and inventory management. Essentially, this shift would turn the attention of agro-dealers to the 'second' sale, or to creating recurrent clients, which would enable a shift from maximizing the per unit margin to maximizing profits over volume. To enable the business strategy, increased customer satisfaction would be necessary, automatically increasing the value of customers' satisfaction in the eyes of the agro-dealer, creating improved incentives for investments in efforts to keep loyal clients through better information and services. MAP works with a range of willing retailers and wholesalers to facilitate their investment in new distribution and promotional tactics/management practices to create this behavioural shift.

Catalysing feedback loops

We assessed a wide range of business practices within various agro-dealers and found that key feedback mechanisms were not in place. 'A Guide to Growth-Oriented Behaviours' (Figure 12.6) would ask questions aimed to explore to what extent feedback loops required for a growth-oriented business strategy were in place. Interesting discoveries were made as to how well the internal management of the agro-dealers was operating. For example, traditional feedback loops related to marketing (tracking of number of sales and new clients in relation, or not, to marketing efforts) and financial controls (balance sheets, income statements, etc.), which serve to create more effective learning and informed decision-making for the dealerships' growth and health, were generally absent, or not effective. Other retail-specific loops related to customer purchase habits were also expected, but seldom observed. MAP's hypothesis and intervention design was built on the assumption that the absence of these feedback loops was an indication of the lack of growth orientation amongst agro-dealers.

1 – No, I have never considered doing this

2 – No, but I would be interested in doing this

3 – Yes, I have trialled and tested some ideas

4 – Yes, I do this but it could work better

5 – Yes, I do this and it works very well

Please tick as appropriate	1	2	3	4	5
Management Systems					
I have invested in developing and expanding the supplier base to get the inputs I need					
I have invested in developing and expanding the distribution channels for my products and/or services					
I have set up policies and procedures and hired admin staff so that I can expand and manage large volumes of business activities					
I have decentralized some management control to high-performing teams and staff members					
I have invested in learning from data on customer, competitors, industry, finance, inventory and staff performance					
I have focused my business model around building a high-performance work culture and strong company brand					
I have coordinated all the business activities so that the profits and investment goes towards growing my business					
Staff Performance Management					
I have invested in staff training and development to cultivate managers for specific parts of the business, such as strategy, customer service, marketing, product development and finance					
I have set up a system that evaluates staff using a competency-based framework, self-initiative and innovation and this feeds into their compensation package					
I have invested in creating a firm identity to build staff loyalty					
I have included staff in firm strategy and performance reviews					
I use a mixture of approaches to motivate my staff especially those that give security, empower, build confidence and encourage innovation					
Marketing Strategies					
I have invested in long-term marketing strategies, such as those that have high short-term investments and longer-term gains					
I have invested in customer service training for all levels of staff and this is continuously renewed					
I use a mixed bag of generic and specialized promotional tactics strategically to capture opportunities and grow market share depending on the market performance and the customer reactions					
I flex the prices of my products/services to take advantage of market opportunities and customer reactions					
I have invested in a customer relationship management (CRM) system that actively encourages staff to collect customer data at all levels of the business					
I have a dedicated team that actively tracks customer data and feeds findings into product development and marketing tactics					
Inventory Management					
I use specialized marketing and promotion strategies to clear stock that is old or slow-selling					
I have a system that manages all activities in inventory management – daily cash intake to receipt collection, maintenance of master inventory list, physical inventory checks, etc.					

FIGURE 12.6 Guide to growth-oriented behaviours

Based on these observations, further assumptions could be made, including that owners of agro-dealers rarely made decisions that would align well with their firms' growth. Instead, decision patterns aligned much more closely with monetization or withdrawing money from the business for personal use, i.e. with those of a 'lifestyle business'. Decision patterns were also found to be informed by cultural factors such as ethnicity and issues around social loyalty.

The lesson to be learned through this process was that internal business practices in agro-dealerships were driven by a much wider set of pressures than those initially scoped for, including social, cultural and regulatory issues. Reframing business goals and helping owners to acquire the tools for managing feedback was paramount to catalyse the shift in behaviour the programme strives for.

When working with Kenyan agro-dealers, one of our core messages was that the growth of a company was defined by its increased value, rather than by its profits (Eric Ries's (2011) 'lean start-up' thinking). The value of a business can be estimated in assets, relationships, a trusted brand or capable staff, in some combination. When promoting business strategies for long-term growth, the distinction between long- and short-term growth was important, as an agro-dealer's internal management strategy varied markedly between them. For example, an agro-dealer who aimed for long-term growth of the value of the firm also understood he or she must make investments in their customers, staff and supplier relationships, i.e. management strategies that may not generate good profits in the short run, but that have the potential to increase value (see Figures 12.7 and 12.8 for feedback loops derived from adopting a customer-oriented growth strategy).

We had to adopt a dynamic learning process to implement these tactics. To initiate the firm's process, focus was placed on feedback loops that could create more powerful, concrete and immediate results, in this case increased direct sales catalysed by promotional events in rural areas. By increasing sales through

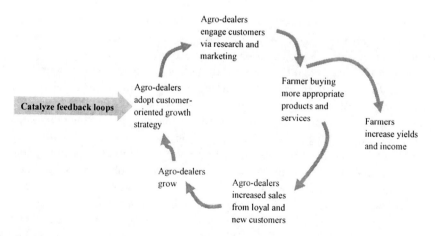

FIGURE 12.7 Causal loop diagram: expected firm-to-firm change

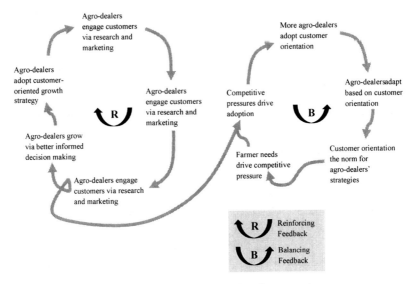

FIGURE 12.8 Causal loop diagram: expected within-function change

direct engagement with customers, the agro-dealer owner would receive immediate feedback from behavioural change, something we were targeting with an eye on greater buy-in to the concept of customer-oriented growth (meeting the needs of the customer).

With selected agro-dealers adopting a customer-oriented growth strategy and increasing their sales and revenues, competitive pressures began to emerge, as similar firms sought to adopt the same sales tactics to increase their revenues and maintain their place in the marketplace. As this process developed, we observed very clear patterns in the firms engaging in competition or cooperation, in that reactions to competitive pressure focused heavily on short-term predatory outcomes. These behavioural patterns supported the perception that firms' perceived growth as a zero-sum game, with other firms' growth necessarily taking place at their expense. This indicated a major systemic weakness.

Specifically, firms when confronted with another firm doing well often reverted to using their network to attack that firm. For example, through personal links to regulators or influential characters within a given social context, the firm feeling threatened would attempt to identify (true or not) irregularities in the other firms that could lead to legal prosecution. Cases of physical attacks on the competing firm's premises also occurred. Instead of cooperating with other firms to improve internal competitiveness, cooperation was also used as a tool to plot against successful firms. Cartel behaviour and political favouritism were common forms of cooperation and were used primarily to ensure win–lose outcomes.

Competitive pressure did not scale up to catalyse system-wide behavioural change as we had initially hoped. It had been clearly observed that traction had been gained with firms to take on a customer-oriented growth strategy with relative ease, and that improved firm performance followed for most partnering firms. However, the competitive pressure from one firm on another firm was not proving sufficient to drive wider change. Market systems seemed to be easily subjected to non-market forces (the influence of MAP) or feedback, but market forces/feedback such as firm performance did not easily affect other firms on a system-wide scale. For wider systemic change, feedback mechanisms with the power to influence firms on a system-wide scale would be imperative as part of MAP's thinking and future strategy adaptations.

Zooming in: three examples of feedback mechanisms

Marketing services firms

We observed that most Kenyan agro-dealers managed their business without a business strategy in place. Little attention was given to how long-term growth could be achieved as focus lay on short-term gains. As a result, occasional attempts by some agro-dealers to grow their business through an expanded network of distributors, partners and customers, often failed as the interventions tend to be isolated from a wider business strategy. Similarly, there was little appreciation for capital invested in staff training, marketing or attempts to create better relations with customers, as benefits they would bring were all long-term and undervalued.

The objective of interventions for improved internal business strategies placed focus on two layers of feedback loops. The first layer of feedback loops was intended to catalyse internal learning and growth by:

1   supporting agro-dealers to better understand their customers by advising on and delivering customer/market research; and
2   supporting agro-dealers in developing and rolling out more effective information-based marketing and promotional campaigns.

By providing the capacity that would allow agro-dealers to more effectively engage and learn about their customers and customer behaviour, we were catalysing feedback loops by encouraging agro-dealers to link their business success to the value their customers placed on the relationship they had with his/her firm. The sustainability of these feedback loops depended on agro-dealers' investment in market research and developed marketing and customer-service capacity to improve responsiveness among staff to customers' interests and needs.

An important lesson in this process was to learn that consumers were generally devalued in Kenyan market systems, something that was even more pronounced in rural areas where consumer protection was almost non-existent. As a result, most firms didn't appreciate the importance of customer care or marketing, and hence the market for specialized services was very weak. We learned that to counter this bias, and to increase the interest in above-mentioned investments, a large part of the project must be dedicated to capacity building and sensitization.

The second layer of feedback loops catalysed was intended to influence marketing and customer service firms to create demand for their services. We hypothesized that these firms would invest in selling to and servicing agro-dealers, once they realized there was an opportunity in the inputs supply sector. The constant cycle of learning and adapting based on customer response was fundamental in driving growth through adaptation and inclusiveness by agro-dealers, which was especially important in weak service markets like these. The intervention and feedback loops here were similar to those in the ICT intervention below in that they aimed to catalyse access, as well as foster the emergence of a robust market for such services (Figure 12.9). This was significant because beyond marketing services being provided to agro-dealers with whom we were working, we wanted to stimulate the uptake of these services more widely among other agro-dealers in Kenya – a potential lever for getting to scale. At the time of writing, three competent marketing firms had emerged that were delivering services to agro-dealers and to firms higher up the distribution channel outside our support.

ICT

Similarly to marketing, ICT was an ever-evolving and powerful tool for feedback, monitoring and, consequently, instigating behavioural change. Through improved accessibility and quality of information about partners, suppliers, customers, financial performance and inventory management, an agro-dealer could make more informed decisions about how to grow a business and what the impact was of given management strategies.

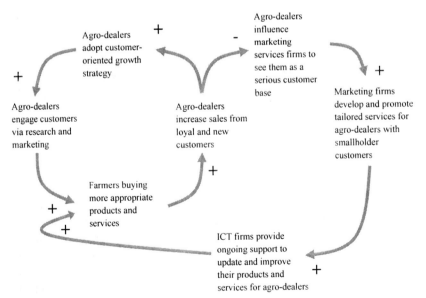

FIGURE 12.9 Expected change with reinforcing feedback from marketing service firms

The MAP team created links between ICT companies and agro-dealers to allow ICT to become part of the inputs sector. Kenyan ICT providers tended to work with more sophisticated businesses and often saw agro-dealerships as enterprises with too low turnover and simple management needs to be a business opportunity for them. To introduce ICT solutions to agro-dealers, it became clear that we had to work with the ICT providers to demonstrate the potential value in working with agro-dealers and the first-mover advantage of entering a market still untouched by ICT firms. On the customer side, there was also a fair deal of sensitization to be done on what benefits the agro-dealers could expect to find should they choose to adopt an ICT platform.

The ICT intervention was designed to test the value of the information that ICT systems could provide for more informed decision-making by managers in agro-dealers. Support was given to a wide range of ICT firms to interact with agro-dealers in order to create a volume of transactions that would allow market pressures (i.e. feedback loops in the form of competition) to emerge that would push the better-performing ICT firms to the forefront and drive out poor performers. Support consisted of skills training in how to market products to new clients, provide post-sale services and training to customers, tailor products to clients' needs and how to handle competitive pressure from other ICT firms. Key to the intervention was hence the component to support ICT firms to learn how to be customer-oriented – integral to the intervention throughout its implementation, but key for leveraging ICT firms' incentives and ability to scale up ICT to a market-wide and sustainable level (Figure 12.10).

Counter to traditional donor project approaches that set out to create solutions to market failures, this process sought to create the necessary linkages for market actors to create their own solutions to the problem of absent feedback loops. After all, a system that is adaptive without donor support is much more highly prized. This process was more cumbersome than designing an ICT platform for an agro-dealer would have been. For example, some of the ICT firms did not invest the necessary time and resources to develop products that met their clients' needs or provide after-sales service at a suitable price point. These firms showed that they were more interested in continued donor support rather than seeking their future in the market. As a result these firms fell by the wayside which we interpreted as a normal churn in the market development strategy. Notwithstanding these challenges, other ICT firms emerged (see Box 12.2) that were able to take advantage of embryonic markets in a more sustainable way. Our perception was that this process catalysed the adoption of a feedback loop on a scale that stands a good chance to stand the test of time long after MAP has ended.

Media

Media is an important social feedback loop through which farmers can voice their opinion on the quality of a product or service to a wider audience through, say,

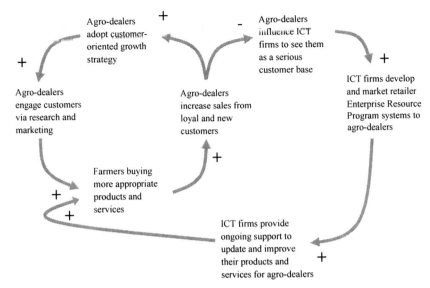

FIGURE 12.10 Expected change with reinforcing feedback from ICT providers

BOX 12.2 THE VALUE OF THE RURAL SMEs FOR ICT FIRMS

There are many opportunities for ICT firms to take advantage of in the rural SME sector. We have learned that if ICT firms can learn how to understand their customers' needs and tailor unique products and services to fit consumer behaviour, agro-dealers and other rural market actors are willing to pay for an ICT platform out of their own pocket.

One ICT firm, EchoMobile, has been working with an agro-dealer chain called Farm Shop. The agro-dealer chain had a need to better communicate with customers, many of which lived far from the shop and who would only procure inputs on one or two occasions per year.

The need identified, EchoMobile provided an ICT platform through which Farm Shop could send SMS messages to customers, marketing new products, promotions and technical advice on usage. EchoMobile took this a step further by scaling up what it was that had allowed a business transaction to emerge between the two firms. EchoMobile now provides close and personal service to rural small businesses, such as regular monthly trainings, feedback sessions and focus group testing of new products. As a result of close collaboration with, and learning from rural SMEs, the ICT provider has been able to develop unique pieces of software that have little competition in the market. For example, where many ICT firms have struggled to set up an 'authentication and rating system', EchoMobile is already in the process of testing this system with dairy enterprises.

radio. The objective of the intervention was thus to create a source of information that could influence farmers' decision-making on a large scale: the radio listeners. However, there was a caveat to engaging radio as a feedback mechanism.

For media feedback to work, the media businesses need to be committed to a growth-oriented, listener-driven strategy. If the media firms believed their growth was tied to the loyalty and influenceability of its listeners then it would have strong incentives to adopt an investigative approach to producing radio content. For example, in Kenya, media firms' typical 'pay to play' business model, where radio content was selected and broadcast in exchange for pay, did not place value on the stations' fundamental assets, its listeners. Value was instead placed on the customer, perceived to be the person to have his or her radio content broadcast. This took place in the form of advertisement or politically biased shows, for example. As a result, our perception was that media firms seldom appreciated their potential and role to pose as an information provider and educator of listeners. Among the three main categories of mass media tools – radio, television and print media – the influence of rural radio at a local level could not be denied. We postulated that by improving the content, listener orientation and proactive advocacy of selected rural radio stations, radio had the potential to create more intensive feedback loops for a more adaptive and inclusive, growth-oriented agro-inputs market system.

The rural radio intervention was designed to create early buy-in from radio stations by demonstrating the value of a listener orientation. With an understanding of the value of listener-oriented content, stations were expected to adopt a more customer-oriented business strategy. Central to this strategy was to foster immediate and localized feedback loops related to agro-dealers. The intent was to support radio stations to develop local agricultural programmes that would 'call out' good and bad agro-dealer behaviour, and hence amplify competitive firm-to-firm pressure (Figure 12.11).

The initial intervention showed some success in that radio programmes were becoming more listener-driven with new formats and with greater listener participation. One immediate observation was that while the relevance of the information was improving, the feedback loops were not as forceful as hoped. One lesson learned here was that access to general agricultural information has not been effective for generating any real pressure for change in agro-dealer behaviour. Thus, more ag-related radio shows per se were not likely to increase radio's influence on the market. Understanding this early on, we reinforced the importance of listener-driven content (content driven by listener demand) and the business strategies radio stations would need to adopt to transform listener-led content into a commercially viable business model.

A key part of listener-led content has been supporting consumer protection programming to increase the power radio can exert on influencing behavioural biases among agro-dealers. With increased belief that radio stations have customers' best interests in mind, we believed the power of what was broadcast would be increased significantly.

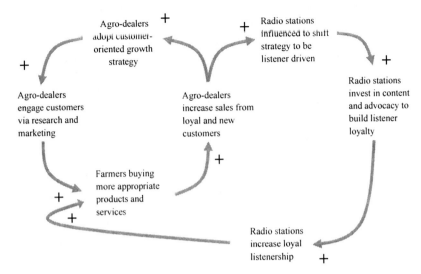

FIGURE 12.11 Expected change with reinforcing feedback from radio stations

Important components of social feedback loops

Nepotism versus meritocracy (proven business models)

The MAP team learned that agro-dealers rarely made decisions that prioritized business growth. Rather, they focused on extracting as much profit from transactions as possible, with little intent on reinvesting the money into the business. MAP identified that in Kenya economic growth was overruled by political and social loyalty. Social pressures were given a higher value than traditional evidence used for management decisions. Such institutional bias saw agro-traders employing friends or family and tolerating behaviour that was detrimental to business growth. For example, a typical narrative featured an owner of an agro-dealership who employed a relative and yet knew that this relative was not performing, or in many cases even hurting his business. In spite of this, the owner would not remove the relative from the business because of family expectations.

Stigma

A Kenyan nickname has evolved known as 'Pull Him Down' (PHD). A PHD individual or community actively seeks to impair people who gain economic success beyond their social status. PHDs can ostracize, start rumours or physically destroy a farmer's or trader's infrastructure if they feel threatened.

The MAP team advised businesses impacted by stigma to re-strategize and adjust their marketing patterns. For example, when we facilitated promotional events, agro-dealers were encouraged to use adjusted promotional tactics that did not single out a farmer, but created groups of winners. Specifically, instead of using a lead farmer or single contest winners as potential demonstrators, we helped agro-dealers work with multiple farmers of different social status to test products and services via trial packs and giveaway contests. We also supported agro-dealers to garner group testimonials rather than individual ones. The combination was important to limit the perception of individual gain, while reinforcing via farmer-to-farmer communication the ease with which any farmer could take on this new behaviour.

Scaling up by leveraging feedback loops

The ability to influence a system is intricately conditioned by a system's institutional biases, as we have seen above. In the case of Kenya, social and political networks, commonly defined by ethnic and social hierarchy, dominate the manifestation and strength of these biases. Hence, the primary mechanism for asserting power in a system is feedback. However, to influence a system on a wider scale to generate systemic change, effective balancing feedback loops need to be leveraged.

As briefly mentioned above, radio is a powerful feedback mechanism with influence to act as a behavioural changer for more inclusive growth when the information broadcast is valued in the right way. We have seen above how individual feedback loops can generate pressure for change among a limited number of actors engaged in a given exchange. When radio programming is culturally valued, it features as a way to leverage on existing feedback loops that have produced change on a small scale. In other words, if a radio station increased its credibility with listeners, farmers would be more sensitive to its influence, and MAP would have a more powerful tool to counter existing social and political biases. Take for example the sale of counterfeit products by an agro-dealer to farmers. If the access to information about the performance of agro-dealers was valued by farmers, a radio station could present itself as a very powerful feedback mechanism generating social pressure with the potential to change agro-dealers' behaviour.

For radio feedback to work, radio stations need to be committed to a growth-oriented, listener-driven strategy. If radio stations believe their growth is tied to the loyalty and influence of their listeners then they will have strong incentives to adopt an investigative approach to producing radio content. MAP determined that by improving the content, listener orientation and proactive advocacy of selected rural radio stations, radio had the potential to trigger a multiplier effect of existing and functional feedback loops for a more solution-seeking and inclusive, growth-oriented agro-inputs market system.

Conclusion

As a programme we have learnt that feedback loops are central to restructuring incentives and hence behaviours in a market system. The agricultural inputs market in Kenya exhibits certain dysfunctional behaviours and market failures that are rooted in social and political norms and result in lost opportunities for an inclusive and adaptable market that promotes pro-poor growth. Manifestations of this include myopic business strategies that tend to be short-term-focused rather than longer-term strategies that add value to the business by becoming more customer-oriented. In order to counter these negative biases and change behaviour we have experimented with a cocktail of other feedback loops. We found that while the demonstration effect of successful business models for agro-dealers created competitive firm-to-firm pressure, the response by other firms was most often not to adopt the practices and to copy these economic successes. More often agro-dealers in the project geography focus area felt threatened by the success of another and they actively used their network to try to impair the gains being made by the customer-oriented agro-dealers. As a result we concluded that firm-to-firm competitive pressure alone could not be the lever for scale-up to catalyse system-wide behavioural change as we had initially hoped. For wider systemic change, multiple feedback mechanisms would need to be employed and aligned to reinforce the competitive pressures for positive change. We experimented with marketing, ICT and media services to create the appropriate ether around which the competitive firm-to-firm pressures would become more powerful and catalytic.

Beyond the learning that the MAP team gained in trying to facilitate this shift in the inputs markets the more important area of learning was among the market actors themselves. Agro-dealers and service providers such as marketing, ICT and media firms learned the importance of being customer-oriented and by working together started to develop a system ability to learn and adapt. In the final analysis a market system that is able to find solutions to future problems without external support is more likely to grow and survive while reaping sustainable pro-poor benefit flows.

References

FAOSTAT. (2013). Web page. Available online at: http://faostat.fao.org/site/291/default.aspx (accessed 28 September 2015).

Meadows, D. (1992). 'Let's Have a Little More Feedback'. Donella Meadows Institute. Available online at: www.donellameadows.org/archives/lets-have-a-little-more-feedback (accessed 28 September 2015).

Ries, E. (2011). *The Lean Startup: How Today's Entrepreneurs Use Continuous Innovation to Create Radically Successful Businesses.* New York: Crown Publishing.

13

CONCLUSION

Duncan Hanks and Roy Steiner

What began as a simple conversation among colleagues and friends has taken on new and significant dimensions based on real-world experiences and wrestling with concepts about

- constituent voice,
- participation,
- accountability and transparency,
- feedback loops, and
- the role of knowledge.

The contributors to this publication have offered insights into how they have been approaching their work in the past years and decades. Each organization, operating from its own reading of reality, has reflected deeply on its experience and the nature of the relationships it is fostering through its work. By reflecting on their actions and consulting with their colleagues, the contributors have provided tangible examples of how certain approaches, methodologies, instruments and technologies, when combined with clarity of vision, values and a spirit of cooperative learning, improve development performance. Furthermore, they share an earnest desire to reframe one significant relationship that consistently seems more remote and disconnected from the work at the grassroots, namely the relationship with the donor or funding organization.

This does not imply that all donor organizations are inherently weak at fostering healthy relationships with their constituents and partners; it does, however, indicate there is room for more research, cooperation and openness to learn.

This chapter will present reflections on three key areas that emerged out of the case studies: (1) the use of new information technologies in feedback and learning; (2) community engagement; and (3) learning and system-level approaches. This is followed by a description of the emerging elements for collective learning in development, which is the expression of the contributor's analysis on the commonalities of their experiences as brought out through consultation about their respective experiences. The chapter concludes with a few closing remarks and recommendations for future research.

Initial observations

1) Reflections on the use of new information technologies in feedback and learning

One key reflection shared by most of the contributors was the importance of learning to *close the feedback loops between all major constituencies*. The challenge is to create environments that enable constituents to address together their often unequal power dynamics. Creating enabling environments in which all constituents participate to close the feedback loops is considered a significant contributing force to addressing unequal power dynamics. In spaces for reflection on action, constituents learn to engage each other in an increasingly transparent and consultative manner, striving to understand each other's perspectives and points of view. Most of the contributors highlighted the importance of how data is presented and handled, and the manner in which co-constituents engage each other to bring meaning to that data.

FIGURE 13.1 Feedback cycles bring meaning to data

The contributors also describe challenges related to translating a good practice into a consistent practice. These challenges included efforts to institutionalize learning processes or to embed certain practices and ways of thinking into the work. A willingness to think and work at both a systemic and grassroots level is part of the growing capacity of constituents to take on greater levels of complexity as their capacity is being built. Keystone, for example, talks about how moving from an occasional, or one-off "useful activity" to a consistent practice that changes organizational culture and practice remains one of its most important lessons learned. Farmer Voice Radio talks about embedding sustainability into the process at the outset, because it impacts the organizational culture moving forward.

Another key lesson identified through reflection on action is the importance and role of information technologies, particularly as they relate to data collection and facilitating feedback. Technologies play a pivotal role in helping to systematize learning from feedback and to diffuse those lessons as well. However, the role of technology and its use cannot be separated from the social and cultural processes by which people engage with each other around technology and its benefits. Technology is being talked about in new ways. There is a shift away from conceiving of technology as a means to give people what they think they want, or merely responding with a technology fix to meet a perceived need. Such action would reinforce the outmoded notion that development is merely about delivering services to the poor. Instead, approaches to technology now place greater emphasis on how technology is used to facilitate learning, to amplify voice and to build capacity. At the heart of this learning is how people engage with data and each other to ascribe meaning that informs and improves action. In this sense, there is a movement away from solutions designed to meet people's needs, because those needs are seemingly endless. Rather, they are using technology to facilitate and enhance learning so that capacity to analyze and solve development problems is built.

It is human interaction with technology that reshapes how that technology can best be used. Whether it is co-creating human-centered design (i.e. IDEO.org) or ascribing meaning to data collected electronically, technology requires conscious and ongoing human engagement.

Technology is never culture- or value-neutral. The introduction and use of any technology are seriously affected by the culture and social constructs assigned by the co-constituents. Learning to introduce the right technology in the right way and embed its use in a collective learning process will significantly impact its eventual uptake and benefit.

Digital Green's shift in values is reflected by its decision to combine technology with social organization to foster collective learning and redefine accountability. By engaging with all its co-constituents, Digital Green has increased the collective capacity to gather timely, appropriate and segmented data and to make it readily available to everyone in the system. Through this approach, *iterative* improvements are made in real time at the project design level, and throughout project implementation and evaluation phases as well. To assign meaning to its data, Digital Green relies on spaces wherein constituents consult. These spaces afford the constituents an opportunity to build trust and align their values to take into account and address unexamined power dynamics. At the heart of Digital Green's approach is a learning process that continually strengthens the relationships within and between co-constituents at the individual and institutional levels. To avoid traditional pitfalls, Digital Green works top-down and bottom-up, by ensuring both formal and informal spaces for reflection on action. One notable feature emphasized by Digital Green and shared by most of the other contributors to this publication, is the cultivation of a humble attitude towards learning. It makes no exaggerated claims about its effectiveness; rather, it focuses on reshaping organizational culture to think in terms of processes that yield mutually beneficial results.

The *Grameen Foundation*'s case study focuses on learning about approaches that cultivate a more responsive organizational culture, by emphasizing rapid learning cycles that are designed to create greater accountability. While the widespread use of technology within the "last mile" is important, it is secondary to developing the analytical capacities needed to derive meaning from feedback in order to make course corrections. Grameen's experience demonstrates the benefits of engaging all co-constituents when identifying indicators in order to optimize outcomes and impacts. It stresses the importance of being able to automate and also visualize the data being tracked, and the importance of participation to ascribe meaning to data. Over time, the participants have a chance to see themselves as part of a collective learning enterprise that: (1) helps them to more accurately read and understand reality; (2) enables them to generate new insights and knowledge by reflecting on action (i.e., closing the feedback loops); and (3) ensures the participatory design of approaches that turns obstacles into stepping stones. The Foundation is learning that progress is made by being consistent, patient and by working through multiple cycles of learning each characterized by formal and informal spaces for reflecting on action.

Farmer Voice Radio (FVR) concludes that at the heart of its quest to be more effective rests its growing reliance on collaboration, particularly with the farmer at every stage of the development process. FVR stresses the importance of two-way accountability, continual feedback loops and collective learning. It articulates that fostering an environment for collective learning represents much more than a utopian or pious ideal; it is a fundamental management principle for results-based development. Without such a management strategy it is difficult—perhaps impossible—to find creative solutions to complicated, real-world challenges. FVR has shown that while it may take longer and require more support for an initiative to become sustainable, it can be accelerated and enhanced if capacity is developed in all constituents simultaneously and deliberately.

Keystone's experience, particularly in Swaziland and Nicaragua, highlights its practical experience testing the use of feedback to manage and improve performance in sustainable agriculture. With its emphasis on constituent voice, Keystone focuses on how the views and experiences of those intended to benefit from development initiatives can meaningfully and systematically influence the way that programs undertaken in their name are designed, implemented, managed and evaluated. It stresses a fundamental shift in thinking that at the heart of development rests not the delivery of services, but the development of capacities of service. It redefines who the protagonists are, and their roles. With refreshing humility, Keystone acknowledges how its methods will continue to evolve in response to what is being learned, to the challenges it faces and the capacity of the constituents. Keystone's approach acknowledges the diverse needs and interests of different constituencies, agencies and participants. It also shows there is real value in 'imperfect data' that can be used effectively to generate collective learning. Perhaps most striking is Keystone's own reflection on how feedback and accountability loops are not merely technical and material in nature but involve social and political dimensions that need to be incorporated into project feedback instruments with great sensitivity to the fears and needs of all constituents.

2) Reflections on community engagement

The impact of new information technologies in feedback and learning takes on added complexity as organizations become increasingly aware of how reimagining their role as an equal partner or co-constituent might impact development outcomes. As this consciousness of co-ownership and co-implementation awakens, there is greater experimentation with new models of community engagement.

PRADAN's work with smallholder farmers in India is predicated on the belief in the capability of every individual to bring about positive change. PRADAN does not allow itself to fall into misconceptions about human nature. Instead, it upholds the fundamental right and obligation (dignity) of all people to actively work towards their individual and collective betterment. But there are obstacles that need to be overcome in order for communities, groups, families and individuals to fulfill their own sense of agency. Among the notable distinctions of PRADAN's work is its willingness and ability to talk about concepts that are frequently discarded by mainstream development agencies because of their perceived lack of ability to be *empirically measured* and easily quantified. Notions of self-efficacy and sense of agency, for example, don't translate into easily recognizable evaluation metrics. By tackling these issues head-on in a transparent learning mode, PRADAN demonstrates the significance of these drivers of change, and it is these drivers that constitute the primary theory of change that governs its approaches, methods, programs and socio-technical interventions. It patiently encourages and accompanies its co-constituents to discover the most harmonious approaches possible by incrementally building their capacities for constructive participation.

In addition, PRADAN also recognizes that change must occur at multiple levels for it to be sustained, and to ensure that any gains achieved are not quickly reversed due to larger societal forces. Working collectively with all the stakeholders (co-constituents) is therefore not an option, but a necessity. All initiatives start small and grow in complexity and expand in scale over time. But the vision is clear at the outset, and the organizational culture to support it is firmly in place before the first step of the learning journey is taken.

CARE puts the spotlight on conceptual coherence, on walking the talk. CARE's Pathways to Empowerment Program places women's empowerment at the center of the program, believing that through women's empowerment, CARE can bring changes in yields and incomes, and food and nutrition security. In systematizing its learning, what is most interesting is the evolution of learning within CARE itself and its network of partners and constituents. CARE's approach addresses questions of change at the level of organizational culture impacting and engaging all of its stakeholders. Following CARE's Women's Empowerment Framework, Pathways builds women's individual agency (skills and capacities as farmers and business-people and their self-confidence in their rights). The Pathways program challenges inequalities in the institutions, including discriminatory policies but also traditional beliefs about men's and women's roles, rights and abilities. Gender-transformative programming examines, questions and changes rigid gender ideas and imbalances of power as a means of reaching both agriculture outcomes and gender equality.

At the outset, CARE knew it needed to invest heavily in its own people and its partners, to ensure conceptual coherence around its empowerment approach. And it needed to make these investments globally, in over eighty countries where CARE works. Thinking systemically and holistically ensured that financial and other resources were made available in order to guarantee organizational integrity and coherence. This is a daunting challenge that requires constant vigilance and investment, and is part of a never-ending learning process. Specific, dedicated learning grants have enabled CARE to bridge the divides between the best thinking from the policy and academic worlds, the interests of diverse donors, and the grounded experience and understandings from its partners and impact groups on the ground. The result of these learning investments is simple (but theoretically grounded) guiding frameworks (such as the Women's Empowerment Framework) and theories of change that provide a structure within which programs can innovate, scale and adapt to new poverty challenges while holding firm to the organization's core beliefs and mission.

One Acre Fund's approach begins with farmer voice, firmly acknowledging that farmers are the best authorities on technologies and services that purport to help them farm better. Joining that voice with other sources of data helps engender support for their approach. By embedding Constituent Voice (CV) and active participation from the beginning, it becomes part of the organizational culture and structure of the NGO, its funders, any partner organizations and farmers. The Fund strives to avoid false dichotomies of "us and them," and requires its staff to engage with farmers at the level of the farm, often hiring farmers to assist with rapid research and development activities. Through its experience, toolkits and methodologies have emerged that drive effective results for farmers. As a social enterprise, One Acre Fund doesn't shy away from the proven tools and approaches used by the private sector and behavioral economics. By effectively engaging farmers and other co-constituents, One Acre Fund demonstrates the centrality of trust as the essential ingredient needed to build equitable and sustainable development among small farmers. When farmers see themselves in key roles and are helping to make strategic decisions about the content of their small farming systems, including direct involvement in service delivery, they become self-motivated to innovate, experiment, learn and engage others.

IDEO.org's approach concentrates on human-centered design and incorporates both qualitative and quantitative research into farmers' behaviors and activities. It goes far beyond typical approaches. Starting with the goal of improving livelihoods, IDEO.org prefers to design holistic solutions that embrace many aspects of a farmer's life. In order to design farmer-centric solutions, IDEO.org directly engages farmers in the design process and builds feedback from the community into the process at all stages. IDEO.org has learned that simplifying the data collection process, focusing on the right data and sharing that data widely is important for wide-scale adoption of best practices. Engaging farmers to assess a program, business, service or product introduced by any supplier or organization can also be accelerated using less traditional means and not relying solely on surveys. IDEO.org uses rough, short-lived tests called "prototypes" wherein farmers interact with the services or products without knowing much about them, and afterwards they are asked probing questions to elicit their perceptions. In this manner, the judgments, needs and values of farmers are directly identified and their perceptions impact subsequent design decisions. They become, in effect, co-designers.

3) Reflections on learning and system-level approaches

The complexity of working in development is vast. The work is multifaceted, multidisciplinary and requires attention from the grassroots right up to the international arena. Learning to manage complexity is part of the challenge of development work, as it requires building synergies with diverse partner organizations.

Synergos supports development initiatives that build trust among and between diverse partners from various levels of government, the private sector, civil society and marginalized populations. This work is done by shifting mind-sets and behaviors of very large, complex and often bureaucratic institutions. When large organizations or groups of organizations have specific and explicit values to support collective learning, then progress is possible. Reliance on hard data needs to be balanced with qualitative learning—indeed they can complement each other. Constituents need to actively participate in the process of generating and refining new knowledge based on their shared experiences, albeit from different vantage points. At the heart of the change process is a commitment to personal learning while working collectively with other like-minded individuals and organizations. To the extent that constituents are engaged in the collective learning process, a greater sense of agency and ownership is engendered. When learning becomes the norm at both the individual and organizational level, then a new culture of learning emerges. In many cases, developing the capacity to bring people together across divides and to work together requires a bridging leadership born from an attitude to advance learning, not control or dominate. Such groundwork establishes new cooperative norms that increase respect for diverse contributions. Constituents are encouraged to both drill down and to have an outward-looking orientation in order to manage the complexity of the whole. They need to observe the system they are striving to change. Capacity is built to identify root causes and system blockages and through consultation to find solutions. Periodic reflection and specific spaces for personal reflection are encouraged, as a means of helping people connect to their personal values and to constantly align their actions and attitudes with those guiding principles. This process encourages the constituents at all levels to be open-minded, open-hearted, trusting and open to learning, and to engage others in an ever-widening conversation about the importance of those values to facilitate learning and advancement. It takes time to build the necessary trust for collaboration and collective learning, as well as patience and perseverance.

FOSCA, as a program of AGRA, builds capacity of farmer organizations to more effectively serve their members. The inherent tensions in the competition for resources that characterize many development initiatives are challenged by FOSCA. They provide evidence that more collaborative strategies prove more effective and durable. Working to align diverse interests towards a shared objective and to foster collective learning allows new capacities for service to be developed. FOSCA uses a wide array of technologies and methods to achieve its aims. Periodic reflection meetings are required to allow consortium members to examine dysfunctional mind-sets that prevent participation, limit voice, reduce accountability and stifle learning. Strict reporting on both qualitative and quantitative data supports learning, particularly when the findings are freely distributed, widely consulted about and wisely used. While different outcomes may be required at different levels of the system, they all should be aligned and coherent. Experience has shown that if achievements at one level impinge on another, then the change is neither effective nor sustainable. Furthermore, while competition has its place, it is not necessarily the best strategy all the time. New learning shows interesting innovations about how to work more cooperatively. The more diverse the consortium members, the more challenging it is to align their respective goals and strategies. However, promoting horizontal accountability and mutual learning makes development planning and implementation work more inclusive. At the outset, it is necessary to overcome the fear or belief that consortium members and co-constituents won't cooperate and learn together. Every journey begins with the first step, and a little faith.

Kenya Markets Trust is learning about how aligning feedback loops between consumers and businesses can be a powerful means to counteract the influence of unexamined social and political systems. These systems are replete with inefficiencies and inaccuracies that undermine collective learning. Behavior is being influenced not by conscious reflection on action and experience, but by the unexamined and controlling influences of outmoded institutional (regulatory, cultural, economic, social, etc.) norms and information flows. These are typically generated and controlled by existing ethnic elites and social hierarchies. In such a society there will be little or no learning, no downward accountability, limited participation and very faint constituent voice. Corrective strategies focus on reframing business relationships away from a preoccupation with short-term gains towards more customer-centric solutions that are developed with consumer participation. Competitive pressure within an economy is insufficient to leverage system-wide behavioral change from within. Instead, for wider systemic change to take place, multiple feedback mechanisms are implemented that make use of competitive pressure for positive change. These feedback loops are essential to comprehensively restructure incentives and behaviors within a market system. Developing the system's ability to learn and adapt is a major focus for Kenya Markets Trust.

Emerging elements for collective learning in development

The case studies provide a rich tapestry of experiences that underscore the positive implications of harnessing the power of feedback loops. When implemented as part of a collective learning process, these feedback loops raise individual and collective capacity for sustainable development. It is premature, however, to draw any hard and fast conclusions, particularly because the story is still being told. When the contributors gathered in Seattle, WA, in May 2014 to share experiences and discuss each other's work, several key elements of a conceptual framework emerged quite naturally out of the free-flowing discussion. These elements were common to all the contributor's stories. Among these elements are the following.

1) Feedback loops and participant voice

Decades of development practice show that enabling participation and ensuring that constituent voices are heard are indispensable features of any successful development initiative. Learning to listen well enables programs to integrate and harness local knowledge, which then increases the likelihood of sustainability and ownership. However, valuing feedback and voice must take into account certain realities on the ground:

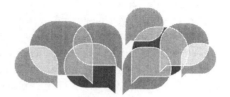

FIGURE 13.2 Valuing constituent participation, voice and feedback

1   Feedback and voice are necessary but not sufficient conditions for collective learning.
2   Listening well does not mean that all voices have to be heard on all issues. This can happen at different times and in different ways. It is unrealistic to expect everyone to participate in everything.
3   Learning requires the acceptance and expectation of failure. Experimentation is a scientific method to discover truth and requires creativity, innovation and humility. Many of the most successful innovations were not planned but evolved.
4   Power imbalances, competing incentives and too many voices within a system can slow or even stop collective learning, yet we still need accountability in complex systems.
5   Technology can enable and magnify voice but spaces for collective and face-to-face interaction are necessary to ascribe appropriate and useful meaning to collected information and data.

2) Making sense of the data

Presenting, collecting and sharing data in a meaningful way remains central to the collective learning process. It is important to collect the right type and the right amount of data with the right frequency. However, this is rarely the case in many development projects where too much data is often collected or where the data only gets into the hands of decision-makers long after it would have been useful for adapting and reshaping the future of a particular project.

Data alone is inadequate. The co-constituents in any development initiative need to make sense of the

FIGURE 13.3 Consultation to ascribe meaning to data generates new knowledge

data together, which requires spaces for reflection on action, and an inclusive attitude of learning. These reflection and consultation spaces can be formal and informal in nature, but are essential for learning to take place. Trust is a key element in the data-gathering and sense-making process. Without high levels of trust it is difficult to act upon the data collected. Where there is no trust, there is marginalization and oppression.

In practice, data can contribute to learning when it is presented simply, frequently and visually. Tools like well-designed dashboards have inherent risks because summaries by their very nature exclude data that might be relevant. Disclosing what details have not been shared is therefore an important act of transparency and legitimacy.

Learning to use data effectively is an incremental, organic process. Capacity to collect and share data increases the more frequently the process is carried out. When the conversation around data collection and its use is contextualized in the perceptions, worldviews and interests of constituents, it becomes increasingly valued and important.

3) Relationships matter

In any relationship, it is necessary to clarify the incentives, roles and expectations of all parties. Questions about voice and power need to be carefully considered when trying to create an enabling environment for collective learning. Voice is not about taking or giving "voice," but recognizing that each constituent has both the right and the obligation to participate in the development process. These rights and obligations need to be safeguarded by all the constituents. It is only when people engage as equals in the consultative spaces that the dynamics of power can be adequately addressed. When the collective voice is heard it can be measured by its impact on decisions about policy, technology choice or actions that impact individuals and communities. If conditions exist whereby constituents can freely express themselves, then there will likely be greater acceptance and understanding when an idea is taken up. Insistence on one's own idea is never helpful, so ensuring that each voice is adequately heard is a collective responsibility.

It is widely recognized that constituents do not work in isolation. Most constituents are part of groups that cooperate and accompany each other. Understanding what mutual support and assistance look like in a learning context requires a humble attitude of learning. Emerging communities of practice and similar collective structures and communal processes that facilitate collective engagement are important.

Strong and vibrant relationships require participants to be both trustworthy and truthful. In many instances, however, a lack of consensus may exist about how to assess truth and trustworthiness. We may lack commonly accepted indicators to measure trustworthiness and truthfulness. In the absence of common indicators, or even a language to discuss them, ineffectual relationships that promulgate self-interest may emerge. The importance of working towards higher degrees of understanding of the implications of trust and truth, however, are an important part of harnessing the power of collective learning.

The process of generating feedback can strengthen or threaten relationships between co-constituents. On the one hand, certain constituents may want to demonstrate that they are effective and can achieve results, or simply need to be seen as valued and competent in their own right. Such thoughts will lead them to act in certain ways. Feedback loops can contribute to enhance honesty and integrity, or obfuscate truth. Thus, there is an inherent tension between them. In order to become more effective it is important to face those things that need improvement even when they make the initiative look bad. This requires, in part, a humble posture and attitude of learning.

In short, effective learning becomes a function of (1) high levels of trust in the relationship + (2) the right data at the right time + (3) a sense-making process that engages all the key stakeholders honestly and as equals.

4) Being systematic ensures coherence

Key among the perspectives shared by the contributors was that learning needs to be systematic. Typically, some form of praxis is introduced, or a cycle of learning that begins with action (experimentation), followed by reflection on experience (and the knowledge and insight of others) and finally a stage of participatory engagement or consultation. Each cycle allows the constituents to make sense of their experience and the data collected, in order to both refine current action and alter future plans. There was a growing awareness among the participants that at every stage of the process (i.e., design, implementation, evaluation, etc.), the active participation of all the constituents was essential to progress. In this sense, participation by all the constituents in the collective learning process was seen to be an essential component to progressing systematically. The continued involvement of the constituents prevented the action from becoming haphazard or serving the vested interests of a small minority of constituents. Deliberately creating spaces for structured reflection and consultation on action allowed for new questions to be explored, and methods and approaches to be examined and reconsidered.

Being systematic implies an appreciation for scientific method, the use of control groups and experimentation of certain hypotheses regarding a theory of change. It also implies a willingness to strive to understand and manage the complexity of entire systems, and not deal with issues in isolation.

The importance of being coherent emerged as another common element. Coherence implies making an effort to learn to apply the stated values and principles of the organization at all times and under all conditions. For example, an organization that values learning, seeks to incorporate feedback loops and mechanisms throughout the project life cycle and beyond. It willingly creates sufficient spaces and allocates sufficient resources to assemble

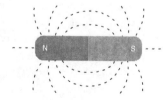

FIGURE 13.4 Collective learning enhances conceptual and operational coherence

constituents in both formal and informal settings and on regular and periodically scheduled reflection gatherings in order to review progress. Similarly, an organization that seeks to ensure gender equality reviews its progress each time it engages in any review of feedback.

With regard to participation, while participation is highly valued, it is impractical to think that everyone should be involved in every decision. Participation occurs at different levels within the system, from and amongst the constituents at the grassroots right up to the highest levels of political decision-making. What emerged out of the discussions of the various case studies was that the principle of participation need not be applied uniformly. Embedding participation in the development process implies a willingness to create spaces for participation at regular intervals wherein constituents can provide input, share feedback and discuss their experience. By engaging in this process, they participate in the ongoing generation of knowledge that will guide and shape the development initiative. Such assurances promote participation, transparency and integrity. It is gradually understood that participation includes being part of an ongoing and purposeful discussion about the work at hand, and that decisions are informed by the discourse as it evolves.

5) Development is learning, and learning is key

The centrality of knowledge (both local and expert knowledge, as well as scientific and cultural) is an essential component of development. The process of collective learning or the collective generation and application of knowledge requires the willingness to allocate resources to help systematize and diffuse knowledge as it is generated through collective engagement. This is a challenge in many organizations. Making data, information and learning readily available to all constituents including the general public takes resources and open-mindedness, both of which may be limited at least initially. The ability to remove these obstacles is significantly affected by the degree to which the constituents are committed to collective learning.

Collective learning does not equate itself with each constituent necessarily learning the same thing. Constituents operating at different levels within the system may learn something different through their collective action, but the lessons being learned at various levels are entirely consistent and coherent with each other.

Any learning process is a challenge. Given the importance of knowledge, learning to apply it is an essential component of development. As constituents refine their capacity to read their reality more accurately, they are more able to produce viable and sustainable development strategies.

The emergence of new language to describe what is being learned is yet another manifestation of the conceptual coherence emerging out of the case studies. Contributors increasingly noted the frequency of the descriptive prefix "co-" to describe what they were learning, using new terms such as co-constituent, co-organized, co-created and co-designed.

6) Sustainability

Every case study touched on the importance of sustainability, principally from the perspective of sustaining action. For some, for an initiative to be sustained the very idea of sustainability needed to be clearly articulated and "baked in" or embedded in the process from the outset, and not something added on later. For others, there was a sense that if the value proposition was significantly attractive, the initiative could be sustained. Common to both perspectives is the idea that sustainability is somehow intricately rooted in human motivation.

From this perspective, most contributors identified the importance of voice, participation, and not only giving feedback, but having the feedback loop closed, as evidenced by their voice having been heard and decisions impacted by that voice. Embedded in the process from the outset, "beneficiaries" move from recipient to co-creator, motivated by what contributes to their personal and community advancement. Participation in this light takes on new meaning. The value proposition, likewise, need not be limited to a material outcome or outputs realized through a specific project. In most cases, the very act of being engaged in a collective learning process contributed to a sense of agency and personal empowerment that resulted in heightened and sustained levels of engagement.

Here again, the authenticity of the relationships among and between the co-constituents is referred to as a key for sustainability. If the relationships among and between the diverse constituents along the spectrum (community member—local organization—partners—networks—grantees—donors—government, etc.) are authentic and trusting, then sustainable progress is possible. Where trustworthiness is lacking, self-interest prevails.

The importance of aligning feedback systems at all levels takes on added importance. If there is transparency and coherence among and between the various levels, then the levels of shared vision and commitment are enhanced, resulting in an improved quality of relationships.

7) Common vision of service/learning attitude and culture

Moving far away from the idea that a shared vision statement of a future condition is sufficiently motivating, the contributors identified several common components that contribute to a deeper appreciation for the need for a common vision and how it serves as a catalyst for

FIGURE 13.5 Vision

participation and sustained engagement. The vision of the desired state or outcome, while important, is only as valid as the strategies, methods and approaches they apply, the attitudes that they engender and their overall coherence with the guiding principles.

Humility is an important aspect to learning and advancement. With the belief that all the stakeholders are co-creators and co-constituents, an attitude of humble fellowship is fostered along with a "we're in this together" attitude. And in the context of enabling a collective learning process, there is an understanding that the work—like the learning—is never complete, it merely takes on greater levels of complexity as capacity is gradually built.

Another common element concerns the evolution in the understanding of the concept of service. Delivering services or solutions to the poor has been replaced with approaches that build capacity for service. This includes working more in an attitude of service, even when delivering products and services. In making this shift, contributors spoke about moving away from approaches that had certain values embedded within them, such as creating a dependency on someone or something, or limiting the role of a constituent to that of a client or consumer who was to be targeted. Chief among these observations was a desire towards co-creating demand-driven approaches that truly respond to all constituent interests, rather than the continuance of albeit well-intentioned approaches that inadvertently impose something on a population. In this instance, it was noted that much learning is required to shift the attitudes and behaviors of key leaders, particularly in government and the private sector.

Concluding remarks and future research

Harnessing the power of collective learning has implications for all the constituents of a development initiative. But the main idea coming out of the workshop is that an invitation needs to be extended to the donor and philanthropic community to accompany other co-constituents in learning more about learning in the context of development.

Donors need to conduct research on several key factors that contribute to development learning. Among these factors is a willingness to build in more time for reflection, to consider longer funding cycles, to encourage timely and relevant feedback loops, to insist on co-constituent accountability, to provide additional funding for organizational learning and to use funding to encourage collaboration rather than competition for resources.

For grantees, lines of inquiry and action include the willingness to support enabling environments that foster learning, both informal and formal, wherein co-constituents can get input and hear feedback from all constituents. Grantees should consider learning more about innovating with timely and more frequent feedback loops. They should also engage in and support lines of action that build trust and that strengthen a culture of learning within organizations.

Community members, both individually and collectively, should strive to voice their concerns, provide timely feedback, hold themselves and others accountable for their actions, organize for sustainability and foster a sense of agency with community members. They should strengthen their resolve to consult more effectively and to appreciate a wide diversity of perspectives.

Academic and research institutions will likely wish to pursue the themes under discussion. The publication "Escaping Capability Traps through Problem-Driven

Iterative Adaptation (PDIA)"[1] introduces an innovative approach that may unlock certain keys to voice and participation as well as accountability and transparency. The list of innovative approaches is likely to increase and lies beyond the scope of this publication.

Organizations, like development approaches, are constantly evolving. The contributors to this publication are learning to see, understand and appreciate the importance of feedback as more than a social science requirement for conducting monitoring and evaluation exercises. They now see learning around feedback and accountability as an integral part of any strategy for generating the knowledge needed to bring about lasting change. The belief now is that this knowledge, when translated into conscious action, can result in greater, more lasting progress, and that being part of a learning community is highly motivating. Focusing on the generation and application of knowledge frees people from the methods, models and approaches of the past. Contributors repeatedly shared examples of approaches that used external rating agencies to assess the validity of alternative development strategies, and measure the quality of the interactions of constituent interactions and responsiveness to feedback. Others spoke about efforts to move away from a traditional "vision—values—modalities and obligation of results" mentality, and to explore alternative development worldviews and approaches. Others examined shortsighted pay to play approaches and the negative impact of short-term results over long-term commitments, and many spoke about an ongoing discourse within their organizations about the limits to learning imposed by insufficient resource allocations for reflection, for systematizing and sharing lessons learned, and for an obsession with results at all costs. And all spoke about how they were learning to address these and myriad other challenges, converting obstacles into stepping stones.

The challenges of development are complex, dynamic and non-linear. We invite donors, grantees and all constituents who are truly concerned with sustainable development to continue the conversation and research on the common elements identified by the contributors to this publication. Harnessing the power of collective learning may be a key to creating the conditions where a sustainable, just and peaceful society that reflects our highest and noblest aspirations can emerge.

Note

1 Andrews, M., Pritchett, L., and Woolcock, M. (2012). "Escaping Capability Traps through Problem-Driven Iterative Adaptation (PDIA)." Working Paper No. 299, Washington, DC: Center for Global Development.

INDEX

0 1341 1660001 3

CPSIA information can be obtained
at www.ICGtesting.com
Printed in the USA
FFOW03n1304080916
27507FF

9 781138 121126